T0385891

The Atheist's Bible

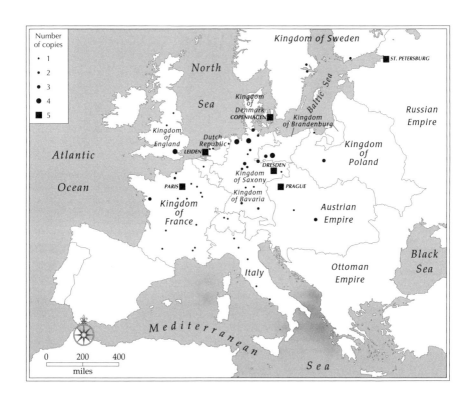

Location of manuscripts of the *Traité des trois imposteurs* in the eighteenth century

The Atheist's Bible

THE MOST DANGEROUS BOOK
THAT NEVER EXISTED

Georges Minois   Translated by Lys Ann Weiss

THE UNIVERSITY OF CHICAGO PRESS   *Chicago and London*

GEORGES MINOIS is the author of *History of Old Age: From Antiquity to the Renaissance* and *History of Suicide: Voluntary Death in Western Culture*, the former published by the University of Chicago Press.
LYS ANN WEISS is an independent scholar in medieval studies who works in book publishing as an editor, indexer, and translator.

The University of Chicago Press, Chicago 60637
The University of Chicago Press, Ltd., London
© 2012 by The University of Chicago
All rights reserved. Published 2012.
Printed in the United States of America

21 20 19 18 17 16 15 14 13 12   1 2 3 4 5

ISBN-13: 978-0-226-53029-1 (cloth)
ISBN-13: 978-0-226-53030-7 (e-book)
ISBN-10: 0-226-53029-9 (cloth)
ISBN-10: 0-226-53030-2 (e-book)

Originally published as *Le Traité des trois imposteurs: Histoire d'un livre blasphématoire qui n'existait pas.* Copyright © Éditions Albin Michel, 2009.

Cet ouvrage a bénéficié du soutien des Programmes d'aide à la publication de l'Institut français. This work, published as part of a program of aid for publication, received support from the Institut Français.

Ouvrage publié avec le soutien du Centre national du livre—ministère français chargé de la culture. This work is published with support from the National Center of the Book—French Ministry of Culture.

Map on page ii: Location of manuscripts of the *Traité des trois imposteurs* in the eighteenth century. Courtesy of Dick Gilbreath, University of Kentucky Cartography Lab.

Library of Congress Cataloging-in-Publication Data

Minois, Georges, 1946–
    [Traité des trois imposteurs. English]
    The atheist's Bible : the most dangerous book that never existed / Georges Minois ; translated by Lys Ann Weiss.
        pages. cm.
    Includes bibliographical references and index.
    ISBN-13: 978-0-226-53029-1 (cloth : alk. paper)
    ISBN-13: 978-0-226-53030-7 (e-book)
    ISBN-10: 0-226-53029-9 (cloth : alk. paper)
    ISBN-10: 0-226-53030-2 (e-book)   1. De tribus impostoribus.
2. Rationalism—History. I. Title.
    BL2773.M5613 2012
    200—dc23

                                                            2012011212

⊗ This paper meets the requirements of ANSI/NISO Z39.48-1992 (Permanence of Paper).

CONTENTS

TRANSLATOR'S NOTE

English translations of material quoted in the text are those of the translator unless otherwise attributed. Numerous historical figures are referred to in the text, some of whose names are likely to be unfamiliar to American readers. Many of these are briefly identified in the glossary of proper names at the back of the book. Of the "three impostors" who are the book's subject, two—Moses and Jesus—are referred to by those names. The third, following the author's varied usage, is referred to as Muhammad, Mahomet, or the Prophet; his followers are referred to as Muslims or Mahometans; the religion he founded is referred to as Islam or Mahometanism. His sacred book is given its correct Arabic spelling, Qur'ān. The treatise on the three impostors is discussed in both its Latin and its French versions. The English title *Treatise of the Three Impostors* or *On the Three Impostors* is used to refer to the work generally; the Latin title *De tribus impostoribus* and the French title *Traité des trois imposteurs* refer specifically to the Latin and French versions, respectively.

PREFACE TO THE ENGLISH-LANGUAGE EDITION (2012)

The *Treatise of the Three Impostors* was an international production, born in the early eighteenth century in European antireligious circles, after a long gestation begun in the Middle Ages. As early as 1796 an American edition appeared, published in Philadelphia. But this was only an additional imposture, as shown two centuries later, in 1996, by Heather Blair of the University of Chicago.[1] The edition was the work of a French publisher, Mercier de Compiègne, who, during the French Revolution, wanted to give the work greater prominence by making people believe that it had reached the New World. The first English translations were published in 1844, in Amsterdam and Dundee, and 1846, in New York.

Although the *Treatise* for a long time enjoyed greater success in Europe than in America, today it resonates more in the Anglophone world. There the question of atheism is debated more freely than in Europe, where the subject still meets with reticence and timidity. While authors like Richard Dawkins, the late Christopher Hitchens, Sam Harris, A. C. Grayling, Daniel C. Dennett, and many others directly confront religious beliefs in works written for the general public, European authors and publishers take a more hands-off approach, practicing self-censorship rather than risking controversy. In Old World Europe, these questions are subject to a consensus, which affirms that all beliefs deserve respect, even when they defy the most basic level of rational thought.

You might say that Europe has forgotten the spirit of the Enlightenment, of Voltaire, Rousseau, Baron d'Holbach, Diderot, and Hume. It still views the *Treatise of the Three Impostors* as a testament of atheist fundamentalism, on the same level with religious fundamentalisms. This refusal to envision a rational critique of the three great monotheistic religions, or even to allow the debate, favors intellectual stagnation, even regression, by abandoning the search for truth. In this context, we may note the striking contrast between European bookstores, where the shelf labeled "Religion" is overly full and relatively homogeneous, and those of the English-speaking world, where books of militant atheism hold an important place alongside religious works, symbolic of a healthy debate.

The *Treatise of the Three Impostors* is an aggressive work, a frontal attack upon religion. Ironically, three centuries after its appearance, it is still viewed in Europe as a dangerous and hard-to-find work. Its combative spirit finds more favorable ground in the more open intellectual environment of the English-speaking world. Developed in Europe, in opposition to the religions whose impostures and totalitarianism it denounces, it has by now lost its impact on a society that prefers social consensus to the search for truth. It is a better fit for the Anglophone intellectual climate, both culturally freer and intellectually more combative. In a Europe that today prizes tranquility more than truth, and doublespeak over clarity, the *Treatise* has only historical value. In an America where Christian fundamentalisms have free play, the vigorous antireligious attacks on the "three impostors," Moses, Jesus, and Mahomet, regain their full sociological and cultural interest.

PREFACE (2009)

The *Treatise of the Three Impostors* is what one might call a mythical work. It's all right there in the title—the supreme provocation, an absolute blasphemy, a direct challenge to the three great monotheistic religions. To call Moses, Jesus, and Muhammad impostors is to assault the faith of billions of people, devout believers. That is precisely why the work's title—a bogeyman, named only in a whisper, whose mere mention evoked fear—was sufficient unto itself for centuries. From the thirteenth to the seventeenth century, this book circulated as a virtual work: nobody had seen it, nobody had read it, but almost everybody believed in its existence. In some ways, its story resembles that of the god it fights against: arising out of human imagination, it became such an obsession that it ended up by existing. There it was, hot off the presses in the Netherlands in 1719, after which time it multiplied, circulating in clandestine fashion throughout Europe, where freethinkers bought up copies at the price of gold.

Its scandalous reputation was ensured by the fact that it not only attacked the founders of the three great religions, and at the same time their respective gods, but, even worse, put all three on the same level, in the same basket—the one full of hoaxes, trickery, and illusions that knock out critical thinking and cause senseless massacres. Yahweh, the Christian God, Allah—these are only words, hot air, and their prophets, Moses, Jesus, and Muhammad, are mere impostors. Their imposture, upheld by rabbis, priests, and imams, has brought about the violent deaths of millions of people, who literally died for nothing. This is the claim of the *Treatise of the Three Impostors*. You don't need to read it to guess the contents, which is precisely why the book was able to circulate for such a long time without ever existing. Anyone could fill it out with his own fantasies. And without ever having seen it, people pointed to its supposed authors, from the Holy Roman Emperor Frederick II to the philosopher Baruch Spinoza, not to mention all those other heterodox, heretics, atheists, or skeptics. In many ways, we might, in our day, call it a psychosis. Without ever having seen the book, people offered large rewards to anyone who would find them a copy. Then one day the notorious treatise materialized.

In the chapters that follow, we shall retrace the story of this mysterious work. Scholars and contemporary historians have managed to reconstruct the broad outline of the tale, although there remain some shady areas, some sources of disagreement among specialists. The story is extremely complex; in the interest of clarity, we have had to do some pruning and simplifying. Citations in the notes will allow interested readers to pursue various aspects of the story in greater depth. It all began in the thirteenth century, much like a historical detective novel, but the crucial episodes took place between the sixteenth and eighteenth centuries.

The story of the *Treatise of the Three Impostors* is inextricably linked with that of atheism and the general theme of religious imposture. Scholars still argue over whether the treatise itself is deist, pantheist, or atheist in inspiration. To us, *atheist* seems the right word to designate a work that denies absolutely the existence of a personal god, a free intellect, the creator of the world, who intervenes in human affairs and assigns punishments and rewards after death. The book is undeniably antireligious, and this is why we have placed its story in a larger context, indispensable for a clear understanding of its origins—that of atheistic thought.

The Origin of a Mythical Theme: The Prehistory of the *Three Impostors* (Up to the Thirteenth Century)

On 1 July 1239, Pope Gregory IX addressed to the monarchs and ecclesiastical dignitaries of all Christendom an encyclical letter accusing the Holy Roman Emperor Frederick II of being "a scorpion spitting out poison from the stinger on its tail." "This pestilent king," he continued,

> has notably and openly stated that—in his own words—*the whole world has been fooled by three impostors, Jesus Christ, Moses, and Muhammad,* two of whom died honorably, while Jesus himself died on the Cross. Moreover, he has dared to affirm, or rather, he has fraudulently claimed, that all those who believed that a virgin could give birth to the God who created nature, and all the rest, were fools. And Frederick has aggravated the heresy by this insane assertion, according to which no one can be born without having been conceived by the prior intercourse of a man and a woman; he also claims that people ought to believe nothing that cannot be proven by the strength and reason of nature.[1]

Thus the theme of the three impostors was launched. At the start, it consisted of a gratuitous accusation, immediately denied by the emperor, who responded by calling the pope himself a heretic. The tension between the two men continued to mount, in the context of what we now call the quarrel of the papacy and the empire, or the Investiture Controversy. Ever since 1075, when Pope Gregory VII proclaimed himself the supreme leader of Christendom and claimed that the emperor held power only through him, the war of the leaders had raged, reaching its heights under Emperor Frederick I Barbarossa (c. 1122–1190) and Pope Innocent III (1160–1216). Between deposition of the pope, on the one side, and excommunication of the emperor, on the other, the spiritual and temporal powers fought each other for 150 years to decide which of the two would exercise supreme power.

On 19 March 1227, Cardinal Hugolin, the comte de Segni, nephew of Innocent III, was elected pope at the age of fifty-seven, and took the name Gregory IX. Austere, stubborn, and energetic, an expert in canon law, and a personal friend of Francis of Assisi, the new pope dreamed of solidifying the supreme domination of the Holy See over Europe and the Holy Land. To achieve this, he needed the submission and collaboration of the Holy Roman Emperor, head of the premier temporal power of Christendom. The problem was, the reigning emperor was one of the strongest and most distinctive personalities of the Middle Ages, and was determined to affirm his independence with respect to the pope. This exceptional emperor was Frederick II, of the Hohenstaufen family. He had ruled since 1215; his states held those of the pope in a vise because, in addition to ruling Germany, he was king of Sicily (which is to say, of all of southern Italy). In the northern part of the peninsula, he imposed his authority on Lombardy by force, intervening frequently in Lombard affairs. In 1227, he led a crusade, which he had to interrupt right at the start due to a sudden illness. The pope excommunicated him. The following year he set out again, and in February 1229, an agreement with the Sultan al-Malik al-Kāmil restored to the Christians Jerusalem, Bethlehem, Nazareth, and a coastal strip from Jaffa to Acre. Frederick II proclaimed himself King of Jerusalem, yet maintained friendly relations with the Muslims, an attitude that cost him dearly when the pope confirmed his excommunication. The excommunication was lifted on 28 August 1230, and a fragile reconciliation took place at Anagni. Nine years later, there was another break: in February 1239, the confrontation in Lombardy polarized, as Frederick led a pitiless campaign, while Gregory federated all the anti-imperial towns and once again excommunicated the emperor. Frederick then directly threatened the papal city. This was the context in which the pope launched his accusation: Frederick was a heretic and a blasphemer who had called the three great founders of the monotheistic religions impostors.

The First to Be Accused: Frederick II and Pierre des Vignes (1239)

Gregory's accusation was likely to be believed, as the emperor already had a demonic reputation.[2] He surrounded himself with suspect characters of heterodox tendencies who did not hesitate to cross religious boundaries. For example, Master Theodore, the court philosopher, was close to Arab circles, and made an extract for the emperor from the *Secretum secretorum*, a work attributed to Aristotle. Michael Scot, a Scottish philosopher, astrologer, diviner, and mathematician, was a member of Frederick's court from 1227 to 1235. While in Toledo, Spain, in 1217, he had translated from the Arabic several works of Aristotle, such as *On the Heavens* and *On the Soul*, and also translated into Latin some works of the Arabic philosopher Ibn Rushd (Averroes). Both of these were rationalist authors; both were considered dangerous. Worst of all, there was Pierre des Vignes, whom the church viewed as Frederick's evil twin. Son of a Capuan judge, he studied civil and canon law at Bologna and became prothonotary of the kingdom of Sicily, and then *logothete* (literally, "he who puts into words"; that is to say, the head of the justice system and the drafter of legislation). It was he who established the written protocol of the court, using ambiguous expressions that referred to the emperor as an emanation of divinity and compared him to Christ. Playing on his own name, Pierre was at once Peter, prince of the apostles of the new savior Frederick, "a new Moses who came down from Sinai bearing the Law," and master "of the vineyard of the Lord." A prelate of the day wrote that "[Pierre] des Vignes is the rock [*pierre*] on which the Church of the Emperor is built when the emperor relaxes at a banquet in the company of his disciples." Mingling the profane and the sacred, and borrowing extensively from ancient Rome, des Vignes masterminded the effective deification of the emperor, as revealed in monumental statuary inspired by the late Roman Empire. Although he was the alter ego of Frederick II, Pierre des Vignes ended up abusing his high office, granting favors for money, and betraying the commands of the emperor. He was arrested in 1249 and imprisoned at San Miniato, where he killed himself by striking his head against the wall. Even his death did not restore his reputation in the eyes of the church, though it did gain him a place of honor in Dante's *Inferno*, in the circle of those who had done violence to themselves—not far from Michael Scot, likewise damned to hell by the Italian poet as a seer and fortune-teller.

Pierre des Vignes, in his capacity as *logothete*, was responsible for answering the pope's accusation, making the emperor's case, and denying the charge concerning the three impostors.[3] His response, however, only served to reinforce the suspicions, and gave rise to a persistent rumor whose repercussions echoed from century to century: Pierre des Vignes was said to have written, in collaboration with Frederick II, a Latin treatise entitled *De tribus impostoribus* [*On the Three Impostors*], denouncing the religious imposture of the three prophets of the religions of the Book: Moses, Jesus, and Muhammad. For hundreds of years, scholars, seekers, collectors, and heretics searched for the notorious accursed manuscript whose title became a damaging label used to stigmatize the heterodox.

No one knew the precise contents of the treatise, of course, but the title was held to summarize the whole work: it was a proclamation and a provocation, the supreme blasphemy, because it not only grouped Muhammad, Moses, and Jesus, but also accused all three of being liars, fabulists, and in short, impostors. At the same time, it was a double-edged blade: on the one hand, each religion hated to see its own founder treated as an impostor; yet on the other hand, each rejoiced to see the other two founders accused of the same crime. No work could have been better calculated to reveal at once the mutual hatred and the solidarity among religions, to the benefit of atheism. Because the work was known only by its title, Christians, Muslims, and Jews could all fantasize about the contents. This helped ensure the continuing notoriety of the work, enriched by the inventions of its enemies and its partisans alike—one of the properties of myth. Everyone interpreted the work in their own fashion, imagining its contents and developing its themes, thus building up this book, whose very existence was uncertain, into a sort of antireligious bible that collected all the arguments hostile to faith. This work, which no one had ever seen, became a powerful weapon for believers of all sorts—one that was timeless because, contrary to logic, people attributed it in succession to any strong mind whom they wanted to bring down. "Author of *On the Three Impostors*" quickly became the ultimate defamatory slogan.

It's no accident that the accusation was first brought against Frederick II. The intent was to blacken the image of this public figure who, in the eyes of the Catholic hierarchy, was guilty of crime piled upon crime: intellectual curiosity, rationalism, syncretism, eclecticism. And in fact there is ample evidence of his wide-ranging interests. Consider the list of philosophical questions he submitted to Michael Scot: Is hell located beneath the earth? Is there something that holds up the earth? How many heavenly spheres are there? What moves them? In which sphere does God have his substance? In what manner do the angels and saints make a crown for him? What is the difference between the spirits that approach God and those that have been cast out of heaven? Can a soul return in this life to speak or show itself? How would the propagation of the human species, which God willed, be possible without original sin?[4] Here was impertinence indeed. For the church, simply posing such questions was the sign of a rash mind, busying itself with secrets that God had not revealed. Even worse, Frederick looked for answers not in the Bible but in Aristotle, and to that end he freely consulted with infidels. During the crusade of 1228–1229, he gave his ambassadors the assignment of asking certain "learned questions" of the Muslim sages; he personally interviewed the Spanish Jew Judah ben Salomon ha-Cohen Matqa, author of the *Inquisitio sapientiae [Investigation of Knowledge]*. To the Muslim philosopher from Andalusia, ʿAbd al-Ḥakk ibn Sabʿīn, himself somewhat unorthodox, he sent a list of leading questions, known as the *Sicilian Questions*. Ibn Sabʿīn himself summarized the list:

> A document containing these questions had been sent by the Emperor to the East, that is, to Egypt, Syria, Iraq . . . and Yemen, but the responses of the Muslim philosophers of these countries failed to fulfill the prince's intent. . . . O prince worthy of being loved, you have said: "Wise Aristotle, in all his writings, clearly states that the world exists *ab aeterno*; no doubt he held that opinion, however, if he proved it, what are his arguments?" . . . O king, you have asked: "What is the goal of theology and what are the indispensable preliminary theories of this science, if indeed it has preliminary theories?" . . . O prince . . . , you have asked about the soul, without specifying what species of soul you were talking about. . . . Moreover, you added: "What is the indication of the immortality of the soul . . . and if it is immortal?" . . . You have requested a material explanation of these words of Mahomet, upon whom be peace: "The heart of the believer is between two fingers of the Merciful One."[5]

These questions reveal the recurring central themes in anti-religious controversies: the eternity of the world, the immortality of the soul, the role of reason in theological speculation. Frederick II was one of those people whose curiosity seems insatiable; he never ceased asking the one question guaranteed to irritate all the clerics of the world: "Why?" This is the question that pushes the theologians' backs against the wall and forces them to pull out their weapon of last resort, the unanswerable argument that reduces such questioners to silence: God's intentions are impenetrable. But Frederick II was not to be placated with an answer that was no answer. He wanted to know, and to know everything, the how as well as the why. Thus, the Franciscan friar Salimbene, in his chronicle composed in the 1260s, accused him of devoting himself to abominable experiments: making a man die in a barrel in order to watch his soul leave the body, disemboweling another to study the workings of the human digestive system, sacrificing divers to explore the gulf of Messina, raising children in total isolation in order to see what language they would speak. For Salimbene, Frederick II showed evidence of "wicked presumption and madness; . . . he was an atheist."

With that, the word was out, the curse, the ultimate accusation. Its indiscriminate use has continued to cause confusion right up to our day, when zealous philosophers try to restore its etymological purity. Some get worked up over how one can class as "atheists" all those who are simply heterodox, pantheists, theists, agnostics, libertines, and freethinkers.[6] In fact, in the history of religious controversy, an atheist is one who does not believe in the existence of the god(s) of his adversary's religion. Use of the term is justified to the extent that, for the accuser, his is the only god; thus, to believe in another god is to believe in nothing—that is, *a-theism*.

Frederick II, however, was viewed as an atheist by all religions. "He was a materialist," wrote Sibṭ Ibn al-Djawzī. Christians could not stand the good relations he maintained with Muslims and Jews, even though this practice followed the tradition of the Norman kingdom of Sicily. The emperor took an interest in the philosophy of Maimonides, as explained to him by Moses ben Solomon of Salerno. At court, the Jew Jacob ben Abba Mari ben Samson Anatoli was a friend of Michael Scot, and the Muslim Ibn Wāṣil described the sovereign as a "distinguished and cultivated man, a friend of philosophy, of logic, and of medicine, and favorable to the Muslims." The story was told that in Palestine he had been in contact with the "Old Man of the Mountain," the chief of the sect of Assassins, who in Frederick's day was painted as a master of imposture—a long-lived myth. He was rumored to recruit young men, who were forced to lead a very hard life for years. Then, they were given a big dose of hashish and left in an enchanting place surrounded by fountains, greenery, and plenty of (willing) virgins. They were told that this was paradise, something they had no trouble believing. Upon their return to "earth," they were ready to take all kinds of risks, including suicide attacks, in order to return to "paradise" as quickly as possible.

In the emperor's eyes, Aristotle, Averroes, and Maimonides were more worthy of belief than Moses, Jesus, and Muhammad, and he had nothing but sarcasm for Christian miracles, such as the Immaculate Conception. "How much longer can such a deception last?" he is said to have remarked at the sight of a priest on his way to administer the last rites. Likewise, he is supposed to have confided to his circle that "the soul dissipates like a breath and rots like an apple, given that fruit, like man, is made up of four essences."

This notorious reputation, in which it is impossible to distinguish reality from fable, was constructed within the emperor's own lifetime by chroniclers, all of whom were clerics, and who repeated the pope's accusations: a man like that, who had no respect for Yahweh, or God, or Allah, could only have seen Moses, Jesus, and Muhammad as impostors. This was repeated in unison by Alberic of Trois-Fontaines, Matthew Paris, and the authors of the *Chronicle of Augsburg* and the *Life of Gregory IX*. According to the last of these, Frederick became convinced of this blasphemy "through trafficking with Greeks and Arabs, who promised him universal rule through knowledge of the stars and made him so infatuated that he believed himself to be a god ... and said aloud that three impostors had come to seduce mankind. He added that his own task was to destroy a fourth imposture tolerated by the simple folk, which is the authority of the pope."[7] In 1245, at the Council of Lyons, the papal representative, Albert Behaim, called Frederick II a "new Lucifer. He has waged an assault upon heaven, to elevate his own throne above the stars, to become superior to the Vicar of God. . . . He has wished to usurp divine rights, alter the eternal alliance established by the Gospel, change the laws and the living conditions of men. . . . This so-called emperor is no more than a Herod, an enemy of the Christian religion, of the Catholic faith, and of the liberty of the Church."[8]

Excommunicated once again by Innocent IV, toward the end of his reign Frederick took on the dimensions of a veritable Antichrist, whose horrific exploits were magnified by the chroniclers of the thirteenth through fifteenth centuries: William of Nangis, Bernard le Trésorier, Philip of Novara, Vincent of Beauvais, and Giovanni Villani. The last of these adds an Epicurean dimension to the portrait: "He was dissolute in the pursuit of pleasure; he had many concubines, according to the custom of the Saracens; he gave himself up to all the pleasures of the senses and led an Epicurean life, calculating that there would be no other life after this one. . . . And this was the main reason why he became the enemy of Holy Church." The atheist, having no fear of hell, can only become a degenerate brute.

Frederick II also took on an eschatological dimension, as he was integrated into the millenarian predictions of the late Middle Ages. Some saw in him the emperor of the last days, whose return would mark the beginning of the third era of the world, after those of Adam and of Christ. An odd posthumous destiny for a man who had condemned religious imposture: to find himself incorporated into a religious mythology.

As for his being the author, or the silent partner, of a treatise called *De tribus impostoribus*, that remains in the realm of pure conjecture. Voltaire, in his *Essay on Morals [Essai sur les moeurs]*, was skeptical, stating that belief in the book's existence was based on the word of Gregory IX. "Men have searched for that book over the centuries, but no one has ever found it." In fact, people claimed to have found it, several times, but without ever proving that it came from Frederick or from Pierre des Vignes. However, some continued to believe in its existence, like Count Mazzuchelli, who in 1741, in his *Life of Pietro Aretino*, attributed the "shameful book *De tribus impostoribus* very plausibly to Pierre des Vignes, secretary to Emperor Frederick II, by whose order it was composed," and stated that copies were "to be found in several German libraries, printed in Holland, with no indication of city or printer or year, from an ancient manuscript that was stolen from the library in Munich."[9] In fact, these copies of the *Three Impostors* appear to be impostures themselves. That is what makes this search so fascinating: seeing the ways that people try to tear down, or to justify, imposture by means of imposture, trickery by means of trickery, in a complex game of deception.

The game began in the mid-thirteenth century with the pope's accusation, which gave birth to what eventually became more than a rumor—the myth of the existence of a blasphemous Latin treatise, the work of Frederick II and Pierre des Vignes, accusing Moses, Jesus, and Muhammad of being liars: *De tribus impostoribus*. The excitement was considerable, because such a treatise tackled all three of the great monotheistic religions. And if its existence was considered at the time to be altogether likely, it is because the idea of religious imposture was already very old. Frederick was by no means the first to suggest that religions, all religions, resting as they do upon unproven affirmations and unwarranted testimony, and thus constituting frauds, allow some people to wield power over a society by playing upon the ignorance, fears, hopes, and imaginations of men.

The Precursors of Imposture: Zalmoxis and Numa Pompilius

As early as the fifth century BCE, Herodotus related how, according to the Greeks, a certain Zalmoxis, a Thracian who had been a slave in the house of Pythagoras, was freed and returned to his country, where he hoaxed his fellow countrymen by passing himself off as immortal, thus creating his very own cult while profiting from the naivete of men:

> After being freed and gaining great wealth, he returned to his own country. Now the Thracians were a meanly-living and simple-witted folk, but this Zalmoxis knew Ionian usages and a fuller way of life than the Thracian; for he had consorted with Greeks, and moreover with one of the greatest Greek teachers, Pythagoras; wherefore he made himself a hall, where he entertained and feasted the chief among his countrymen, and taught them that neither he nor his guests nor any of their descendants should ever die, but that they should go to a place where they would live for ever and have all good things. While he was doing as I have said and teaching this doctrine, he was all the while making him an underground chamber. When this was finished, he vanished from the sight of the Thracians, and descended into the underground chamber, where he lived for three years, the Thracians wishing him back and mourning him for dead; then in the fourth year he appeared to the Thracians, and thus they came to believe what Zalmoxis had told them.[10]

Thereafter, says Herodotus, the Thracians believed in immortality, and when they died, they believed they were going to rejoin Zalmoxis.

Here we have the prototype of the impostor who founds a religion. All the elements are there: a credulous people, a skilled char-latan who promises eternal happiness in a future life to the faithful, whom he subdues by a fake miracle, which permits him to control their minds through the intermediary of his clergy. This anecdote was not forgotten: Zalmoxis would be incorporated into the arsenal of the adversaries of Christianity as the precursor of religious im-posture. Replace the three years by three days, followed by a resurrec-tion, with the promise of eternal salvation, and we have, so they said, the model for the Christian imposture. Zalmoxis was a skilled orator, just like Jesus, and it is not surprising that we find mention of him in all the texts denouncing religious imposture.

If Zalmoxis prefigures Jesus, to the extent that he presents him-self as a god, Numa Pompilius, in contrast, is the precursor of the founder-legislators, like Moses or Muhammad, in claiming to re-ceive signs directly from the divinity, and in making use of them to give out the law. The episode occurs in Livy's *History of Rome*, and takes place about 710 BCE. According to the Roman historian, King Numa Pompilius made use of a subterfuge that gave a sacred char-acter to his legislation:

> And fearing lest relief from anxiety on the score of foreign perils might lead men who had hitherto been held back by fear of their en-emies and by military discipline into extravagance and idleness, he thought the very first thing to do, as being the most efficacious with a populace which was ignorant and, in those early days, uncivilized, was to imbue them with the fear of Heaven. As he could not instil this into their hearts without inventing some marvellous story, he pretended to have nocturnal meetings with the goddess Egeria, and that hers was the advice which guided him in the establishment of rites most approved by the gods, and in the appointment of special priests for the service of each.[11]

Numa Pompilius became a textbook case in antireligious argument.

With the ancient historians having reported on these two fa-mous impostors, it was up to the philosophers to develop a theory of religious imposture and to study its workings. The Greek soph-ists were the first to come up with an explanation—those thinkers, like Protagoras, who believed that "man is the measure of all things." Moreover, according to Epiphanius, Protagoras used to say that nei-ther the gods, nor any individual god, existed. Most were skeptics or agnostics, and Critias held that the gods were invented by a "very skilled" man—that is, an impostor—in order to guarantee the virtue of individuals through fear of punishment. For others, the gods were simply famous men of the past who had been deified. It was the sophist and mythographer Euhemerus (fourth-third century BCE) who, in his *Sacred Narrative*, pushed farthest the theory that now bears his name (euhemerism).

Epicurus (341-270 BCE) and his disciple Lucretius (c. 94-55 or 51 BCE) elaborated the most radical critique of religion, so that for future Christian theologians, atheism and Epicureanism would be closely linked. Epicurus affirmed that "the gods exist; the knowledge that we have of this is clear and evident," but this affirmation was purely formal. In his view, the gods, composed of subtle atoms, are absolutely indifferent to what happens in this world, which they did not create. They make no promises of either reward or punishment to men, whose soul, being material, ceases to exist at the moment of the body's death. There is no difference between this and atheism. For Epicurus, religious belief was based on fear. By playing on this feeling, priests maintained their imposture. Fear and ignorance, added Lucretius who, in his *De natura rerum [On the Nature of Things]*, furnished the first global explanation of the origin of religions: "Besides, whose mind does not shrink up with fear of the gods, whose limbs do not crawl with terror, when the scorched earth quakes with the shivering shock of a thunderbolt and rumblings run through the mighty sky? Do not nations and peoples tremble ...?"[12]

The Greco-Roman world thus elaborated a theory of religious imposture that contained all the classical elements of debunking: religions are human inventions that some skillful individuals use to manipulate the people by playing on their fear and ignorance. An authentic atheism was propagated at the heart of this society, denouncing every form of religion. Men like Theodorus of Cyrene and Diagoras the Atheist, in the fifth century BCE, openly expressed their lack of belief. Others would only admit it privately—like Bion of Borysthenes, who, when someone asked him if the gods existed, responded: "First, get rid of the crowd," or Stilpon, a friend of Diogenes, who chided: "Don't ask me that on a public street, you idiot, wait until we're alone."[13] As early as this, the authorities were already vigilant: religion was an essential pillar of the social order and of patriotism. There was fear that open disbelief might lead to chaos, and the organized repression of atheism began. Thus, at Athens, the decree of Diopeithes in 432 BCE provided for action against those who did not believe in the gods recognized by the city. The philosopher Anaxagoras became the first victim, for having dared to offer a scientific explanation of supposedly supernatural phenomena.

What was important was that the common people should believe. Greco-Roman intellectuals had greater freedom of opinion with regard to religion. Most were not duped. Cicero, in his *De natura deorum* [*On the Nature of the Gods*], revealed the variety of opinions on this subject, and this multiplicity was itself cause for skepticism: "Surely such wide diversity of opinion among men of the greatest learning on a matter of the highest moment must affect even those who think that they possess certain knowledge with a feeling of doubt."[14]

Celsus: Moses the Impostor

The Christian apologists were confident that pagan religions were impostures, and they glorified Theodorus of Cyrene for having rejected such fables. To Clement of Alexandria, for example, a devout pagan was an atheist twice over: both because he did not know the true God, and because he worshiped false ones. But for a long time suspicion weighed heavily on Moses as well. In his work *Against Apion*, written in the first century of our era, the historian Flavius Josephus related Hellenistic stories that spread the tradition of imposture of the famous founder of the Jewish religion. Supposedly, Moses had been initiated into the secrets of Egyptian magic, which enabled him to fool the people. According to the Egyptian priest Manetho, the pharaoh Amenhotep once wanted to see the gods; the priests allegedly told him that would only be possible after the expulsion of the lepers and all those who were impure. The pharaoh accordingly forced the lepers to work in the quarries, before establishing them at Avaris. With the aid of strangers, called "shepherds," they revolted under the command of a priest of Heliopolis, Osarsiph, who, after changing his name to Moses, used magic to impose a cruel religion, with a mighty god enacting terrible vengeance.[15]

The reputation of Moses as a magician-impostor was born in Hellenistic circles, possibly in reaction to the sectarian character of the Jewish communities of the Diaspora. These traditions were picked up in the second century by the philosopher Celsus, whose work

The True Doctrine, composed between 176 and 180, was an authentic treatise of religious imposture, aimed mainly at Moses and Jesus. The fanatical zeal of the Christians having succeeded in destroying all copies of his book, we know it only through the work of Origen, *Against Celsus*, compiled in 248, seventy years after *The True Doctrine*. This in itself tells us that Celsus' book was well enough known by that time to constitute a danger for Christians. Origen undertook to refute it, and to that end he cited entire passages, thereby making himself, despite himself, the propagator of the ideas he condemned.

Celsus presented Moses as the great impostor who borrowed all his knowledge from the pagans and who invented monotheism, which he taught to his ignorant compatriots: "The goatherds and shepherds who followed Moses as their leader were deluded by clumsy deceits into thinking that there was only one God." "They worship angels and are addicted to sorcery of which Moses was their teacher."[16] He made fanatics of them, and caused them to "swallow" old wives' tales: "that a man was formed by the hands of God and given breath, that a woman was formed out of his side, that God gave commands, and that a serpent opposed them and even proved superior to the ordinances of God—a legend which they expound to old women."[17]

Celsus and the Talmud: Jesus the Impostor

As for Jesus, Celsus made him a bastard, the son of a Roman soldier named Panther who applied to himself the prophecies of the Old Testament. Anyone so "inspired," he said, might have had the same pretensions. Here Celsus takes up in his turn the accusations that circulated among the Jews. This Jesus, "because of his simplicity and his utter and complete lack of culture, conquered only the simple." In fact, his "miracles" were only magic tricks learned in Egypt, and the Egyptian magicians were capable of doing just as much: "Since these men do these wonders, ought we to think them sons of God? Or ought we to say that they are the practices of wicked men possessed by an evil daemon?"[18]

"Jesus told great lies" and uttered many stupidities. "These were the actions of one hated by God and of a wicked sorcerer."[19] Christians characterized the Greek myths as impostures, but affirmed that their own myths were true. Why should anyone believe them?

"Many others of the same type as Jesus have appeared to people who are willing to be deceived." If the imposture of Jesus succeeded so well, it was because he addressed himself to the most ignorant: "Their injunctions are like this: 'Let no one educated, no one wise, no one sensible draw near. For these abilities are thought by us to be evils. But as for anyone ignorant, anyone stupid, anyone uneducated, anyone who is a child, let him come boldly.'"

The height of the imposture was this tale of resurrection: "While he was alive he did not help himself, but after death he rose again and showed the marks of his punishment and how his hands had been pierced. But who saw this? A hysterical female, as you say, and perhaps some other one of those who were deluded by the same sorcery, who either dreamed in a certain state of mind and through wishful thinking had a hallucination due to some mistaken notion (an experience which has happened to thousands), or, which is more likely, wanted to impress the others by telling this fantastic tale, and so by this cock-and-bull story to provide a chance for other beggars."[20]

Celsus was a redoubtable debater. If Jesus was not an impostor, said he, why this ambiguous attitude, these sibylline remarks, these affectations of mystery? "If he wanted to be unnoticed, why was the voice from heaven heard, proclaiming him as Son of God? Yet if he did not want to be unnoticed, why was he punished or why did he die?" Before being arrested, he preached publicly, without great success; and after his "resurrection," although such an exploit might have convinced the whole world, he hid himself, and "appeared secretly to just one woman and to those of his own confraternity." "If Jesus really wanted to show forth divine power, he ought to have appeared to the very men who treated him despitefully and to the man who condemned him and to everyone everywhere."[21] "But what messenger that has been sent ever hid himself when he ought to be delivering the message that he had been commanded to proclaim?"[22] "After his resurrection from the dead he ought to have called all men clearly to the light and taught them why he came down."[23] Instead of which, he hid himself and disappeared! This surely seems like a trap: "Or was his purpose in coming down that we might disbelieve?"[24] If he was really the son of God, he had every means to convince all men, instead of covering his tracks and speaking in riddles, as if he wanted men to damn themselves by not believing in him. Why work miracles publicly, and then hide the greatest miracle of all? At least, wrote Celsus, we find among the priests of Cybele, Mithra, Sabazios, and others an internal logic, while here they ask us to believe something absurd and then brag about it. "For just as among them scoundrels frequently take advantage of the lack of education of gullible people and lead them wherever they wish, so also . . . this happens among the Christians. . . . Some do not even want to give or to receive a reason for what they believe, and use such expressions as 'Do not ask questions; just believe,' and 'Thy faith will save thee.'"[25] And Origen agreed: it's true, we ask people to believe without understanding, which does a real service to those who don't have the time to seek to understand. "I have to reply that we accept it as useful for the multitude, and that we admittedly teach those who cannot abandon everything and pursue a study of rational argument to believe without thinking out their reasons."[26] For Celsus, in contrast, one must "follow reason and a rational guide in accepting doctrines . . . anyone who believes people without so doing is certain to be deceived."[27] In this case, "people" meant Moses and, above all, Jesus, clearly presented as impostors.

The same sentiments were expressed in the same period, the second half of the second century, by Lucian of Samosata, who laughed at all charlatans, false prophets, and their gods. His laughter was rueful, set off by the lamentable spectacle of "the immense stupidity of men," who let themselves be convinced by the first dreamer to come along. In his works *Sects at Auction*, *Hermotimus or the Sects*, *The Assembly of the Gods*, *Dialogues of the Gods*, and *Dionysus*, he ridiculed all the founders of philosophical schools and myths, starting with Homer, "that blind man, that charlatan who relates in detail what happens in heaven while he couldn't even see what was happening on earth." Christians received special treatment in his treatise *The Death of Peregrinus*, where Jesus was presented as "the man who was crucified in Palestine for introducing this new cult into the world," an impostor who seduced a band of naive folk and persuaded them "that they are immortal and will live forever." "Moreover, their first lawgiver taught them that they are all brothers of one another, when once they have sinned by denying the Greek gods, and by worshipping that crucified sophist himself and living according to his laws. . . . Accordingly, if any quack or trickster who can press his advantage comes among them, he can acquire great wealth in a very short time by imposing on simple-minded people" (*Death of Peregrinus*, 11-13;

English translation by C. D. N. Costa, *Lucian: Selected Dialogues*, Oxford
World's Classics [New York: Oxford University Press, 2005], 76–77).

Jesus the impostor is similarly the central theme of the work of
Julian the Apostate, *Against the Galileans*, composed in 362–363. This
emperor, who had been a Christian before returning to paganism,
believed that Christianity was actually atheism, because the disciples
of Christ betrayed the religion of Moses, which itself had betrayed
polytheism to spread fables of intolerance. Jesus knew how to exploit the attraction of the human mind for the irrational: "I allowed
myself to be convinced that the hoax of the Galileans is a human
fiction, motivated by malice; that it contains nothing divine, but has
turned to advantage the penchant for fables, the childish and non-
sensical side of the mind, in order to transform a fantastic tale into
a truthful testimony."[28]

Like Celsus' *True Doctrine*, Julian's *Against the Galileans* has totally
disappeared. But his treatise was sufficiently noteworthy that seventy
years later one of the fathers of the church, Cyril of Alexandria, felt
it necessary to compose a work *Against Julian*, in which he gave long
quotations from Julian's own treatise, thus helping to make known
Julian's ideas, just as Origen had done with those of Celsus.

The character of Jesus as an impostor was fashioned from the start
by rational, skeptical minds, as well as by the adherents of paganism.
It was equally diffused under the name of the defenders of another
religion, Judaism. For the Jews, in effect, this Jesus was a hateful mys-
tifier who betrayed the religion of Moses. While Christians venerate
Moses as a great prophet, the Jews reject Jesus as an impostor, a false
messiah. This accusation was formulated in the Talmud,[29] an encyclopedia of rabbinical knowledge compiled by the fifth century CE.

The Talmud avoids calling impieties by their name, so it is difficult to determine which passages really target Jesus. A number of
false messiahs and impostors are mentioned in passing, such as a
Ben Pantera and a Ben Stada, but the chronological and geographical indications one can glean from the text only rarely agree with the
texts of the Evangelists. For the Talmud itself, compiled in a Persian
cultural environment, Jesus is only one impostor among many, and
the most precise accusations are aimed at those among the Jews who
follow him. Only later, in the context of medieval Europe, were these
passages reinterpreted in an anti-Christian sense, especially by Jews
converted to Christianity, who manipulated talmudic citations in

order to persecute their former brothers. These accusations, which presented the Talmud as a blasphemous book and as the principal obstacle to the conversion of the Jews, gave rise to condemnations. In Paris in 1242, for example, "Saint" Louis (King Louis IX) caused cartloads of copies of the Talmud to be burned. When the papacy authorized (always on an exceptional basis) the printing of the Talmud, it did so on the explicit condition that all expressions that could be read, even distantly, as allusions to Jesus or to Christians be suppressed. Not until the end of the twentieth century did uncensored editions of the Talmud see the light of day.

The spectacle of the church's intolerance confirmed the Jewish communities in their vision of Jesus as a corrupting influence to be avoided. The allusions in the Talmud, along with a good dose of popular imaginings and borrowings from Celsus, were quickly assembled into a collection called *Sefer Toledot Yeshu [Book of the Life of Jesus]*. This text never became part of the canon of rabbinical writings, as it emerged from popular literature, with the whiff of scandal and secrecy appropriate to its theme, given the very real danger of condemnation by the ecclesiastical authorities. In the sixteenth century, Martin Luther amused himself by translating the *Toledot Yeshu* into German, in order to offer up the Jews to the vindictive Christian population.

In this work, Jesus was presented as the illegitimate son of the hairdresser Miriam of Bethlehem and the legionary Joseph Pandira, or Panthera. Ambitious, jealous, and violent, he made use of the sorcery he learned in Egypt to penetrate into the Temple of Jerusalem and gain access to its secrets, which permitted him to perform fake miracles and to fool the crowd. At his death, his body was stolen by the gardener, who buried it in his garden.[30]

But it was undoubtedly the philosopher and rabbi Maimonides, in the twelfth century, who expressed most clearly the theme of Christian imposture and its eschatological function:[31]

Jesus of Nazareth who aspired to be the Mashiach and was executed by the court was also alluded to in Daniel's prophecies, as *ibid.* 11:14 states: "The vulgar among your people shall exalt themselves in an attempt to fulfill the vision, but they shall stumble."

Can there be a greater stumbling block than Christianity? All the prophets spoke of Mashiach as the redeemer of Israel and their savior who would gather their dispersed and strengthen their observance of the mitzvot. In contrast, Christianity caused the Jews to be slain by the sword, their remnants to be scattered and humbled, the Torah to be altered, and the majority of the world to err and serve a god other than the Lord.

Nevertheless, the intent of the Creator of the world is not within the power of man to comprehend. . . . Ultimately, all the deeds of Jesus of Nazareth and that Ishmaelite who arose after him will only serve to prepare the way for Mashiach's coming and the improvement of the entire world, motivating the nations to serve God together. . . .

How will this come about? The entire world has already become filled with the mention of Mashiach, Torah, and mitzvot. These matters have been spread to the furthermost islands to many stubborn-hearted nations. They discuss these matters and the mitzvot of the Torah, saying: "These mitzvot were true, but were already negated in the present age and are not applicable for all time."

Others say: "Implied in the mitzvot are hidden concepts that can not be understood simply. The Mashiach has already come and revealed those hidden truths."

When the true Messianic king will arise and prove successful, his position becoming exalted and uplifted, they will all return and realize that their ancestors endowed them with a false heritage and their prophets and ancestors caused them to err.

From the birth of Christianity, and consistently thereafter, it is evident that for the Jews, Jesus was an impostor, a dissident who used magic and sorcery to pass himself off as the long-awaited messiah. This interpretation was well known at the time of Frederick II in the heterodox circles of the emperor's entourage.[32]

Mahomet the Impostor in Christian Literature (Ninth to Twelfth Centuries)

At the beginning of the seventh century, there arose out of the Arabian deserts another founder of a religion: Muhammad, or Mahomet.[33] The origins of Islam are much better known than those of Christianity, and, of course, than those of Judaism, which are lost in the mythical mists of antiquity. With Mahomet, the historical element of the character increases, although unfortunately there is still enough of the unknown for irrationality to rush in, especially because we have no independent source of information. The first biographies, those of Ibn Hishām, who died at Bassorah (modern Basra) in 834, and of Al-Bukhārī, who died in 870, were composed long after the events they recount, and are really works of hagiography.

From the start, many Arabs viewed Mahomet as an impostor. The Qur'ān alludes discreetly to the Prophet's credibility problems. Surah 53 finds a need to reaffirm: "Your companion [Muhammad] has not erred and has not gone astray; nor does he speak from desire. It is just an inspiration with which he is inspired: one strong in power taught him, one full of intelligence. . . . His mind did not imagine what he saw; and yet you argue with him over what he sees?" (English translation by Thomas Cleary, *The Qur'an: A New Translation* [Starlatch Press, 2004], 260–61).

For the Qur'ān, the impostors are evidently the adherents of the old polytheistic religion, while Moses and Jesus are considered authentic prophets. Moses, who receives divine revelations, is a guide and a legislator for the people, is cast out and sometimes misunderstood, and prefigures Mahomet's destiny. As for Jesus, the Qur'ān accords him a miraculous birth, an inimitable life, miracles—while Mahomet is not credited with any—but he remains a man. He is not considered as an impostor insofar as he did not present himself as the son of God, this blasphemy being, for the Qur'ān, the invention of the Christians.

For Christians, in return, Mahomet is the impostor par excellence. From the ninth century, theologians present an image of him whose extreme negativity mirrors the hagiography of the Muslim accounts. The West and the East were mutually ignorant of each other, with rumor, calumny, and malevolent imagination filling in for the absence of objective information. The Prophet was presented, in an ambiguous fashion, as at once a dangerous impostor and (from an apocalyptic perspective) an instrument of God to punish the sins of men. He was the Beast of the Book of Daniel, the precursor of the Antichrist.[34] Scandalized by his polygamy, Christian authors portrayed him as someone lewd and lustful whose doctrine was seductive because of the sexual license it permitted. The oldest Christian writings about Mahomet come from regions in contact with Muslim countries, but this proximity did not prevent them from demonstrating the extent of their ignorance about the Prophet.

The Crusades, beginning in the late eleventh century, contributed to blackening Mahomet's image in the West. In 1109 Guibert of Nogent wrote in his *Dei gesta per Francos [The Deeds of God through the Franks]*:

> Popular opinion has it that there was once a man whose name, if I formulate it correctly, was "Mahomet." He had completely turned the Orientals away from belief in the Son and the Holy Spirit; he taught that only the Father was God, the only and the creator; he used to say that Jesus Christ was a human being. To sum up his doctrine, after having instituted the practice of circumcision, he gave rein to all the shamelessness of men. In my opinion, this impious being lived not too long ago, but I have no other reason to believe it than the fact that I have never found anyone, among the doctors of the Church, who has written against his infamy. Since I have never seen a text to inform me about his ways or his life, no one should be surprised if I limit myself to reporting what I have heard tell of here or there by well-informed men.... One runs no risk of maligning a man whose wickedness far surpasses any evil one might speak of him.[35]

This is an astonishing text, which reveals the unbelievable ignorance of the Christians with regard to Mahomet, after a half-millennium of Islam! And it was written by a learned man. We can only imagine what must have been the awareness level of the average Crusader. However, the accusations of Guibert of Nogent correctly circumscribe the essential doctrinal differences: the Muslim rejects the Trinity and the divinity of Christ, and he permits greater sexual license for men. Guibert admits his ignorance concerning Mahomet, who, he says, can only be a heretic.

This image was refined over the course of the twelfth century, in a series of texts issuing from the Mozarabic environment of Toledo. In that Spanish city, cohabitation among Christians, Muslims, and Jews favored a better knowledge of rival faiths. This did not at all signify a spirit of goodwill and tolerance, as an idyllic view of the past might make one believe. The three communities lived separately, were suspicious of each other, and got along with some difficulty.

It was here, around 1109, that Petrus Alfonsi composed his *Dialogue against the Jews*, which included a chapter against Muslims. The Jew asks the Christian why he doesn't believe in Islam. He replies that it is because Mahomet "pretended to be a prophet, by a shameless imposture," in order to spread a "foolish doctrine."

The writings of Petrus Alfonsi were widely read in the West, where they contributed to the spread of the image of Mahomet the impostor. Up to the present, seventy manuscripts of the *Dialogue against the Jews* have been found. Humbert of Romans, in his *Treatise on Preaching the Crusade*, strongly recommended reading Petrus Alfonsi's work in order to better understand Islam.

From Peter the Venerable, the respected abbot of the famous French monastery of Cluny, one might have expected more reserve. Not so. After having read the treatises of Petrus Alfonsi, he went to Spain in 1142-1143 with a team of translators and then wrote two treatises against Islam: *Summa totius haeresis Saracenorum [Summation of the Entire Heresy of the Saracens]* and *Contra sectam sive haeresim Saracenorum [Against the Sect or Heresy of the Saracens]*. In these works he presented Mahomet as a poor illiterate manipulated by the devil, who made use of greed and violence to spread his foolishness. For him, Mahomet was above all a heretic, in the lineage of Arius, who denied the divinity of Christ.

The image of Mahomet in the medieval Christian imagination was thus multiform: a magician, a heretic, a morally corrupt person, an instrument of God or the devil, the Beast of the Apocalypse—in any case, an impostor who seduces the naive masses and leads them to hell.

Politico-Religious Imposture in the Middle Ages

In a general way, medieval Christians understood the idea of imposture. From the beginning of the Middle Ages, false messiahs had been periodically heralded and pitilessly executed. As early as the sixth century, Gregory of Tours mentioned several in his *Historia francorum [History of the Franks]*.

In his classic study of the phenomenon of false messiahs and false prophets, Norman Cohn outlined the general traits that explain their proliferation:[36] a time of frequent catastrophes, famines, and epidemics, which could appear to be divine punishments, exacerbating the apocalyptic expectations spread by some intellectuals, who interpret in their own way the twists and turns of the Book of Daniel or the Book of the Apocalypse. The excitement is brought to its peak by the start of the Crusades at the end of the eleventh century. The false messiahs have a minimum of culture and a great deal of charisma, which allows them to seduce the ignorant masses, living in an atmosphere full of superstition where profane and sacred, natural and supernatural currents mingle. Most of these characters are not, properly speaking, impostors, to the extent that they themselves believe in their role—rather, they are unbalanced individuals. But the clergy do not distinguish. People are all the more willing to believe because the phenomenon was announced by the scriptures: according to 1 Timothy 4:1-2 (*RSV*), "Now the Spirit expressly says that in later times some will depart from the faith by giving heed to deceitful spirits and doctrines of demons, through the pretensions of liars whose consciences are seared." The false messiahs, presented as agents of the devil, use the same texts to get back at the clergy, whom they accuse of betraying their mission. Thus everybody cooperates in accusing each other of imposture and maintaining a climate of generalized suspicion.

To religious imposture is added political imposture, which assumes new proportions in this same period,[37] facilitated by the so-called Prophecy of the Last Emperor. This prophecy originated in Greece, then passed to the West in the eighth century. It predicted the return of an emperor—Roman? Eastern? Western?—who would seize Jerusalem, banish the Antichrist, and inaugurate an era of prosperity. Some bold individuals were greatly tempted to insinuate themselves into the role of this character, especially in a climate of struggle between the emperor and the pope, starting in the eleventh century. For some, it would be Charlemagne, who would only be sleeping, not dead, in his tomb at Aix-la-Chapelle. But there were numerous interpretations of this myth. In the twelfth century, Emmerich, count of Leiningen, in the Rhine Valley, claimed to have received divine revelations and presented himself as the heralded "last emperor." He was killed in 1117. In 1224, the affair was more serious: a hermit from the area around Tournai claimed to be Emperor Baldwin IX, whom the Crusaders had set on the throne of Constantinople after the Crusade of 1204, and who had been killed by the

Bulgarians at Tsarevets. The impostor claimed that he had spent several years in the East. Some members of the nobility of Flanders and Hainaut granted him recognition. Supported by the textile workers, who were going through a difficult time, he was crowned at Valenciennes as emperor of Constantinople and Thessalonica, and Count of Flanders and Hainaut. Soon undone, he was arrested and hanged at Lille that October. But for seven months, the pseudo-Baldwin had managed to keep the north of France in suspense and to sow trouble in people's minds. In this case, the imposture was obvious. The fake emperor was a serf from Burgundy, Bertrand de Ray, who had taken part in the Fourth Crusade as the minstrel of a lord, and put to good use his exceptional gifts as an impersonator and a charlatan.

The myth of the last emperor did not die with Bertrand/Baldwin. In 1251, a defrocked monk named Jacob presented himself, bearing a letter from the Virgin Mary calling all shepherds to come together to help the king of France, Louis IX, to take Jerusalem. He was said to have come from Hungary, and soon he was venerated as a special envoy of God. The queen mother, Blanche of Castile, treated him with respect and offered him gifts. The troop of shepherds and herdsmen committed so many crimes that it was necessary to wipe them out; Jacob was drowned at Bordeaux, and his imposture was revealed. According to rumor, he was an agent of the sultan, sent to Europe to bring back to the East young people who would then have been reduced to slavery.

In the mid-thirteenth century, Christianity seems to have gone through a sort of psychosis of politico-religious imposture. This psychosis was fed by the proliferation of prophets announcing the coming of an extraordinary personage, who would accomplish God's plan as laid out, however enigmatically, in the Book of Apocalypse. These prophecies, extravagant and contradictory, opened the door to all those, enlightened or charlatans, who imagined themselves to be the long-awaited personage, or who took up the role consciously, in the knowledge that the public would be predisposed to follow them. The prophecies of Joachim of Fiore, the Calabrian hermit who died c. 1202, were especially prized. Claiming to have discovered the key to reading the Book of Apocalypse, he announced the approaching advent of the Age of the Holy Spirit, an era of happiness and love, succeeding the Age of the Father and the Age of the Son. A divine guide would initiate this happy period, but first, for three and a half years, the Antichrist would rule. Now there were two roles to fill: that of the good and that of the evil.[38]

In the first half of the thirteenth century, among members of the more excitable spiritual movements, the predictions of Joachim of Fiore began to mingle with those that concerned the last emperor. Everything now focused on the character of Frederick II. Some saw in him the emperor of the last days, the reincarnation of Barbarossa; for others, he was the guide, the herald of the Age of the Spirit; for still others, he was the Antichrist. The events of his reign nourished all these hypotheses: he recaptured Jerusalem; he was excommunicated as a blasphemer; he scolded corrupt priests and fought against the pope, who had betrayed his mission; he was cruel and pitiless. Was he good or evil? Who was the Beast, the Antichrist—the pope or the emperor? For German Joachimites, Frederick II was the savior; for Italian Joachimites, he was the Antichrist. And when he died brutally in 1250, rumors circulated: he had left secretly on pilgrimage, or he was merely sleeping; he would return, he would awaken. As early as 1262, a false Frederick attracted crowds on the slopes of Mount Etna. Other impostors appeared in the 1280s, at Worms, at Lübeck, in the Rhine Valley. Each time, it was the poor who were the faithful supporters of the pseudo-Frederick, in the hope of seeing the arrival of an era of abundance. Despite setbacks and executions, hope was renewed, as new impostors tried their chances.

In some sense, medieval civilization can be called a civilization of imposture, to the extent that the general belief in the permanent intervention of supernatural forces of good and evil made the world a shadow theater where everyone and everything could be suspected of being a diabolical illusion. Satan is the master of deceit, and his agents try to seduce men by presenting themselves under false identities. Any event even slightly out of the ordinary is susceptible of two contradictory interpretations: diabolical or divine. Every man who is too knowledgeable, too good-looking, too strong, too persuasive— or too evil, too cruel, or too ugly—has to be something other than what he appears to be. And since the criteria for deciphering were themselves enigmatic, opinions varied, oscillating from utter credulity to extreme mistrust. It was this coexistence of two diametrically opposed attitudes that allowed imposture to proliferate.

This cultural situation was grafted onto a receptive combination of social circumstances. Social unrest in the urban environments that were undergoing change in the thirteenth century, along with the periodic return of crises that plunged the lower classes into misery, favored the emergence of charismatic leaders who claimed to have been inspired directly by heaven to reestablish justice. These bold individuals, in a world that did not separate the profane and the sacred, were at one and the same time political revolutionaries and messianic founders of sects. To challenge the established social order was simultaneously to challenge established religion, the church being the sole guarantor of an order commanded by God. In the eyes of the authorities, every political impostor was also a religious impostor.

The Arabic Origins of the Theme of the Three Impostors (Tenth Century)

The novelty, in any case, is that the idea of imposture began to contaminate the very origins of religion. The drift was inevitable. In the context of a civilization that has reached an equilibrium and has achieved a broad consensus with regard to its fundamental values and beliefs, innovators and heretics are branded as impostors, just like the founders, whether mythical or historical, of the competing great religions. For the Christian intellectual of the thirteenth century, it was evident that Zalmoxis, Numa Pompilius, and Mahomet were impostors; for the Jew, Jesus was an impostor. The Muslim was less categorical, because he considered Moses and Jesus as prophets, preferring to accuse Christians and Jews of having falsified the scriptures and betrayed the message of the prophets—which is another form of imposture, this one collective. If Moses was thus relatively spared, because all three religions venerated him, Jesus and Mahomet, in contrast, were each the object of accusations of imposture on the part of the other two groups. Mahomet was the most often targeted, since Jesus had gained a special intermediate status among the Muslims. But these controversies and anathemas inevitably led some individuals to cast doubt on *all* the founders of religions, speaking in terms of religious imposture in general. This blasphemous extremism was still in the process of gestation among some particularly bold thinkers. But the idea saw the light of day, and the accusation made by Pope Gregory IX in 1239 was the proof:

for some, Moses, Jesus, and Mahomet were three impostors, and if these three were impostors, then it was evident that *all* founders of religions were impostors. To reject this "trinity of lies" was to reject all religion—that is, to establish atheism.

Was this still a specter that existed only in the minds of horrified believers, or were there truly men willing to uphold this blasphemy, as the pope believed? The origins of the idea of radical religious imposture are obscure. Obviously, its defenders, if any existed in the Middle Ages, could not proclaim it openly, no matter what their environment—Jewish, Christian, or Muslim. They expressed themselves only by the indirect means of the dialogue, the absurd hypothesis, or fiction—which makes the interpretation of their personal thoughts very problematic.

We seem to uncover the first traces of it in the Arab-Muslim milieu. Arabic philosophy, from its origins, was strongly influenced by Neoplatonism and by a current of thought, widespread in the East, called "the metaphysics of light,"[39] which envisioned the presence of the divine spirit in the world as the radiation of a light that, in traveling farther from its source, grows dimmer little by little. This was a form of pantheism: God is present in all things, and each person can know him through meditation; there is no need for the prophet or messiah who would come to reveal the word of God to man. God is far away and diffuse, beyond reach of any intermediary. For Islam, in contrast, divine revelation was concentrated on a few historical characters, of whom the last and greatest was Mahomet, the indispensable intermediary. Philosophers were thus regarded with mistrust in the Muslim world as early as the ninth century, and closely reasoned discussions took place at Baghdad in this period and the next century, between Christians, Jews, Arab philosophers, and Muslims— "a kind of philosophical conference, in which even atheists participated,"[40] according to one of the most knowledgeable scholars of medieval philosophy, Émile Bréhier. To deny prophets their capacity as privileged intermediaries with God is to make them, in some sense, impostors.

Some even say it explicitly. This is the case with the Karmate movement and its principal representative, Abū Ṭāhir al-Djannābī, born in 907. The Karmates were a dissident sect, an outgrowth of the Ismaelians, themselves an esoteric branch of Shi'ism. Their beliefs were a mixture of Manichaeism, Neoplatonism, gnosticism, esoterism, and savage opposition to existing religions. They preached the doctrine of communally held goods and the subversion of Muslim society, and rejected the founders of the great religions as impostors. An initiatory text, sent toward the middle of the tenth century to Abū Ṭāhir, and published in 1920 by Louis Massignon, showed how to refute Moses, Jesus, and Mahomet by making use of their contradictions.[41] Some think that on this point the Karmates were inspired by Mandaeism—another sect, this one deriving from Judaism and Christianity, that considered Jesus as a false prophet. A second text, likewise published by Massignon, is even more explicit. Composed around 1070, it reports the following proposition, attributed to Abū Ṭāhir: "In this world three individuals have corrupted men: a shepherd [Moses], a doctor [Jesus], and a camel-driver [Mahomet]. And this camel-driver was the worst conjuror, the worst magician of the three." Here we have, chronologically, the first expression of the theme of the three impostors. And this is indeed how Massignon interprets it: "This is the very basis of the legend of the three impostors, fixed in place toward 1080 at the latest, at least one hundred fifty years before its appearance in Western Christianity." In fact, if this is indeed a statement of Abū Ṭāhir, then the idea goes back to around 950.

Certain Arab-Muslim philosophers show evidence of an absolute relativism, which is not far from invoking the idea of the triple imposture, such as Abu 'l-ʿAlāʿ al-Maʿarrī, who wrote: "The Christians take a wrong turn here and there, and the Muslims have lost their way altogether; the Jews are no more than mummies, and the Persian wise men are dreamers." Or again: "Jesus came, and abolished the law of Moses; Mahomet followed him, and introduced the five daily prayers. Tell me now, since you live under one of these laws, do you enjoy more or less of the sun and the moon?"[42]

The historian Ibn al-Athir (1160-1233) told how the founder of the Almohad dynasty, Ibn Tūmart, had men hidden in a well, pretending that they were divine spirits whom he consulted and who sanctioned his deeds. Later, he had the well covered over, burying the men alive, in order that no one might discover his subterfuge.[43] This story, which exists in several versions, was put down to the black legend of Mahomet, who was said to have had recourse to the same procedure, as we shall see abundantly in what follows.

But the name that comes up most often in research on the origin of the three impostors is that of Ibn Rushd (Averroes, 1126–1198), the Muslim philosopher of Córdoba, translator, commentator, and disciple of Aristotle: "This great man, who had no religion, used to say that he preferred that his soul should be with the philosophers than with the Christians. Averroes called the Christian religion impossible because of the mystery of the Eucharist. He called that of the Jews a religion of children, because of the various precepts and legal obligations. He admitted that the religion of the Muslims, which looks only to the satisfaction of the senses, was a religion of swine."[44] Thus spoke Giles of Rome, in the thirteenth century. In reality, as Ernest Renan showed in 1852, we need to distinguish Averroes from Averroism. The philosopher Averroes, a savage defender of Aristotle, undertook to justify the philosophers, such as Al-Farabi and Avicenna, in the face of the attacks of the theologians, such as Al-Ghazali. This led him to uphold, following Aristotle, the eternity of the world, the impossibility of God knowing the particular, and the improbability of the resurrection of the body—all this with many nuances of meaning.[45] This sufficed to carve out for him a reputation for disbelief, and to make him a convenient scarecrow to whom one might attribute the origin of the most subversive ideas: "Each one glossed in his own manner, and attributed to Averroes what he did not dare to say in his own name," wrote Renan. Notably, they put on his shoulders the thesis of the "double truth," which consisted of saying "that certain things are true according to philosophy, which are not true according to the Catholic faith, as if there were two contrary truths, as if the truth of the Holy Scriptures could be contradicted by the truth of the texts of those pagans whom God had damned," wrote the bishop of Paris, Étienne Tempier, in 1277. Averroes had said nothing of the sort, but rather had attempted to reconcile faith and reason. This was a dangerous exercise that permitted him to be interpreted in two different directions. Reformist Muslims saw in him the defender of a rational Islamic religion, an agent of social emancipation; the materialist thinkers made him a champion of rationalism, of freethinking, against the fanaticism of the religious. This was the case with the Syrian Marxist Tayyib Tizini.[46]

Averroes had written that "the revealed religions, Jewish, Christian, Islamic, contain no truth unprovable by philosophical reasoning, but only the symbols of the highest truths," a statement that, far from separating faith and reason, instead associates them. But Averroism is a construction of the thirteenth century, the work of Christian theologians who found in Averroes an ideal scapegoat: the infidel Muslim could freely be charged with all sorts of crimes, and notably with the paternity of the three impostors. Giles of Rome was the one mainly responsible for this reputation, writing that Averroes "criticizes the law of the Christians and that of the Saracens, because they allow for creation *ex nihilo* … and what is worse, he calls us—us and all those who advocate for a religion—talkers, chatterers, people deprived of reason. In the eighth book of the *Physics*, he again criticizes religions and calls the opinions of the theologians fantasies, as they conceived them by caprice and not through reason."[47] Raymond Lull, Duns Scotus, and Nicolás Eymeric drove the nail in further. Jean Gerson, toward 1400, openly attributed the idea of the three impostors to "this cursed man, this mad dog, this most bitter enemy of the Christians."[48] Benvenuto da Imola, commenting on the fourth canto of Dante's *Inferno*, was surprised that Dante showed himself so indulgent in his regard, because Averroes was a notoriously impious man who not only treated Moses, Jesus, and Mahomet as impostors, but moreover said that Jesus was the lowest of the three, because he died on the cross. Petrarch has no words harsh enough to stigmatize the Latin Averroists, those atheists who "despise everything that conforms to the Catholic religion." They are libertines, hypocrites who "when there is no threat of punishment, and there are no witnesses, … attack the truth and piety, and in their private dens they secretly mock Christ. They worship Aristotle, whom they don't understand."[49] Even painters got into the act: at the Campo Santo in Pisa, in 1335, Andrea Orcagna placed Averroes in hell with Mahomet and the Antichrist. Francesco Traini and Agnolo Gaddi followed suit.

In the Jewish world, one philosopher was equally suspect: Moses Maimonides, a contemporary and compatriot of Averroes, who was born at Córdoba in 1135 and died in Egypt in 1204. He also used philosophy in the service of faith: "The science of the law is something apart, and philosophy is something apart; the latter consists of confirming the truths of the law by means of true speculation." This approach had some major problems, such as that of the eternity of the world, presupposed by the philosophers contrary to the teaching of Genesis. Maimonides was rather embarrassed by this question, and his rabbinic contemporaries were distrustful of him. His name has occasionally been advanced, although completely erroneously, as one of the upholders of the triple imposture.

The First Mention in Christianity (Twelfth Century)

In Christianity, until the thirteenth century, we find few traces of this blasphemy. However, slightly unorthodox echoes reach us from the twelfth century, despite the efforts of the church to wipe out all trace of blasphemous propositions. These rumors came from student circles, especially the famous Goliards, which historiography has had difficulty pinning down: wanderers, no doubt, cultivated or semicultivated, using Latin, sometimes also described as minstrels, buffoons, dissolutes, or vagabonds. They formed gangs, they were troublemakers; their name comes from the Latin *gula*, "throat," meaning "noisy." In their songs, collected under the title *Carmina burana*, they attacked the religious authorities, castigating their vices, their greed, their incontinence, in an openly obscene way, and they espoused blasphemous propositions that, if taken literally, reveal a true atheism: "The soul is mortal, I care only for my body!" I am "more greedy for passion than for eternal salvation." "I want to die in a tavern, where wine is close to the mouth of the dying man." Are these no more than the words of drunkards? There is no way to know. The multitude of condemnations concerning them shows in any case that they were considered a dangerous element that could not be ignored. Honorious of Autun called them "ministers of Satan" and denied them any hope of salvation.[50] For these young challengers of the status quo, all religions were impostures.

The professors, however, could not allow themselves such deviations. This did not prevent them from showing considerable intellectual audacity, in the course of the exercises in formal argumentation and rhetoric called *disputationes*. The *disputatio* involved presenting both the pros and the cons of an idea or a hypothesis, before offering the solution. Certain professors, like Peter Abelard, excelled in these highly esteemed exercises in which dialectic ruled. To be sure, the orthodox, official truth always won, but the search for contrary arguments and their public airing could lead on the unsure, and might give rise to doubt, because the subjects of debate included the thorniest propositions, such as "the world is eternal," "the soul is mortal," or even "God does not exist." Some professors made use of this in order to adopt an ambiguous attitude, which led, in the thirteenth century, to what has been called the "double truth." This in turn led to nominalism, the separation of reason and faith, whereby it was legitimate to uphold according to reason a proposition that was insupportable according to faith.

These propositions were difficult to condemn, because they were presented purely as exercises in dialectic. In the twelfth century, a professor in Paris suggested disputing the following thesis: Moses, Jesus, and Mahomet are three impostors, each of whom seduced the people. This professor was Simon of Tournai, born c. 1130, who taught at Paris from 1165. He was well known for the dialectical virtuosity of his *disputationes*,[51] which had earned him a sulfurous reputation. The chronicler Matthew Paris, in the thirteenth century, reported that he flattered himself that he, like the sophists, was capable of proving everything and its contrary. After a beautiful discourse on the truth of the Christian religion, he is supposed to have said, "O little Jesus, little Jesus, how I have lifted up your law! If I wanted to, I could tear it down even better." His contemporary Thomas of Cantimpré reported the episode concerning the three impostors: "Master Simon of Tournai was a regent of theology at Paris, and was excellent in his time; but—something very inappropriate to his office—he was intemperate and proud. And because he had more students than all the other doctors of Paris, and having made a disputation in the school, he publicly addressed the question of the humility of the very high doctrine of Christ, and finally, going beyond the bounds of acceptability, he began to presumptuously utter hateful blasphemies against Jesus Christ. . . . Those who have subjugated the world by their sects and teaching are, he said, three: that is, Moses, Jesus Christ, and Mahomet. First Moses made the Jewish people mad; second, Jesus Christ with the Christians; third, Mahomet with the gentile people."[52]

Here we have the first mention in the West of the theme of the three impostors, which had already been circulating in the Muslim world for two centuries. From this point on, it would appear as the prototypical blasphemy, a total negation of all divine revelation. To put the three prophets on the same level, and to envelop them in the same condemnation as a lie, a deception, and an imposture, was in fact to denounce the religious phenomenon in itself. If one rejected the Old Testament, the New Testament, and the Qur'ān, the three sacred books of the three monotheistic religions, what faith could one fall back on? Pagan polytheisms had long since been reduced to the status of improbable stories; all that remained was pantheism and atheism. But didn't both simply affirm that only the world of the senses exists? Whether or not it is inhabited by some divine spirit that in any case does not communicate with man was not a fundamental difference. The world is eternal, the death of individuals is total, and there is no hell or paradise: such were the implications of the thesis of the three impostors. This radical challenge to the three great religions of the Book could rightly be called atheistic. And it was so called, by Jews, by Christians, and by Muslims. Their position was uncomfortable, for while each religion admitted the imposture of the two others, it refused to acknowledge it for itself, which made them the sport of atheists.

The accusation of the triple imposture thus was known from the twelfth century. It was in the Christian world that it would achieve the greatest success. There are two basic reasons for this. One concerns the nature of the dominant religion. Official Christianity had always proclaimed the necessary alliance of reason and faith, despite the existence of fundamentalist currents. Thus it had a need to consolidate faith through proofs, or at least convincing signs. This made it more vulnerable than Judaism or Islam, which considered the existence of God as evident, something that went without saying and which it was not even useful to discuss or seek to prove. In these conditions, there was no need at all to try to refute the accusation of imposture; it was considered a gratuitous insult, arising from insane or demonic provocation. Thus they did not allow themselves to be drawn into the controversy. Christians, in contrast, wanted to prove something.

There is another reason for the diffusion of this theme in Christianity: it is manipulated by the adversaries, as well as the defenders, of the church. On both sides, it is an offensive weapon. The former use it to attack religion, and the latter to attack the heterodox by accusing them of upholding the idea of the three impostors, or even of being the authors of a treatise bearing this title. The accusation of Gregory IX against Frederick II in 1239 marked the beginning of the trial. It was indeed the pope who started it, and it was he who let loose the idea of the three impostors. If he had not mentioned this theme in his attack on the emperor, perhaps it would never have known the diffusion that it achieved. From 1239 on, the accusation became ritual: as soon as a thinker became dangerous, he was suspected of having written a treatise of the three impostors. The rumor was circulated in order to discredit him, and thus the church itself maintained the myth and nourished a serpent. The church made use of the specter, until the day when it would become flesh. Until the beginning of the eighteenth century, the *Treatise of the Three Impostors* was a phantom treatise that escaped all efforts to research it. Did it really exist? Repeatedly, people would think they were on the point of uncovering it, of knowing who was the author, and each time it was only an illusion. It was an effective scarecrow, because its title alone created fear. One did not have to read it to be horrified; merely mentioning it sufficed. *De tribus impostoribus*—because, of course, it was supposed to be in Latin, like all philosophical and religious literature. But even if the title carried the full ideological weight, people were curious to know the contents: what revelation would it contain? what arguments might it develop? The church tracked it to destroy it, while heretics and atheists chased after it to read and make use of it, and still others sought it out of simple curiosity. Every time hope was dashed, curiosity grew.

In the mid-thirteenth century, the hunt for *De tribus impostoribus* began.

The Hunt for the Author of a Mythical Treatise (Fourteenth to Sixteenth Centuries)

The last centuries of the Middle Ages, from 1300 to around 1500, were a period of intense religious fermentation. In addition to repeated catastrophes, including famine, the Black Death, and the Hundred Years' War, there were the internal problems of the church—the Great Schism, conciliary crises, and the growing Turkish threat. Everything combined to create an apocalyptic climate that favored prophetic ravings and the appearance of saviors, messiahs, Antichrists, and false prophets of every stripe. In the general confusion, the boundary between true and false, divine and diabolical, became blurred. Superstitions, irrational fears, and credulity encouraged deceptions of all kinds, to the point that one might speak of these two centuries as a veritable "culture of imposture."[1]

A Culture of Imposture

Impostors were everywhere: a false Baldwin IX, a false Alfonso I, a false Frederick II, a false Henry V, a false Conradin, a false Edward II, a false Richard II, a false Valdemar II, a false Warwick, a false York, a false Joan of Arc, false popes, and even a false female Pope Joan. It was in the fourteenth century that the word *impostor*, used in the chronicles of the *Continuation of Martin of Cologne* and of the *Continuation of Guillaume de Nangis*, came into use at the expense of its less inflammatory predecessors: *trufator* (faker), *falsidicus* (liar), *tricator* (trickster), *seductor* (seducer). This is an indication both of the growing diabolization of the idea of imposture, and of the growth of belief in sorcery. All these impostors were agents of the devil, sent to sow chaos and confusion in the world.

At the same time, imposture became a political weapon, intentionally manipulated by certain parties. "The ranks of active or passive partisans of factitious kings are composed essentially of hardened cynics or victims of a shared illusion," writes Gilles Lecuppre.[2] This fact is of capital importance, because it helped spread the idea of the association of political and religious imposture, with founders of religious movements being viewed as calculating men whose teachings were rooted in a divine "revelation" in order to confer upon them the force and prestige of the sacred. The great politicoreligious impostures multiplied and made the notion of the impostor commonplace. Thus, the number of false Frederick IIs increased. In 1368, Konrad Schmid, in Thuringia, claiming to be the resuscitated emperor, found enough credulous folk to form a community of flagellants, inspired by a millenarian spirit. Others came along in the fifteenth century. Among the most successful impostures were those of Hans Böhm, in 1476, at Niklashausen, near Würzburg. Manipulated by a hermit, this young shepherd, armed with a drum, began to preach: the Virgin Mary appeared to him and told him that Niklashausen would be the New Jerusalem, and that it was necessary to come there on pilgrimage, if possible with offerings. Later he conceived a hatred of the wealth of the clergy and announced an egalitarian society. The faithful flocked toward the "holy boy" right up to the moment when the bishop of Würzburg had him arrested and burned.

This was only one example among dozens. False messiahs and false prophets rose up almost everywhere; some were unbalanced, some inspired and convinced of their mission, others authentic charlatans profiting from the credulity of the people and the climate of eschatological suspense; still others were instruments manipulated by the politicians, such as the shepherd of Gévaudan used by the lieutenants of Charles VII as a substitute for Joan of Arc. Joan herself, classed among the impostors by the ecclesiastical tribunal that condemned her, had imitators of her own, such as Pierrone la Bretonne or Jeanne des Armoises. Pseudo-Antichrists roamed the countryside; in the 1490s Savonarola, an especially erratic monk, announced the coming of an "angelic pastor" to Florence, before he ended up on the stake. In the sixteenth century, the movement was particularly active in Germany and the Low Countries. In 1524–1525, Thomas Müntzer and the "prophets of Zwickau" stirred up Saxony, Thuringia, and Bohemia with their talk of an Edenic communism, before being slaughtered. In 1530, the messiah Hans Hut was beheaded at Stuttgart; according to him, his predecessor Jesus was only an ordinary man. The same year, Augustin Bader and his band were arrested. Bader in some ways played the role of Joseph; his son, born in 1529, was the Christ who would rule for a thousand years. In prison, he demanded that they not execute him before Pentecost, the day when the truth would be made clear. The authorities did not grant him this favor, and he was put to death on March 30. Another fanatic, a furrier of Schwäbisch Hall, Melchior Hofmann, announced the return of Christ for 1533, then for 1535, then 1539, and finally died in prison in 1543. At Münster, at the same time, Bernard Rothmann foretold the imminent coming of God and worked out an extravagant psychodrama mingling David, Goliath, Abel, Cain, Gog, and Magog. In the same city, Jean de Leyde and Jean Matthys in 1534 presented themselves as Enoch and Elias. Jean de Leyde, a tailor's apprentice, a smooth talker, an excellent actor, a megalomaniac, and a schizophrenic, proclaimed himself prophet and king over all the earth. Seated on a throne, adorned with jewels, wearing two crowns, holding a globe with two swords, the king of the entire world imposed his law at Münster, before ending up like the others, captured, tortured, and executed.[3]

The multiplication of impostors tended to generalize the idea of imposture, to make it commonplace, and to make people's minds receptive to rumors of trickery. If Jean de Leyde and the others were impostors, why not Jesus, Moses, and Mahomet also? The message of Jesus was the same as that of his imitators, and he ended up like them, executed. Historians are beginning to discover, in the surviving judicial archives of the late Middle Ages, numerous traces of popular skepticism, carefully hidden by the official history controlled for a long time by the clergy. Thus, the British historian John Thomson cites several cases in the fifteenth century: in September 1422, a man was tried at Worcester for having denied the resurrection of the dead. In the same city, in 1448, a certain Thomas Semer denied the divinity of Christ, the existence of heaven and hell, the immortality of the soul, the Trinity, and the divine character of scripture. In 1491, a fuller was tried at Newbury for thinking that the soul dies at the same time as the body, as a flame is extinguished when blown out. In 1499, at Salisbury, four men and one woman admitted that they went to Mass only out of fear of others and to escape the dangers that would threaten them if they failed to do like others. How many may have done the same? In 1502, authorities tried a man at Windsor who did not believe in the resurrection, and in 1508, a woman of Aldermanbury for the same reason. In 1493, a woman of London declared that she had her paradise in this life, and that she had nothing to do with a paradise in the other world.[4]

The importance of popular skepticism in England at the end of the Middle Ages was confirmed by G. G. Coulton[5] and by Keith Thomas, who stated in his now classic work, *Religion and the Decline of Magic*: "A wide range of popular scepticism was uncovered by the fifteenth century church courts. Much of it has been wrongly bracketed by historians under the general title of 'Lollardy.' But it was not Wycliffite or proto-Protestant theology which underlay this reluctance to accept some of the most elementary doctrines of Christianity.... [T]he actual volume of disbelief may have been much greater than that which the surviving evidence indicates."[6]

The same finding could be made in France, where sermons denounced the presence among the people of several categories of strong-minded and argumentative individuals. In 1486, at Troyes, a preacher distinguished four categories of "believers," the last of which seems very close to atheism in practice: they "believe not by reason nor by experience nor by sentiment but by custom, and they do not think or understand anything with regard to the things presented to them. And they are very far from the faith of the Christians."[7] Around the same time, a preacher of Auxerre mentioned the presence of skeptics whose doubts appeared to go very far indeed:

> They wish to experience their faith and do not want to rest content with the word of God. And when you speak to them of God and of his Paradise and of his judgments, they respond: "And who was it who returned from the dead? And who was it who came down from Heaven? There is only being. One knows very well where one is, but one does not know where one is going and what will become of one." ... They wish to have signs and miracles from God, neither his passion nor his resurrection suffices for them, and they have no more faith than devils.[8]

The preacher also noted that the conformity of many people served to conceal unbelief and atheism: "There are plenty who, whatever foolishness they commit, have not a drop of faith in them and all

of whom are depraved and outcasts." The same observations were
made by a preacher of Bayeux. "We want proof": this demand sums
up the recriminations of these skeptics. In short, the troubled times
gave rise to a growing number of doubters whose minds were receptive to the thesis of the three impostors.

The Rumors of the Late Middle Ages

From this point on, the thesis of the three impostors was openly
spread by a few daring intellectuals, while others were accused of
this blasphemy for having adopted positions that were suspect. All
of this contributed to the spread of the theme. In 1335, the theologian Alvaro Pelayo, in his *Collyrium fidei adversus haereses [Dose of
Faith against Heresies]*, an inventory of known heresies, mentioned
a certain Thomas Scoto, a Dominican and then Franciscan friar
teaching in the school of the decretalists in Lisbon at the beginning
of the fourteenth century; Scoto was said to have taught that three
impostors had fooled the world, Moses, Jesus, and Mahomet. To this
he added that souls are mortal, that the Virgin was not a virgin, that
there were men before Adam, that Jesus had lived with prostitutes
and been hanged for his sins, that his miracles were magic tricks,
that Aristotle was worth more than Moses, and other blasphemies.
The inquisitor Pelayo had Scoto arrested, and no doubt he ended up
being burned to death.[9] In 1459, still in Lisbon, Alphonso de Spina,
in his *Fortalitium fidei [Armor of Faith]*, declared that the doctor Alvarao Fernandez had denounced to the Inquisition one Diego Gomez,
a young unmarried man, who "had spoken to him of a Hebrew book,
in which, among other libertine and impious matters, we find that
the three principal religions are no more than vagaries of the human spirit; they teach only fables so puerile and ridiculous that it
was surprising that people should believe such foolishness; that a
saturnine spirit, evoked by the effusion of his blood that Abraham
had caused in his circumcision, presided over the Mosaic religion,
just as Mercury presided over the Christian religion, and Mars over
the Mahometan religion."[10] The same year, at Rome, a doctor in
canon law, one Javinus de Solcia, was condemned by the pope for
having declared that "Moses, Jesus, and Mahomet had governed the
world according to their fantasy."[11]
Some folk did not hesitate to own the theme of the three impos-

tors. Others were suspected, and the religious authorities sometimes attributed to them the paternity of the *De tribus*. Among the suspects was Giovanni Boccaccio, of whom Prosper Marchand wrote in his *Dictionnaire historique [Historical Dictionary]* of 1758: "As for religion, I believe that Boccaccio had none, and that he was a perfect atheist, which can be demonstrated by some chapters of his *Decameron*, especially that in which there is mention of a diamond that a father of a family left to his three sons."[12] Marchand is speaking of the famous story of the three rings, which Boccaccio relates in the third story of the first day of the *Decameron*: Saladin, representing Islam, asks the Jew Melchisedech: "I would gladly know of thee, which of the three laws thou reputest the true law, the law of the Jews, the law of the Saracens, or the law of the Christians?" The Jew responds with a parable, that of the father who had three sons, of equal merit, and who declared that his heir would be the one to whom he gave a very beautiful family ring that had been handed down from father to son. But because he loved his three children equally, he had two copies made, and he secretly gave a ring to each one. That way, no one could judge among them. The conclusion is quite daring: "And so, my lord, to your question, touching the three laws given to the three peoples by God the Father, I answer: Each of these peoples deems itself to have the true inheritance, the true law, the true commandments of God; but which of them is justified in so believing, is a question which, like that of the rings, remains pendent" (English translation by J. M. Rigg, 1903). This puts all three religions on the same plane. Not to know which holds the truth is to suspect each of the three of imposture. The story is all the more suspect because it comes from *Il novellino*, a work compiled in the thirteenth century at the court of Emperor Frederick II.

But that's not all. In his *De genealogia deorum [Genealogies of the Gods]* (about 1360), Boccaccio, taking up once again the idea of Euhemerus, showed how the ancient gods were only the result of the deification of heroes or the personification of physical phenomena. He pushed his audacity so far as to suggest that the first Christians had begun to do the same thing with Paul and Barnabas. His *Decameron* presented an image of Christian society that was scarcely flattering, characterized by breathtaking credulity, for example, in matters of the cult of saints and their relics. In the tenth tale of the sixth day, a friar convinces "the simple folk that were in the church" that he is going to show them a feather of the archangel Gabriel, and in another case he has the coals on which Saint Lawrence was roasted, not to mention a finger of the Holy Spirit, a fingernail of one of the cherubim, or a phial of the sweat of Saint Michael.

In the fifteenth century another suspect, according to Prosper Marchand, was Poggio Bracciolini (1380–1459). A Florentine humanist, apostolic secretary, and a churchman who fathered fourteen children, he mistreated monks in his *Facetiae*, translated Lucian, made fun of the credulity of believers, and praised Pierre des Vignes as a "man full of knowledge and skill." This was enough for him to be suspected, if not of having written *De tribus*, at least of having spread its ideas.

The church was quick to mistrust any hint of relations among religions. Simply to compare religions was suspect: one does not compare incomparables. To compare is to bring together, to suggest points in common, and that was intolerable. This is why all ecumenical or peace-loving people who dreamed of a reconciliation or at least a simple rapprochement among the three monotheistic religions were looked on with suspicion, even cardinals of the church such as Pierre d'Ailly, the fifteenth-century author of the treatise *On the Three Sects*, or Nicholas of Cusa, whose *De pace fidei [On the Peace of Faith]* of 1453 evoked a concord among the three religions under the aegis of Abraham, the common ancestor. In his *De cribatione Alcorani [Sifting the Qur'ān]*, he listed common points between Islam and Christianity. Before him, Raymond Lull (c. 1232–1315) had crisscrossed the Muslim world in the hope of converting it. These were misguided attempts, severely criticized, just like the attitude of the King of Castile Alfonso X the Wise (1221–1284), who surrounded himself with Arab, Christian, and Jewish scholars, with whose help he produced his famous astronomical treatise, the *Alfonsine Tables*. Settled at Toledo, he nicknamed himself the "emperor of the three religions," which unfortunately recalled the cosmopolitanism of Frederick II and gave rise to rumors concerning his relations with the idea of the three impostors. A famous anecdote, reported by Sanctius, illustrated the bad reputation of the sovereign: "The king often repeated the blasphemy that, if he had been present with God at the creation of man, some things would have been better ordered than they were."

Among the Christians, the tendency was rather toward the growing diabolization of Mahomet, the Qur'ān, and Islam. Ricoldo Pennini composed a new *Confutatio alcorani [Refutation of the Qur'ān]*, while Dante placed Mahomet in the depths of his hell, the body open "from the neck to the ass" with all the organs hanging out, intestines and excrement between the legs. He is there in his role as a schismatic—that is, as the divider of the unity of believers, inspired by Satan.[13] In the sixteenth century, Luis de Camões (c. 1524-1580), in his *Lusiads*, presented Mahomet as the incarnation of the devil, who manifests himself to an imam to push him against the Portuguese; he then assimilates him to Bacchus. The German Salomon Schweigger, a Lutheran who stayed in Constantinople from 1578 to 1581, was the first translator into German of the Qur'ān, under the title *Al-Koranum Mahumedanum: Das Ist, Der Türcken Religion, Gesetz, und Gotteslästerliche Lehr [The Muslim Qur'ān, Or, The Turks, Their Religion and Superstition]*. For Schweigger, Mahomet was an agent of the devil.[14]

Any attempt at rapprochement between Mahomet and Jesus was considered an unspeakable blasphemy, and responsibility for the theme of the three impostors was thrown back on the Muslim world, particularly on Averroes, as Renan showed in his 1852 study:

> It is not without reason that opinion charged Averroes with the term "the three impostors." It was by their claimed impossibilities, and not by their common divine origin, that one brought together the various cults in this period. This thought, which haunted the thirteenth century like a bad dream, was the fruit of Arabic studies and the result of the spirit of the court of the Hohenstaufen. It hatched in anonymity, with no one daring to admit to it; it was like a temptation, like Satan hidden deep in the heart of the century. Adopted by some as a blasphemy, gathered by others as a calumny, the term "the three impostors" . . . became a book. . . . One arrived at the result that there were three religions in the world, founded on similar principles, and all three mixed up with fables. It was this thought that betrayed itself in popular opinion by the blasphemy of the three impostors.[15]

Thus, for Renan, the Latin book *De tribus impostoribus* was a medieval chimera, born in the minds of theologians who were scandalized by the cohabitation of the three worlds in the courts of Palermo and Toledo. They attributed its paternity either to Frederick II and

Pierre des Vignes or else to Averroes, and accused any intellectuals who were too original or heterodox of spreading the central theme. During the last two centuries of the Middle Ages, it was a question only of confused rumors. The few cases of individuals who were directly accused of having defended the idea of the triple imposture all centered on southern Europe, in the zones at the border of the Christian and Muslim worlds: Sicily, Spain, Portugal.

As for the manuscript itself, it remained a myth. No one claimed even to have seen it.

The Renaissance: A Receptive Context for the Idea of Imposture

The mystery rebounded in the Renaissance; it solidified and took shape. For the first time, some people claimed to have seen the famous treatise. But the more its existence was sworn to, the less sure they became of its author. The multiplication of cases of heterodoxy, the religious conflicts within Christianity, the resurgence of esoteric and astrological currents of thought, as well as of the rationalists of classical antiquity, served to spread confusion. The *De tribus*, a curse for some, a standard-bearer for others, acquired the status of myth, exacerbated by the failure of all efforts to lay hands on the manuscript. It became a sort of grail for atheism, and the quest for it spread from Italy toward Switzerland, France, the United Provinces, northern Germany, and England. Most of the sixteenth-century humanists were involved with it.

The cultural context of the Renaissance and the Reformation largely explains the interest taken in the phantom treatise. The rediscovery of ancient philosophical currents, such as Epicureanism; the rereading of Greek and Roman histories that revealed pagan religious impostures; the controversies between Catholics and Protestants, which gave rise at one and the same time to fanaticism and to relativism in matters of faith; the humanists' passion for ancient texts, classical works as well as alchemical manuals or kabbalistic or esoteric works; and finally, the longing felt by many original thinkers for greater freedom of mores as well as of thought: all these formed a strange ensemble stimulating interest in a book with a sulfurous reputation, which had the attraction of both the mysterious and the forbidden.

The critical attitude with respect to religion—a notable trait of the Renaissance—was accompanied by a loosening of mores, tied to the resurgence of a distorted form of Epicureanism that retained above all the desire for the enjoyment of life. For example, consider Pietro Aretino (1492-1556), whose obscene *Sonetti* were both a public scandal and the private delight of the cardinals and great men of the day, including King Francis I of France, Emperor Charles V, and even the pope. In his comedies, Aretino showed himself to be disrespectful toward religion, miracles, and Jesus; he scarcely seemed to believe in the immortality of the soul. We die in our nests, "like spiders," in the words of one of the characters in his *The Courtesan*, a play in which "Master Andrew" explains that to be an accomplished gentleman, one must fool around, blaspheme, act like a whore, be a heretic, and make fun of Lent by giving up baptism. Of course, he claimed that all this was intended to unmask hypocrites, and some churchmen believed him, such as one Gnatio de Fossembrune, who wrote: "Aretino unites the morality of Gregory the Great, the profundity of Jerome, the subtlety of Augustine, and the written style of Ambrose. You are a new John the Baptist, discovering, taking up, and courageously correcting malice and hypocrisy."[16] The majority, however, were not fooled, and the commentators of the seventeenth century did not hesitate to attribute the *De tribus* to him. This was the opinion of Marin Mersenne, W. E. Tentzel, and T. G. Spitzel.

The accusation was unfounded, but it revealed how the *De tribus* was by then commonly used to stigmatize the overly free spirits whose numbers were proliferating. This period saw the multiplication of suspect works, arriving by cartloads in a clandestine commerce that flooded the great cities of Europe and submerged the official censors.[17] Blasphemy became a current practice and veered more and more toward a direct attack on faith, a denial and negation of God. The renewed outbreak of blasphemy is attested by too many sources for us to doubt it. The printer Henri Estienne, in mid-century, in his *Apology for Herodotus*, evoked "the blasphemies that contain statements showing great impiety, even ... true atheism." Bernard Palissy testified: "All I heard was blasphemies, assaults, threats, tumult, and they did not content themselves with mocking men, but also made game of God." Ambroise Paré spoke of "soldiers who were blasphemers and deniers of God." It was necessary to strengthen repression: fines for the first four infractions, being put in the pillory for the fifth, and having both lips cut off for the sixth were the penalties specified in the laws of 1510 and 1514 against those who "shall deny, curse, and blaspheme the sweet name of God." But sanctions were in vain. In 1544, the Parlement of Paris declared that "several grave and hateful blasphemies ... have begun once again to swarm about this kingdom." The litany of complaints continued under Henri II, Charles IX, Henri III, and Henri IV. Innumerable cases of blasphemy were reported in contemporary memoirs, the decisions of the sovereign courts, and in judicial archives.[18] In addition, there were instances of sacrilege, profaning of the Host, and destruction of holy images, especially the crucifix. These deeds can often be traced to Calvinist propaganda, but they contributed to the devaluation of the holy in the eyes of the faithful, who were horrified and disoriented, astounded by the lack of divine reaction: "Where is your God? ... let him save you, if he can!"[19] the hoodlums of Orléans taunted their victims. In a play performed at the beginning of the century, the *Morality of the Blasphemers of God*, which placed on stage the Insulter, the Blasphemer, and the Denier of God, we hear responses that must have made devout hearers' skin crawl. "I deny God the creator, and also his litany." The Blasphemer insults the church: "You fill our ass with abuses." The Insulter accuses the clergy of using religion "in order to have goods and honors." All of them, of course, are punished at the end, but such remarks bear witness to the circulation of these ideas and also helped propagate them. They made people's minds receptive to the idea of religious imposture.

There is another contributing factor as well: the growth of pantheistic naturalism inspired by antiquity. Nature has a soul; she acts purposefully and watches over man like a providence. The God of Moses, of Jesus, and of Mahomet is replaced by the god Pan. Even the greatest minds were seduced, including Leonardo da Vinci, who, according to Vasari, "arrived at such a heretical conception of these matters that he would not subject himself to any religion, considering himself to be much more a philosopher than a Christian." It's true that Renaissance pantheism espoused the irrational as much as classical religions, because it led to magical and animist practices, but since it rejected any notion of revelation, it relegated even the prophets to the rank of impostors. Christ is "the supreme impostor," a resident of Orléans confided to Gabriel Dupréau, who wrote in 1559: "Some years back, when I was on my way to Poitiers for my studies, I passed through Orléans. A resident of that city, a well-known

Latinist and Hellenist ... told me in confidence that numerous adepts of that sect [the atheists] had reached such a degree of madness, that not only did they have bad feelings for Christ, but they went so far as to doubt the existence of God and his Providence."[20]

"Fables and impostures": such are the messages and gospels of all these founders of religions, say the impious of today, reported François de Foix in 1579. The diversification of vocabulary that occurred in the mid-sixteenth century reveals the refinement of antireligious criticism and the importance of the movement of unbelief. It is striking to note that the French word *athée*, or *atheist*, first began to flourish during the first half of the sixteenth century. This cannot have been a matter of chance. At the very beginning of the century, the term appeared only in Greek and in Latin, in glossaries like that of Ambrogio Calepino (1502), in the context of ancient doctrines: "*Atheos*, he who does not believe in any god, *Atheus* and *Atheos*, he who has neither god nor religion (*atheista*)." Similarly, Rabelais used the Greek word in 1532 concerning Julius Caesar Scaliger. In 1552, Guillaume Postel used it in Latin, and Joachim Du Bellay in French in 1549.

Everyone agrees that atheists were numerous. In 1570, the theologian Melchior de Flavin, in his treatise *De l'estat des ames trepassees*, declared that there had never before been so many atheists in Europe, among wise men as well as "brutes." In 1563, the Lutheran historian Jean Sleidan wrote that in Germany "some are becoming atheists at present," and that "many refuse to worry about things and do not believe in anything at all."[21] They were also referred to as "strong minds" (*esprits forts*), a term that appeared in Latin around this time, and that Abbé Cotin would define this way in 1629: "They profess to believe nothing except that which they can see and touch." And then there were the "libertines" (*libertins*), a term that had been used since the Middle Ages to refer to the adherents of free thought. Geoffroy Vallée, author of *La Béatitude des chrétiens ou Le Fléau de la foy [The Beatitude of Christians, Or, The Scourge of Faith]*, who was burned at the stake at Paris in 1574, was undoubtedly one of them. This odd character, born at Orléans to a well-to-do family, was an Epicurean. His little work, also known under the significant alternate title of *The Art of Believing in Nothing*, was a deist pamphlet, which brought its author to be executed at the age of twenty-four. With Pierre Viret, Nicolas de Nancel, and François de La Noue, the term *libertine* took on its meaning of unbelief. In any case, for Henri Busson, if much of the vocabulary concerning unbelief grew and achieved brutal precision around 1540, it was a sign that this state of mind had hardened into a conscious system. He concluded: "Not only do we not accept this paradox that unbelief is impossible in the sixteenth century; we would say, rather, that it has always existed."[22]

Moses the Machiavellian

Moses, who had been relatively spared until this point, was placed in the first rank of impostors by numerous humanists in the sixteenth century, thanks to a phenomenon unrelated to religion: the evolution of political thought. Paradoxically, what was a compliment in political matters became a reproach in religious matters. Moses was praised for his political skill, as a liberator and organizer of the Hebrew people, but this political ability rested on a religious deception. Like Numa Pompilius, he based his law on a claimed revelation, which made it sacred and rendered it untouchable. It evidently was up to Machiavelli to give this ambiguous homage. He thereby established one of the bases of the theory of religious imposture as an instrument for the manipulation of people.

By the seventeenth century, Machiavelli's reputation was such that some people did not hesitate to attribute the *De tribus* to him. This was stated in 1688 by Nicolas Lefèvre.[23] This text, known to the Florentine, would tend to justify these suspicions. Let us pass over his Epicureanism and the fatalism of his moral tales. The most daring of these, *The Golden Ass*, took up an idea of Lucretius and Celsus: that animals are superior to men in their physical capacity; and that human beings, who spend their time tormenting themselves with vain questions and killing each other over chimeras, have need of religion to maintain order. One must leave people to their illusions and their prayers: "Prayers are no doubt necessary, and anyone would be mad who would prevent the people from following their ceremonies and carrying out their devotions" (canto 5). His letters confirm his naturalism and his fatalism, but it is his historical and political works that clearly develop, on a factual basis, his theory of religion as a necessary imposture. In *The Prince*, he states that it is essential for rulers to maintain "the appearance" of piety and religion, and he gives Moses as an example to follow for having known how to combine religion and the use of force. He places Moses on the same level as Cyrus, Romulus, and Theseus. Some two centuries later, an attentive reader of Machiavelli who was also his best student, Frederick II of Prussia, saw clearly the sense of this statement: for Machiavelli, Moses is "an impostor who made use of God."[24]

In his *Discourses on the First Decade of Titus Livius* (1516), Machiavelli built up this mode of conduct into a model to be imitated: "As the observance of the divine cult is the cause of the greatness of republics, so disdain for it is the cause of their ruin. For where the fear of God fails, it must be either that the kingdom comes to ruin or that it is sustained by the fear of a prince, which supplies the defects of religion." This is why "wise men who wish to take away this difficulty have recourse to God. So did Lycurgus; so did Solon; so did many others who have had the same end as they." "And truly there was never any orderer of extraordinary laws for a people who did not have recourse to God, because otherwise they would not have been accepted."[25]

The ancients understood this principle perfectly, and made skillful use of religion:

> For every religion has the foundation of its life on some principal order of its own. The life of the Gentile religion was founded on the responses of the oracles and on the sect of the diviners and augurs. All their other ceremonies, sacrifices, and rites depended on them; for they easily believed that that god who could predict your future good or your future ill for you could also grant it to you. From these arose the temples, from these the sacrifices, from these the supplications and every other ceremony to venerate them. . . . As these latter began to speak in the mode of the powerful, and as that falsity was exposed among peoples, men became incredulous and apt to disturb every good order.[26]

For Machiavelli, it is really a question of a "fraud," that is, an imposture. When pagan religion lost its credibility, it was replaced by another, which filled the same function:

> Thus, princes of a republic or of a kingdom should maintain the foundations of the religion they hold; and if this is done, it will be an easy thing for them to keep their republic religious and, in consequence, good and united. All things that arise in favor of that re-

ligion they should favor and magnify, even though they judge them false; and they should do it so much the more as they are more prudent and more knowing of natural things. Because this mode has been observed by wise men, the belief has arisen in miracles, which are celebrated even in false religions; for the prudent enlarge upon them from whatever beginning they arise, and their authority then gives them credit with anyone whatever.[27]

The question, then, is not the truth of religion, but its usefulness. And it is essential to complete it with an army: this is the theory of the sword and the aspergillum. The two are complementary: "For where there is religion, arms can easily be introduced, and where there are arms and not religion, the latter can be introduced only with difficulty."[28] Moses was a master of this game of combining force and faith: "And whoever reads the Bible judiciously will see that since he wished his laws and his orders to go forward, Moses was forced to kill an infinite number of men who, moved by nothing other than envy, were opposed to his plans."[29] Similarly, he did not hesitate to "enter with violence into the countries of others, kill the inhabitants, take possession of their goods, make a new kingdom, and change the province's name" (book 2, chap. 8; p. 144). In that respect, he is no different than Mahomet, whose success Machiavelli admires, praising "that Saracen sect ... which did so many great things" (book 2, pref.; p. 124). In contrast, Jesus failed miserably. Of the three impostors, he was the least clever, because his religion made men weaker. Christianity became the religion of submission, because of the "cowardice" of the men who interpreted the religion. In any case, all religions are mortal, which is proof of their imposture:

> It is a very true thing that all worldly things have a limit to their life.... I am speaking of mixed bodies, such as republics and sects.... And it is a thing clearer than light that these bodies do not last if they do not renew themselves. (Book 3, chap. 1; p. 209)

Machiavelli was not alone among his contemporaries in thinking that Moses was an impostor. But for him, this was a compliment—imposture is justified by its success—while for others, it was a stain. Many denounced the supposed founder of Judaism. Calvin testified to this in his *Institution of the Christian Religion*. Doubters of his day, he said, demanded to have it proven to them "by reason, that Moses and the prophets were inspired by God to speak." They referred to the content of Mosaic law as "a jumble of childish games," accusing it of inhumanity and "falsity." Some even doubted the historical existence of Moses, contesting the notion that "there ever was a Moses."

The same complaint came up in the *Catechism* of the Protestant writer John Brenz, which was translated into French in 1563. This work also testified to the denunciation of Moses and the conception of religion as an imposture. We hear the same in the *Anti-Machiavelli* of Innocent Gentillet (1576): Moses was "a robber and usurper . . . who took over the country of Judea just like the Goths and the Vandals" in France. He was a military chief, who ruled by means of his *virtù* (a natural quality that had nothing to do with providence), and he forged a "vigorous, well-designed" religion, "disguised with beautiful ceremonies," in order to keep better hold of his people.[30] Moses? He was a spinner of tales, or at least that's what one hears every day, wrote Florimond de Raemond at the end of the sixteenth century in his *Histoire de l'hérésie [History of Heresy]*. He also testified to the progress of unbelief all over Europe, from the Palatinate, which spat out "mockers of religion, . . . lost souls who hold holy books as fables," to Poland, where some said that "after death, the soul is no more," while passing by Switzerland and Bohemia. Raemond recognized that the multiplicity of religions was a factor in skepticism and unbelief, and held that for this reason one must ban them all, except for the true one, his own. This Catholic magistrate, who was a friend of Montluc, successor to Montaigne in the Parlement of Bordeaux, and an admirer of the sweet sonnets of Ronsard, preached by example in his zealous pursuit of Protestants.[31]

Moses was only a magician, and his prophecies only an illusion. These tales were also heard by Duplessis-Mornay, who in 1581 published a long apologetic work, *De la vérité de la religion chrétienne contre les athées, épicuriens, payens, juifs, mahumédistes et autres infidels [On the Truth of the Christian Religion against Atheists, Epicureans, Pagans, Jews, Mahometans, and Other Infidels]*. That men should have found it necessary to compose apologetic works to defend Christianity after fifteen hundred years of existence (just as they had done in the third century) is revealing in itself. Duplessis-Mornay's book recounted the arguments of the strong minds of his time, who contested every revelation: How can these vulgar texts, about which the classical authors say nothing, be the word of God? Can we believe that men used to live for seven hundred years, or even nine hundred? That from seventy Hebrews who came into Egypt, there came a hundred thousand? That these primitive men could have undertaken such colossal works as Noah's Ark or the Tower of Babel? That a serpent could speak, and other such fables? Moses was no more than a magician, and prophecies are only illusions. As for Christ, "what did he do in his whole life that was worthy of being remembered?" What is he next to the great men of antiquity, he who "left us no written record, neither of his life, nor of his doctrine"? Born from a virgin?—that's really "strange"! And as for being the son of God, that is inconceivable, and people can't understand "why God sent his dear son to earth at one time rather than another, and why not earlier or later." As for the resurrection, it's likely that "someone stole the body."

Appeals to the Holy Union of Religions

Attacks against religious imposture multiplied to such an extent that certain Christian intellectuals began to suggest the necessity for a holy union among religions: Moses, Jesus, Mahomet—the fight was the same. The danger had to be very pressing to arrive at such a step. Pierre Le Loyer, a friend of the poet Ronsard, felt that in the face of accusations made by atheists, one had to defend even Mahomet against those who, in his own camp, called him an impostor. One such was that "mad dog" Averroes, who denied the supernatural and the immortality of the soul, thereby placing himself in the lineage of Epicurus, Lucretius, Celsus, or Porphyry, and in the same category as Pomponazzi or Cardano.

Another theologian, Melchior de Flavin, who traveled to Palestine in 1570 (where he had the opportunity to converse with "Christians, Jews, or Muslims"), felt that in order to face up to the "stinking and pernicious cesspit of atheism," or to "the swine of Epicurus," or to the materialists, one had to make use of all religious forces, even those "of the Jews and Mahometans." Atheists, he wrote, "deny God against common sense," they "call into question whether there even is a God." Thus, all three religions are concerned, and need to make a common front, calling in as reinforcements such auxiliaries as "the philosophers whom they hold to be the wisest," such as Plato, Hermes Trismegistus, Plutarch, Orpheus, and Pythagoras. This is a strange coalition of spiritual forces, which reveals the disquiet of the defenders of religion.[32]

The feelers put out by Pierre Le Loyer and Melchior de Flavin in the direction of the Muslims were too discreet, and they themselves were too insignificant to be heard. Instead one had to simultaneously make a defense against atheists and attack Mahomet in the name of Jesus (Moses remaining neutral in this bout). The accusations of imposture in Christianity, while they did not spare the Jew or the Muslim, focused principally on Jesus and Christianity. But through this, they were aimed at the entire religious phenomenon.

Italy and the Specter of the Three Impostors

At the start of the century, the idea of religious imposture still circulated mainly in southern Europe, and especially in Italy. In 1506, Vivaldo de Mondovi related that some people dared to put Moses, Jesus, and Mahomet on the same level and in competition, and would discuss which of them had had the greatest success.[33] On 22 June 1534, Fausto da Longiano wrote to his friend Aretino: "I have begun another work entitled 'The Temple of Truth,' a strange undertaking that perhaps I shall divide into thirty parts: it will show the destruction of all the sects, the Jewish, the Christian, the Muslim, and the other religions."[34] This project's aim was very close to that of the three impostors. Unfortunately, no further trace of it has been found.

Still in Italy, the Sienese Bernardino Ochino made such a reputation for himself through his writings between 1550 and 1560 that in the following century Thomas Browne launched this famous accusation against him: "That villain and secretary of hell that composed that miscreant piece of the three impostors, though divided from all religions and was neither Jew, Turk, nor Christian, was not a positive atheist."[35] This accusation was taken up in 1640 by Sir Kenelm Digby: "Bernardinus Ochinus was a developed and manifest atheist who, having been the founder and patriarch of the Capuchin order, of a zealous and ardent spirit, became a heretic, and then a Jew, and finally a Turk. After all that, he showed a vindictive spirit and wrote against all three, whom he called the greatest impostors of the world, among whom he counted Christ our savior, Moses, and also Mahomet."[36]

Why these accusations? What shocked Ochino's readers was the great freedom of tone in his writings, notably in his *Disputa intorno* (published at Basel in 1561), where he dared to say that all religions could be mistaken, and that it was best for each person to keep to his own faith, even if it was found to contain errors. This was his own case: he expressed great reservations concerning the Eucharist, and raised the question of the Trinity, affirming that the Father is clearly superior to the Son. From this arose the rumors of his conversion to each of the three religions, then of his denial. Such rumors were absurd, like the accusation of his having written a work called *De tribus impostoribus*, when he wrote only in Italian, not in Latin. For Bayle, on the other hand, "Some have wrongly concluded that he was the author of the book *De tribus impostoribus*."

Ochino, however, opened himself to criticism, not only for his eventful life, but also by reason of his *Dialogi triginta [Thirty Dialogues]* of 1563. This ex-Capuchin, who "carried with him a lovely young Italian girl, whom he had seduced under hopes of marriage" (according to Florimond de Raemond, writing toward 1600 in his *Histoire de la naissance . . . de l'hérésie*), had actually held some highly suspect opinions. In his *Thirty Dialogues,*

> he caused a Jew to speak in debate, blaspheming against the doctrine of Jesus Christ, and he refuted only weakly the arguments made by this Jew. . . . He collected all the heresies against the Holy Trinity and against the divinity of Jesus Christ on pretext of countering them and then, far from condemning them, he appeared to favor them while watering down the passages of Scripture that prove the divinity of the son of God. . . . The goal of these thirty dialogues was to call Christian doctrine into question, to provoke quarrels, and to cause scandal.

Thus spoke the censors who, on 21 November 1563, examined the *Thirty Dialogues*, the original Italian text of which had been translated into Latin by Sébastien Chateillon (Castellion). They denounced his classical procedure of expounding with forceful and vigorous argumentation the thesis that one claims to oppose, while countering it with a "refutation" that is scarcely convincing. The subterfuge did not fool the theologians. Here, Ochino was attempting to establish whether Jesus was indeed the messiah announced by the prophets, and he used the arguments of Jews and Muslims to deny it. Yet again, we are not far from the thesis of the three impostors.

If it is in Italy that, in the sixteenth century, the rumors concerning the *De tribus* were the most insistent, it was due in large part to the University of Padua. In this center of studies that escaped the Roman Inquisition daring speculation flourished, in the tradition of Latin Averroism. Its scholars upheld theses denying the existence of miracles and the immortality of the soul, and separating faith and reason; many suspect intellectuals spent some time there, as students or as instructors. One of the most famous was Pietro Pomponazzi (1462-1525). His famous *Treatise on the Immortality of the Soul*—published in 1516, duly burned, and later put on the *Index librorum prohibitorum [List of Forbidden Books]*—upheld one of the central theses of the three impostors: the three religions, being put on the same level, all affirmed the immortality of the soul, with the sole aim of keeping the people obedient by making them fear the pains of hell and hope for the rewards of paradise. This idea, according to Pomponazzi, was a betrayal of Aristotle, the guiding light of the Paduans. In his lifetime, his book found its place in the tradition of the double truth: the natural light of reason often teaches us the contrary of faith, but still we must subject ourselves to faith. The work caused a scandal. To defend it, Pomponazzi composed two anonymous treatises in which he returned to the same idea: the greatest ancient sages—Simonides, Homer, Hippocrates, Galen, Pliny, Seneca, Alexander of Aphrodisias, and Al-Farabi—all denied the immortality of the soul, and the concept was only a means used by lawmakers to keep the people under control. He also manifested great skepticism with regard to miracles, recalled that Moses had been labeled as a magician, and thought, like Ochino, that the best way to live was for people to remain faithful to their religion, even if they thought it contained a lie, since this pious lie was what guaranteed the social order. Pomponazzi covered his traces so well that historians, even today, can't decide for certain if he was an atheist or a Christian. Protected by Cardinals Bembo and Giulio de' Medici, he died peacefully, still holding his chair at the university. At the very least, his insinuations contributed to keeping up doubt.

One could say as much of Girolamo Cardano (Jerome Cardan, 1501-1576), the mathematician, physicist, doctor, and philosopher, who was born at Pavia and died at Rome, and whose baffling theories closely approached the thesis of the three impostors. In his *De subtilitate* (1550), a kind of encyclopedia of the "subtle sciences," he put on stage a representative of each of the three monotheistic religions and a defender of ancient polytheism, and had them compare "the laws of the idolators, of the Christians, of the Jews and the Mahometans." This comparison initially highlights the hatreds among religions: "The worshippers of Mahomet have no esteem for Christians, and the Jew has no more regard for either of them than for a mad dog," and all three detest the rational philosophers. The Muslim accuses the Christian of polytheism and a cult of images, while praising the piety of his coreligionists, along with their moral sense, the chastity of their women, and the victories of their armies (a sign of divine protection). The Jew accuses the Christian of hypocrisy, since he has assimilated "the fables contained in Mosaic law"; the pagan defends the use of reason; and the Christian makes but a pale figure in the discussion. So, which of them holds the truth? "Let chance decide the victory!"—a barely disguised way of treating all four as impostors.

Cardano's compatriot Francesco Pucci, of Florence (whose work was also placed on the *Index*) got no better press. Pucci was known for his religious nomadism—a sign of skepticism. First a Catholic, he became a Calvinist, then returned to Catholicism. The censors of the seventeenth century accused him of upholding the thesis of the three impostors because he had written that redemption would be universal, gathering together those faithful to Moses, Jesus, and Mahomet in the same paradise.[37]

The century came to an end in Italy with the resounding execution of Giordano Bruno at Rome, in 1600. Born at Nola, near Naples, in 1548, this Dominican friar and doctor of theology was an original spirit, thus baffling, for his thinking lay outside all established religions. It is not surprising that he should have been accused of composing the *De tribus*, but these accusations came late and were essentially groundless. More than a century after Bruno's death, John Toland wrote in the *Spectator*: "The work known for so long under the title of *De tribus impostoribus* is nothing other than the *Lo Spaccio de la Besta trionfante*," one of Bruno's works. A little later, Prosper Marchand, referring to Toland's article, took up the accusation in his turn: "After having taken the opportunity ... to compare the dogmas of paganism to those of Judaism, Christianity, and Mahometism,

[Bruno] readily reviled the latter as childishness and foolishness, and their respective founders as notorious impostors, all under the pretense of combating vice and commending virtue."[38]

Bruno had never held such opinions, even if for him, necessarily and implicitly, Moses, Jesus, and Mahomet were ordinary men, whose message, however important, contained only a small part of the truth. The Dominican's vision went far beyond debates on imposture. Affirming the infinity and eternity of the world, he could be considered a pantheist. The world is an infinite Whole. Two infinities could not exist with one outside the other, or one next to the other. God thus is not separate from the world, but rather exists in it: He is immanent. Bruno's writings allow us to understand some of the nuances of his pantheism. In *The Infinite Universe*, he suggested a separation of a logical order between God and the world, which do not coincide absolutely.[39]

As for the founders of religions, Bruno is reported to have said some harsh things in the course of his interrogation before the Inquisition. He called Moses a magician who pretended to speak with God on Sinai in order to justify his law; pressed by the inquisitors, he corrected himself to say that Moses, who knew the magical secrets of the Egyptians, could have made use of that knowledge.[40] As for Jesus, he was probably a liar, adored by ignorant believers, who died a miserable death.[41] According to Caspar Schoppe, writing in the wake of Bruno's execution, Bruno held that "Moses worked his miracles by magic.... The holy Epistles are a fable.... Jesus Christ is not a god, but a notorious magician."[42]

In 1661, Jean Henri Ursin repeated how Bruno used to say that "all of Moses' miracles were the result of magic, and that they were superior to those of other magicians only because he had made more progress than they in the art of magic; that he himself had forged the laws that he gave to the Israelites; that Holy Scripture was no more than a fantasy."[43]

Then, in 1711, Veyssière de La Croze hammered home the nail, making a clear link to the three impostors. "In *Lo Spaccio*, abominable comparisons are made between the fables of the poets and the stories that are believed in the religions that succeeded paganism. The Gospel is turned to ridicule. The term impostor is repeated several times, and applied to the three legislators, that of the Jews, that of the Mahometans, and even to our Savior."[44]

As François Berriot has shown, these authors appear not to have really known the works of Giordano Bruno, and merely to have repeated each other. Influenced by the idea of the three impostors, they applied it artificially to Bruno, which testifies to the obsession with this theme among the defenders of religious orthodoxy.

If Italy was a particular focus, we may attribute it to, among other factors, the popularity at that time of systematic doubt in exercises of formal argument, which kept alive the medieval method of the twelfth-century *Sic et non*. This practice was studied as early as 1939 by Delio Cantimori[45] and more recently by Silvana Seidel Menchi: "The inquisitorial archives serve to prove the penetration of doubt in the most diverse milieux of dissidence, and of its tendency to become much more than an instrument of communication, a habit of the mind."[46]

Typical of the damage the method could cause is this deposition, taken in 1559, of an Augustinian friar of Catania, Andrea Ursio, who was summoned to explain himself on the subject of heterodox opinions he had expressed on the real presence of the Eucharist. According to him, these opinions dated to the time "when I was a tutor, and every morning I had to argue against the truth in the disputations that we held in the monastery, as an exercise."[47] In some monasteries there were colloquia, in the course of which two speakers would compete in upholding opposite theses on passages of scripture and even on items of dogma. In this way doubt insinuated itself and was archived in inquisitorial records: doubt over differences in ritual, doubt over the afterlife, doubt about the sacraments, doubt about the authenticity and sincerity of the founders of religions. Thus, the monk Giulio Basalù confessed in 1555: "I have read some of the commentary of Erasmus, and I admired him for denying, as it seemed to me, the divinity of Christ." He arrived at the idea that with the death of the body, the soul died as well, that God did not exist, and that all religions were a human invention to get people to lead an honest life.[48]

The Obsession Spreads

So founders of religions were impostors. From Italy, the idea spread rapidly into other parts of Europe, by means of wandering monks such as Tommaso Campanella (1568–1639) and Lucilio Vanini (1584–

1619), whom we shall meet again later. We hear echoes even in the works of Erasmus, who wrote in his *Praise of Folly* that "the Turks and that whole horde of barbarians pride themselves on their religion and ridicule Christians as superstitious. The Jews are even more happily deluded between constant expectation of their Messiah and a tenacious hold on their Moses."[49] This is a rant on his part, of course, since it is Folly who speaks, but for the guardians of the faith, it amounted to a declaration of atheism. Many of his propositions were indeed adjudged "scandalous, blasphemous, and heretical" by the Sorbonne in 1526-1527. The Jesuit Francis Garasse called him a falcon of atheism, and Étienne Dolet called him "Lucian" and "without God."

This same Dolet was burned alive at Paris in 1546 as a "relapsed atheist," an "Epicurean and a Sadducee." This shows yet again the difficulty of discerning the real religious opinions of these audacious intellectuals who were constrained to a continual dissimulation, alternating between provocation and recantation, false front and ambiguity. Dolet, born at Orléans in 1509, studied at Padua, which was scarcely the best school for piety. Arrested several times, at Toulouse and then at Lyon, he escaped only by royal grace, but at the age of twenty-six, he smelled of sulfur.

Dolet was a publisher in Paris—a genuinely suspect profession, which put him in contact with dangerous authors and manuscripts. Rumor had it that another Parisian printer, Christian Wechel, had, around 1550, published the *De tribus*. The famous treatise that nobody had yet seen gave rise to a veritable psychosis among theologians, who made use of it to accuse the heterodox. While this phantom book had initially been supposed to have been written by Emperor Frederick II and Pierre des Vignes, theologians now attributed it, in an incoherent fashion, to all the unbelievers of whom they wished to rid themselves. These included the Dutchman Herman Ristwyk, burned in 1512 at The Hague for having mocked the Jewish and Christian religions; the German Thomas Salzmann, executed at Strasbourg in 1540 for having called Christ an impostor; and the humanist Muret, another Ciceronian, run out of Paris for homosexuality and unbelief, then condemned to the stake at Toulouse in 1554 as a Huguenot and sodomite (he fled to save his life), suspected of heresy and of "crime against nature" at Venice and Padua, before being ordained as a priest. A winding path if ever there was one! At the beginning of the eighteenth century, Bernard de La Monnoye told how the jurist Henri Erntius had said in 1636 that Campanella had told him that Muret had written the *De tribus impostoribus*—a vague attribution, even if one adds to it Joseph Scaliger's assessment: "Muret would be the best Christian in the world, if he believed in God as well as he persuaded people of the necessity of believing." Muret was an admirer of Aristotle, Cicero, and Pliny, but his greatest fault, in the eyes of the theologians, was sodomy. The *De tribus* was only added on for good measure. The amalgamated notion of unbelief and homosexuality was almost systematic at the time. Interrogations for heresy were routinely accompanied by investigations into the sexual preferences of the accused, and conversely, sodomites were automatically suspected of heresy. Muret, Gruet, Vallée, Dolet, Servetus, Bruno, Vanini, La Chalade, Des Barreaux were all victims of this double accusation, and were all suspected of having written a *De tribus*, or at least of having had the idea. It was even attributed to "someone named Merula, a false Mahometan," wrote La Monnoye, no doubt recalling a certain Ange Merula, who was burned in 1557 at Mons.[50]

Geneva, Birthplace of the Three Impostors?

In the mid-sixteenth century, it was at Geneva that one found the most serious candidates for the paternity of the *De tribus*. Calvin thought he had identified the author in the person of one Jacques Gruet, whom he consigned to the flames in 1547. Gruet, a clerk, was known for his dubious morals, his dangerous opinions, and his spirit of opposition in politics. He was arrested following the discovery of a poster attacking the Reform ministers of the town, especially Calvin. The basis for his condemnation was mainly the content of his private conversations, but two years after his execution, a brief memoir, handwritten in Latin, was discovered in his house. This manifesto of absolute unbelief was authenticated, by request of the Council of Geneva and of his own friends, as the product of Gruet's own hand. Calvin caused it to be burned in a public bonfire, which served as a warning to other unbelievers in the town. This memoir has not survived, but a summary was given in the register of the Council of Geneva in order to justify the condemnation and, in the eighteenth century, a clerk recopied the contents of a letter entitled "Clarissime

lector" ("Most Illustrious Reader") attributed to Gruet, who had denied its authorship while admitting that he had it in his possession.
These two documents, if authentic, allow us to glimpse Gruet's
thinking. François Berriot examined this point at length:[51]

> It is thus altogether reasonable to affirm that there was at Geneva,
> in the first half of the sixteenth century, an odd character named
> Jacques Gruet, who ... said to himself that "whatever Moses wrote
> and taught was only done to bring order among humans," "that
> there was one law of nature by which one was to be guided," and that
> "concerning the mysteries of the universe, if we referred to Plato
> and Aristotle, we would see a bit of the truth."[52]

The fragments of the two documents cited by Berriot are eloquent. Christianity was rejected with remarkable finality; the prophets were "lunatics, dreamers, crazy people"; the apostles were "rogues
and rascals, apostates, louts, harebrains"; the Virgin, "a wench."
"The Gospel is nothing but lies; all of Scripture is false and wicked,
and has less sense than Aesop's fables; it is a false, mad doctrine." As
for Christ,

> Jesus was a beggar, a liar, a madman, a seducer, a wicked and miser-
> able man, unfortunate, crazy, a vainglorious lout who deserved to
> be crucified. . . . He played the hypocrite, having been hanged as he
> deserved, and having died miserably in his folly, a crazy man, out
> of his senses, a notorious drunkard, a wicked and detestable traitor,
> whose coming brought to the world nothing but misfortune, . . . and
> all sorts of disgrace and outrage that it is possible to invent.[53]

The attack was not limited to Christianity. "God is nothing," "men
resemble beasts," we read in the memoir, while the letter to the "Most
illustrious reader" is as explicit as it can possibly be.

> I don't know what men have said and written, but I believe that ev-
> erything that has been written about divine power is falsity, dream,
> and fantasy. . . . Truly, I believe that the world is without beginning or
> end. Who was it who described truthfully the circumstances of the
> beginning of the world? None other than Moses, who described the
> first generation, and this same Moses wrote about things that had
> happened two thousand years before his time; and for everything
> that he wrote, he wrote out of his own head, lacking any author-

ity other than his own for what he said, and claiming that it had been revealed to him. As for me, I deny his authority because many men have contested it. . . . The same Moses affirmed, as I have said, that the stories he told had been revealed by God, something that I am ignorant of. After him came other men, who invented even more and added other fables and wrote them down, such as Job, Isaiah, and the other ancients. Then the moderns, such as Jerome, Ambrose, Bede, Scotus, Aquinas, and other barbarians who invented other falsehoods. . . . As for me, I believe that when a man is dead, there is no hope of life.[54]

Six years later, they burned another heterodox at Geneva: Michael Servetus, likewise accused of having authored the *De tribus*. In his *De orbis terrae concordia [On the Harmony of the World]* (1543), Guillaume Postel—himself under suspicion—wrote that "there is a general tendency to convince men that they must live in impiety and, like brute beasts, let themselves go to whatever is forbidden. Some even make a profession of their impiety. I need no other proof than the hateful *Traité des trois prophètes* of Villeneuve, the *Cymbalum mundi*, the *Pantagruel* and the *Nouvelles Indes*, whose authors were once leaders of the Lutheran party."[55] The *Traité des trois prophètes* is surely the *Treatise of the Three Impostors*, and "Villeneuve" is the other name of Michael Servetus. This Spanish doctor and theologian certainly was no atheist, but his thought was sufficiently baffling that neither Catholics nor Protestants would accept it, and consequently, he was seen as having rejected all religion. They could not forgive him for being antitrinitarian, which caused him to be suspected of favoring Moses and Mahomet over Jesus. After all, had he not written, in his *Christianismi restitutio [Restoration of Christianity]*, that the doctrine of the Trinity was a "degenerate theism, a thousand times inferior to that of Mosaism and the Talmud, and even to the theology of the Qur'ān"?[56] Even worse, he had visited Africa and had read the Qur'ān. For Florimond de Raemond, this unbeliever was capable of upholding the thesis of the three impostors: he considered Jesus to be only a prophet; he supported several heresies, as well as Mahometism; and he had lived in Africa with the Mahometans.[57] What else would he have done down there, if not fraternize? According to Moréri, he traveled to Africa to gain a more perfect understanding of the Qur'ān, and at his trial the Genevan judges dwelled on this point, asking him if he had studied the Qur'ān, which he admitted. But "didn't he know that the Qur'ān was an evil book full of blasphemies? Why should he cite passages from it to support his own doctrine and excuse the Turks?—He answers that he confesses that the aforesaid Qur'ān is wicked, but that he only took from it what was good, and that, in a wicked book, one can find things that are good; he alleges that the Qur'ān is full of good for Jesus Christ and makes him greater than Mahomet."[58]

Three Impostors or Three Prophets? (Guillaume Postel)

The case of Michael Servetus illustrates that, for the religious authorities, both Protestant and Catholic, the search for the author of the *De tribus impostoribus* involved everyone who, in one way or another, touched on the question of the three religions, whether to approve or to criticize them. Taking up the defense of Moses, Jesus, and Mahomet was no better than accusing all three of them of lying. What could not be permitted was to place all three on the same level. To make them into three authentic, divinely inspired individuals was as serious as making them a trio of charlatans, because in either case the Son of God was worth no more than the Arab camel-driver.

And to add to the confusion, the suspects themselves accused each other. To be sure, they did this partly out of a desire to turn the attention of the censors away from themselves, because they were each risking their lives, but also, often, out of a sincere conviction that they were defending what they believed to be the truth. Far from being all potential atheists, many were themselves mystics ready to see revelation everywhere, even in Mahomet.

The case of Guillaume Postel offers a blatant illustration. As we have just seen, Postel accused Servetus of being the author of the *De tribus*, yet he himself was accused of the same thing by Henri Estienne and by Petrus Ramus, who was himself implicated. Any original or far-out thinker (of the sort that abounded in the Renaissance) was a potential suspect, and Guillaume Postel was first in line. This Frenchman from Normandy, born in 1510, was a notable orientalist who mastered not only Latin but also Greek, Hebrew, and Arabic, and who seemed destined to interest himself in the three religions. Sent to the East by Francis I to look for manuscripts, on his return in 1539 he was named professor at the Collège de France. He translated the New Testament into Arabic, with the goal of converting Muslims. At Rome, he sought to become a Jesuit, but Ignatius of Loyola found him too peculiar and somewhat too ecumenical. In 1547, at Venice, he met Mother Jeanne, a mystic who believed she had been sent by the Holy Spirit to help regenerate humanity. He was astounded by the "new Eve," this "new Joan of Arc," this "Mother of the world," this "spouse of Jesus Christ," and when she died, he declared that "the substance of her spiritual body" descended into him, and he began to prophesy in her name. Pastor Lambertus Danaeus, writing in 1562, had a more prosaic explanation: Postel forged a "female messiah from a certain prostitute named Jeanne, whom he incestuously called his mother."[59] In any case, from this time on, Postel wandered about Europe, was imprisoned by the Inquisition at Rome for some time, then was cloistered in the monastery of Saint-Martin-des-Champs at Paris, where he died in 1581.

Guillaume Postel was a prolific writer, but his style and his ideas were both so unusual that his work is difficult to interpret. His work is not terribly orthodox and is open to accusation concerning the three impostors, in the positive sense, to the extent that he pleads for re-uniting the three monotheistic religions. Thus, in *Absconditorum clavis* [*Key to Hidden Things*], which appeared at Basel in 1547, Postel affirmed that "neither nature, nor Moses, nor Mohammed" represents the complete truth, but that each has part of the divine spirit as revealed in Jesus. All will be saved, "the good Christians, the Jews, the Muslims who want to be called successors to the law of nature in observing the law of Abraham."[60] He pays ambiguous homage to Mahomet because "although he is the second Antichrist ... while we remained inactive ... he purged almost the entire universe of idolatry," and he received from God "a great blessing and a great power."[61] As for Moses, he brought the law, which permitted the world to pass from the age of polytheism to monotheism; Jesus inaugurated the adult stage of humanity.

In his *Orientales histoires* (1560) Postel advocated for "human reconciliation," by bringing together Christians and Muslims, which would happen through a rehabilitation of Mahomet, who came to complete the work of the other two. Moses brought the tables of the law, Jesus the gospel of peace and love, while Mahomet was charged with eliminating the infidels. "God gave men, through Moses, a law mingling good and evil, but they had no wish to observe it, and they engaged in idol worship. Then he sent another by Issa or Jesus

Christ, filled only with kindness, and they did not observe that one any better. So he sent Mahomet with a sword to make people believe in God by force or else to kill them."[62] Finally, they will all go to paradise: "Paradise is like Paris: people enter by different gates, Judaism, Christianity, Mahometanism." Only atheists have no right of entry.

We can imagine that such an open mind must have horrified the theologians. Not only were Postel's works placed on the *Index*, but both Catholics and Protestants accused him of having composed the *De tribus impostoribus*. According to La Monnoye, Ramus, another suspect, attributed the work to Postel, as did Erntius and Henri Estienne. Estienne reproached this "madman" for having made "a mixture of the Mahometic religion and the Judaic religion, if they can be called religions, with that of the Christians," and for having "publicly preached and upheld heresies that were not only full of blasphemy, but repugnant to natural honesty, even of pagans." Estienne also recalled "the propositions that [Postel] upheld one time at Venice to several people, myself among them, in the Rialto, that to make a good religion, it would have to be made up of three religions, Christianity, Judaism, and Turkish religion, and that the religion of the Turks had good points if one considered it closely."[63] Theodore Beza went in the same direction, while Du Verdier, in his *Bibliothèque françoise* of 1585, declared that "[Postel's] brain was not well put together," a statement that may have some truth. Postel was often accused of having studied, and even practiced, Kabbalah, and Moréri wrote that he paid too much attention to the imaginings of the rabbis. Campanella accused him formally of being the author of the *De tribus*, and an anonymous monk even claimed to have seen the work—or at least so it was reported by Prosper Marchand, who did not believe it. "To come back to Postel, Campanella clearly attributes to him the *Book of the Three Impostors*, and a lying monk swore to Nicolas de Bourbon that Postel was the book's author; that the work had been printed; that he had seen it in the library of Buxtorf at Basel; that it was written in Latin; and that the Latin style resembled that of Postel, all things that Bourbon denies and rejects in his *Borboniana*."[64] Florimond de Raemond likewise gave no credit to this story. For him, Postel's mind had been disturbed by religious conflicts, so that "he no longer knew what to believe. He therefore went wandering all over the place, sounding out Turks, Jews, Greek Christians, German Christians, and others, and attentively reading their books." His opinion was shared, at the end of the eighteenth century, by Sabatier de Castres, who stated that Postel's "goal was to gather together all the peoples in the world into the Christian religion, an idea as chimerical as the projects of the good abbot of Saint-Pierre (Charles-Irénée Castel), but one that ought to clear Postel of the accusation of having authored the *De tribus impostoribus*."[65] In any case, Postel never made use of the term *imposture* when referring to the three men. For him, they were prophets, and this is the word he used when he himself turned the accusation toward others. We have already seen him targeting Servetus, but he also put François Rabelais and the author of the *Cymbalum mundi* into the sights.

As for Rabelais, accusations of atheism were often made against him, and his books achieved the honor of the *Index*, but it is hard to see the author of *Pantagruel* writing a Latin pamphlet stigmatizing Moses, Jesus, and Mahomet. The *Cymbalum mundi*, which appeared anonymously in 1537 but whose author was quickly identified, made a better target. The author was one Bonaventure Des Périers, a valet of Marguerite of Navarre and a skeptic who decided that human reason was incapable of attaining truth, and who held a grudge against all those who, since antiquity, had claimed to have penetrated the secrets of the universe, whether by means of religion or of astrology or alchemy. He denounced as impostures miracles, the immortality of the soul, the existence of providence, and the idea of creation. All these gospels were in reality only fables, tricks, and deceptions that served the purposes of the rich and powerful. His attacks against Christianity were barely masked. Anyone who claimed to decide the truth of things, such as the heavens, the Elysian fields, vice or virtue, life or death, peace or war, the past or the future, was either a madman or an impostor. Placed on the *Index*, condemned by the Sorbonne, the *Cymbalum* nearly disappeared; today only two original copies remain. The author himself committed suicide in 1544. Clearly, for him our trio were impostors, but there is nothing to prove that he set this down in a treatise.

Who Actually Saw the Treatise?

So, did this notorious treatise actually exist? Everyone seemed to believe that it did. At least no one expressed the slightest doubt on the subject during the sixteenth century. But curiously no one seemed to be in a hurry to find it. They looked for the author without ever having seen the object itself; they sought the criminal without having ascertained that a crime had taken place. The theologians had no need to see in order to believe. Nor were they disturbed by the thought that they were accusing sixteenth-century men of having written a phantom work that supposedly dated from the thirteenth century. They probably did not even wish for the work to be discovered, for, like the devil, it was more useful while remaining invisible, so that they could make use of it as an appropriate accusation to discredit heterodox individuals.

Toward the end of the century, for the first time, some voices were raised to say, "I've seen it!" But the witnesses had about as much credibility as those who later claimed to have seen the Loch Ness monster. Let us pass over Guillaume Postel, who in 1543 mentioned the treatise with no further qualification, as if its existence were taken for granted. Likewise, let us pass over the gratuitous affirmation of Campanella, who, in order to exculpate himself, wrote in the preface of his *Atheismus triumphatus* that the book had been written around 1538, thirty years before his birth. Instead, let us reread what Florimond de Raemond wrote at the end of the century:

> Jacques Curio in his chronology of the year 1556 says that the Palatinate was filled with mockers of religion, called Lucianists, lost souls, who called the holy books fables, especially those of the great lawgiver of God, Moses. And did we not see a hateful book, forged in Germany, though printed elsewhere, at the same time that heresy was flourishing, which spread this doctrine and carried the horrible title *On the Three Impostors*, mocking the three ruling religions which alone recognize the true God—Jewish, Christian and Mahometan? The title revealed its hellish origins, and what century gave it birth, which could produce such a monster. I wouldn't have mentioned it if Hosius and Genebrard before me had not spoken of it. I remember that as a child I saw a copy of it in the Collège de Presles in the hands of Ramus, a man noteworthy for his great knowledge, but who mixed himself up in researches into the secrets of religion, which he mixed with philosophy. They passed the book from hand to hand among the most learned, who all desired to see it.[66]

The testimony is categorical. Florimond de Raemond, a historian of heresy, died in 1601. His *Histoire de la naissance, progrez et décadence de l'hérésie de ce siècle* ... was published in Paris in 1610, but had been written at the end of the sixteenth century. The author was a serious man, and he made reference to a specific episode. While a student at the Collège de Presles, he saw one of his teachers—the famous Pierre de la Ramée, or Petrus Ramus, who was assassinated during the St. Bartholomew's Day Massacre in 1572—holding the *De tribus* in his hands. This must have been around 1570. The testimony, however, requires caution. Can we trust a fleeting childhood memory going back thirty years? Moreover, La Monnoye, who cited the passage in his *Menagiana* at the beginning of the eighteenth century, simultaneously discredited it in recalling that "Florimond de Raemond" was the frequently used pseudonym of Father Richeome, a Jesuit, in his writings against the Protestants. Richeome was more an orator than a historian, and he might well have made up the story with the goal of discrediting Ramus. This interpretation is hardly more convincing than the testimony itself, and yet most historians accept it, using the argument that Ramus, an original yet sincere Christian, would not have risked attracting attention to himself by walking around in front of his students carrying the infamous treatise, reading it secretly, and passing it surreptitiously to his colleagues.

Some lines of Genebrard, written in 1581 in a letter to Lambertus Danaeus, also allude to the "wicked author" of the "little book of the three impostors,"[67] but do not prove that he had seen it. Similarly, Claude Beauregard, who was a professor of philosophy at Paris, Pisa, and Padua, cited in his *Circulus pisanus* a passage from the *De tribus* where the miracles of Moses were attributed to his demon. For La Monnoye, that did not seem probable; if Beauregard had truly had the book before his eyes, he said, he would have described it in detail.

Rare were the theologians, polemicists, and apologists of the sixteenth century who doubted the existence of the treatise, whose central thesis appeared more and more credible to the most rational authors. For Montaigne, the imposture of Mahomet had not a shadow of doubt: "When Mahomet promised his followers a paradise decked out with tapestries and carpets, with ornaments of gold and precious stones, furnished with voluptuous nymphs of outstanding beauty, with wines and choice foods to eat: I realized that ... [he was] laughing at us, stooping low to tempt our brutish stupidity with sweet allurements, enticing us with notions and hopes appropriate to our mortal appetites."[68] A prudent man, the author of the *Essays* spared Moses and Jesus, which did not prevent him from affirming that "religion" is an instrument in the service of our passions: "It is evident to me that we only willingly carry out those religious duties which flatter our passions. Christians excel at hating enemies. Our zeal works wonders when it strengthens our tendency toward hatred, enmity, ambition, avarice, evil-speaking . . . and rebellion. On the other hand, zeal never makes anyone go flying toward goodness, kindness, or temperance, unless he is miraculously predisposed to them by some rare complexion. Our religion was made to root out vices: now it cloaks them, nurses them, stimulates them." He concluded from this that men manipulate faith to satisfy their passions, and they make use of religion when matters ought to be otherwise.[69]

From there to saying that all the founders of religions are impostors requires only a step, yet it is a step that Montaigne did not take. A different case is that of his contemporary Jean Bodin (1529/30–1596), who made use of the classic subterfuge, the dialogue form. The famous jurist embodied all the ambiguities of the religious controversies of his century: he was an economist and savvy political theorist, and simultaneously a committed partisan of the witch hunt, a rational skeptic preaching tolerance and at the same time an adversary of atheism. In his *Méthode de l'histoire [Historical Method]* he made a comparative study of religions, underlining the role of climate in explaining the differences among them, and suggesting in a relativist spirit that someone should write a history of impiety. Yet in his *La République* he wrote that "little by little, out of contempt for religion, there has grown up a hateful sect of atheists . . . , from which there follows an infinite number of murders, parricides, and poisonings."

Bodin expounded his religious ideas most fully in his *Colloquium heptaplomeres*, composed around 1590. This curious book, which libertines came to admire very much, made use of seven sages representing seven religious attitudes: a Catholic, a Lutheran, a Calvinist, a Jew, a Muslim, a deist, and an agnostic. They are all on good terms and debate the merits of their respective positions, unanimously condemning atheism, which entails immorality and reduces man to a bestial state. They are equally hostile to religious discussions, which weaken faith and lead to doubt. Their own conversation is an illustration, because no criticism is spared against the different religions, especially Christianity, which is attacked with extraordinary vehemence by the Jew, the Muslim, the deist, and the agnostic. The character of Jesus is bitterly contested: his immaculate conception, his divine nature, his miracles, his temptation by Satan, his tardy vocation, and his resurrection are all denied with arguments drawn largely from Celsus and Julian. The Trinity, the Holy Spirit, and original sin are considered as defying both reason and the laws of nature. Anthropomorphism, the sacraments, the ceremonies, the mournful character of this religion; all are passed through the crucible of a pitiless critique.

Salomon, the Jew, is the most bitter with regard to Jesus, in whom he clearly sees an impostor comparable to Apollonius of Tyana and Simon the Magician. The deist Toralba dwells on the improbability of his conduct and on his weakness on the Mount of Olives. "By that," he says, "does he not show sufficient evidence of a low soul, whereby he himself recognizes that he is nothing like a god?" In any case, Toralba continues, why should we believe all this nonsense? "Where are the sufficient witnesses and the authorities who will go bail for them, and who will post bond that they will give them a firm and assured credence that will leave no uncertainty?"[70] The response of the Catholic Coroni is pathetically weak, which only serves to reinforce the skepticism.

Mahomet is no better treated, having imposed his "fables" by "violence and force of arms" after being unable to win "by force of reasoning." By comparison, Moses is somewhat spared, but in any event all messiahs and prophets are characterized as "impostors" who "promise more than they can deliver," and all the founders of religions are dismissed: "What need of Jupiter, of Christ, of Mahomet?" Religion is "a doubtful opinion suspended between the true and the false." Each person holds to his own: "The Jews root for theirs, the Mahometans on the contrary, the Christians award it to themselves, and the pagans of all the Indies want to win by sheer antiquity." Senamy, who plays the role of the agnostic in the discussion, puts all the credos on the same level: "I think that all the religions of the world, whether the natural religion that Toralba follows, or that of Jupiter, or the gods of the Gentiles that the Eastern Indians and Tartars worship, or that of Moses, of Christ, and of Mahomet ... are all agreeable to God."

The conclusion is that the best way is for each to keep to his own religion while tolerating the others, because reason, which ought to be our sole guide, cannot determine which is the true one. Senamy expresses his skepticism by a sibylline formula: "Amid so great a number of religions, it may be one of two things: either that it is nothing, or that one is no more the true religion than another."[71] We might translate this as: Either religions are all false, or else they are all false.

This is of course the implicit message of the *De tribus*, which Jean Bodin himself might well have written. Thus, the sixteenth century produced a plethora of potential authors of a book that probably didn't exist, but that visibly haunted their spirits. Until the dawn of the seventeenth century, the *Traité des trois imposteurs* was above all a scarecrow, used by religious apologists to discredit unbelievers, skeptics, and atheists, whose numbers increased greatly with the interconfessional conflicts. Atheist, pederast, and author of the *De tribus*: the amalgamated insult was practically a matter of ritual. This reinforced the general certainty that the notorious, blasphemous treatise existed, even if no one had seen it. Because so many people were supposed to have written it, it had to exist. There was no need to go and search for it.

What changed in the seventeenth century was the transition from the search for the author to the search for the treatise. This reversal of priorities was gradual, and it formed part of a global intellectual evolution. The age of Descartes required written documents for proof. Fontenelle and the gold tooth[72] are not far off: first let us prove that the treatise exists, before we look for its author; let us put the horse ahead of the cart. The new spirit was accompanied by a geographical displacement: while the sixteenth century had sought the author mainly in Italy and Switzerland, the seventeenth century searched for the manuscript farther north, because the center of gravity of disbelief had also become displaced.

CHAPTER THREE

The European Elites and Religious Imposture (Seventeenth Century)

Right from the start of the seventeenth century, attention turned toward Germany. In 1610, a Spanish Carmelite monk, Geronimo de la Madre de Dios, stated in his *Miserable estado de los ateista [The Miserable State of Atheists]* (published in Brussels) that manuscripts of the *De tribus impostoribus* were circulating in Germany.[1]

On the Trail of De tribus *around the Baltic Sea*

Two years later, in 1612, an anonymous pamphlet, the *Magot genevois, découvert es arrests du Synode national des ministres reformez tenu à Privas l'an 1612 [The Genevan Hoard, discovered in the decrees of the National Synod of Reformed Ministers held at Privas in the year 1612]*, accused a doctor from the Dauphiné, Nicolas Barnaud, of having "made an abominable book, whose title alone causes one's hair to stand on end, titling it *De tribus impostoribus, Moses, Christ and Muhammad.*" Barnaud was a friend of the heretic Faustus Socinus. The name Barnaud appeared at the same time in Holland, at Gouda and Middelburg, where a Ferdinand Barnaud was said to have offered to make copies of the notorious treatise.[2] There is no doubt that Ferdinand and Nicolas were one and the same person, who also made an appearance at Prague. In 1614, still in Holland, a certain J. C. Nachtegael was banished for having distributed copies of the *De tribus* to Alkmaar. He confessed that he was encouraged in this by a Frenchman who claimed to be an illegitimate son of King Henri IV, a type that proliferated at the time. Here again, it was a question of a Nicolas Barnaud. This obscure individual, officially a Huguenot, was in reality a distinctive heterodox like so many others. In 1583, he had dedicated to Henri IV a deist work, the *Trois perles dans le cabinet du Roy de France [Three Pearls in the French King's Cabinet]*; in 1592, he had translated the *Livret de l'authorité de la Sainte Écriture [Booklet on the Authority of Holy Scripture]*, by Faustus Socinus. The latter, a nephew of Laelius Socinus, was the source of the antitrinitarian heresy, and "Socinianism" was spreading throughout the United Provinces at just this time.

The affair remains murky, because the accusations date to 1612, while Barnaud died around 1605. François Berriot thought there might be some confusion with the Pastor Bansillon who was condemned by the synod of 1612.[3] In any case, starting in the 1610s, rumors of the existence of the treatise *De tribus* increased and became focused on northern Europe. In 1621, Jacques Severt mentioned it several times in his *De atheismo et haeresibus [On Atheism and Heresies]*,[4] as did Marin Mersenne in 1621–1624 in his *L'Impiété des déistes [The Impiety of Deists]* and his *Quaestiones celeberrimae in Genesim [Famous Questions on Genesis]*. It was taken up again by an Englishman, Robert Burton, who in his *Anatomy of Melancholy* (1621) mentioned "that pestilent booke *de tribus mundi impostoribus, quem sine horrore (inquit) non legas [which, he says, you could not read without being horrified]*."[5] Burton did not claim to have read it, or even to have seen it, but, citing Mersenne, he listed the names of all those who, since Frederick II, had been accused of having been its authors. As for Mersenne, he affirmed that one of his friends had recited passages of the work to him, and he summarized the contents: an impious book, which turned "Moses, Christ, and Mahomet into impostors" who had sought to impose their own law.[6] Some years later, the Italian Tommaso Campanella was more categorical and more precise. In his *De gentilismo non retinendo [Concerning Gentilism Not to Be Retained]* (1631), he stated: "There came from Germany the book *De tribus impostoribus*, conforming to the doctrine of Aristotle and Averroes, according to whom all lawgivers were impostors, principally Jesus Christ, Moses, and Mahomet according to Averroes."[7] Germany was clearly designated as the country of origin of the treatise. Florimond de Raemond had already said so. Campanella repeated it in the 1636 edition of his *Atheismus triumphatus [Atheism Conquered]* and added that he himself had read a copy of it belonging to a Florentine heretic, Francesco Pucci.[8]

In 1643 the Englishman Thomas Browne of Norwich, in his *Religio medici [A Doctor's Religion]*, spoke of "that villain and secretary of hell that composed that miscreant piece of the three impostors."[9]

In the same year, Beauregard alluded to the treatise in his *Circulus pisanus*, already mentioned. It seems that by this time manuscripts of the *De tribus* were circulating in Europe. The basic idea of the treatise had become commonplace among unbelievers, as the Parisian clergyman Paul Beurrier testified. In his *Memoirs* covering the years 1650–1670, this clergyman, who had been curé of Saint-Étienne-du-Mont for more than twenty years, told how he had often had dealings with unbelievers, such as a lawyer for the council, who had told him, outside of confession, that religion was a collection of fables and "that God, if he exists, does not meddle in human affairs, and many other blasphemies that he uttered against Jesus Christ, whom he believed to be an impostor, just like Moses and Mahomet."[10] There was no need to mention Moses and Mahomet in this context; their intrusion can only be explained by the spread of the idea of the three impostors. The lawyer had added: "I am not the only one holding these views, for there are a good twenty thousand of us in Paris who feel this way. We all know each other, we meet secretly, and we strengthen each other in our opposition to religion, believing that religion is only a political strategy invented to keep people under the yoke of the rulers through fear of imaginary hellfire. For in good faith, we don't believe in it, any more than we believe in paradise. We believe that when we die, everything is over for us." Beurrier likewise cited a homosexual unbeliever colleague, for whom "the Christian religion was only a fable and only little minds believed its teachings, because it taught things that were impossible and ridiculous." Or again, there was the doctor, Basin, who, in good scientific style, had experimented with all three religions, converting in turn to Judaism, to Christianity (Protestantism), and to Islam, and who eventually "convinced himself that all religions were only fantasies and political institutions set up by the rulers to keep their subjects in line through the lure of religion and the fear of God." He categorically rejected all revelation: "Your Bible is a real novel, in which there are a thousand stories to put you to sleep, contradictions and foolishness, impossible things, imaginary notions that are poorly conceived, poorly digested, and even more poorly written." His credo can be summed up as: "I believe the three articles of my religion of philosophy: first, that the biggest fable of all is the Christian religion; the second, that the oldest novel is the Bible; third, that the greatest of all cheats and impostors is Jesus Christ."[11]

This brings us to the middle of the seventeenth century. It is clear that at this precise moment the *De tribus impostoribus* is in the process of becoming a reality. Several people claimed to have seen it, and some even claimed to have read it. Even better: in Wittenberg there is the earliest printed copy that has so far been found, and scholars date it to around 1650.[12] Of course, the printed book must have been preceded by a manuscript, but that seems to have disappeared. Research has been directed primarily along the Baltic, as well as toward Hamburg, in connection with the affairs of a Swedish diplomat, Johan Adler Salvius. At this time, Sweden was at the center of European affairs. The military genius of King Gustavus Adolphus had allowed him to rule the Swedish Empire until his death in 1632 at the battle of Lützen. In the Thirty Years' War (1618-1648) Sweden, allied to France, extended its conquests around the Baltic. In 1648, through the Peace of Westphalia, Sweden obtained western Pomerania, the bishoprics of Bremen and Verden, and the city of Wismar. On the home front, Gustavus Adolphus's daughter Christina was one of the most striking individuals of the century. Free in her behavior, she had a skeptical and inquiring mind, reminiscent of Frederick II. Surrounded by unbelievers, she showed complete independence with regard to religion. Her teacher and librarian, Isaac Vossius, was a strong mind who died an atheist. Christina also had with her, for two years, Pierre Bourdelot, Condé's doctor and a notorious atheist. He was the author of a *Catéchisme de l'athée [An Atheist's Catechism]*, which he sent to the head pastor of Stockholm, and in which he maintained that heaven was empty, and that in Italy as well as in France no intelligent man believed in God.

In 1654, at the age of twenty-eight, Christina abdicated and began to crisscross Europe in a search for artworks and manuscripts, especially heterodox works, such as the *Colloquium heptaplomeres* and the *De tribus impostoribus*. Courted by the philosopher Descartes as well as by literary figures like Pascal and La Rochefoucauld, she traveled in the Low Countries, in France, and then settled in Rome. She offered a large reward to anyone who could find her a copy of the *Three Impostors*. In 1653, a French courtier at Stockholm, Philippe Bourdon de La Salle, wrote that he had heard the queen talking for three or four hours about providence and the divine essence, treating the Incarnation as a fable. He added that she was looking for "a manuscript that no one has ever seen, the *De tribus impostoribus*."[13]

The following year, Christina wrote to the widow of the Protestant pastor Saumaise, to reproach her for having burned her husband's papers at his death. According to Andreas Colvius, Saumaise was said to have owned a manuscript of the treatise.[14] She had no better luck upon the death of her diplomat, Salvius, in 1652. It is extremely likely that he had possessed a copy, as we shall see, but Christina knew he would refuse to give it to her. So she waited until his death, on 23 August 1652, then sent Bourdelot to ask the widow for the precious document. She was too late, however: on the eve of his death, seized by remorse, Salvius was said to have burned the book in his bedchamber. La Monnoye, who reported the affair, did not believe the story. Again in 1661, Christina went to Hamburg, and asked first a Dominican monk and then a certain Giulio Cesi to obtain for her, at any price, a German "manuscript book," which might have been the *De tribus.*

In vain did Christina rummage through all the libraries of Europe to find her manuscript. Her envoys were recognized, but sometimes lacked diplomacy; for example Alexander Cecconi, who in 1652 went to the Biblioteca Laurenziana in Florence and calmly demanded to see the manuscript, reputed lost, of the fifteen books of the *Kata christianon* of Porphyry, in order to make a copy of it. Porphyry, who died in 304, was supposed to have mentioned "three chatterboxes" who "had attracted the world"—Moses, Jesus, Simon the Magician, or Apollonius of Tyana. The library's curators refused the request.

But if Christina's hopes were frustrated, her diplomat Salvius may have had better luck. Johan Adler Salvius, the queen's personal advisor, was a cultivated man who took an interest in the different aspects of power. His rhetorical studies at Rostock, in 1612, convinced him of the importance of communication for those who rule—the image one presents of oneself is more important than what one really is. He composed an erudite doctoral dissertation in law, *Sciagraphia universi iuris feudalis,* and in 1620 he married a rich widow of Gothenburg. He participated in the war in Poland, where he was taken prisoner by the Cossacks in 1625. Ennobled in 1629, he soon settled in Hamburg. In 1635, he led the negotiations in Germany concerning trade with Persia. His diplomatic role became dominant by 1637, when he attempted to persuade the northern German states to enter the Thirty Years' War. He then went to Paris to discuss a French alliance. He was one of the principal negotiators at the conferences held at Osnabruck in 1645–1648 that resulted in the Peace of Westphalia. During this whole period, he stayed in close contact with Queen Christina and made use of the many meetings involved in international conferences in order to search out rare books and manuscripts. Thus in 1645 he promised Per Brahe that he would find him a copy of the very rare European atlas of Joan Blaeu, *Atlantem majorem*. Ambassadors were wealthy aristocrats, many of whom were collectors and men of culture; in the intervals between diplomatic sessions, they traded art objects and valuable books. International conferences and congresses were especially favorable for these contacts, especially when they went on for a long time, as was the case at Münster and Osnabruck and later at Utrecht.[15]

In his search for the *De tribus*, Salvius (in 1635) approached a Jew of Hamburg, Bendito (Baruch) de Castro (who later became Christina's physician). He was a strange character, with a strong interest in the esoteric, in Platonism, and in the Kabbalah. A supporter of the mystical messiah Shabbetai Ẓevi, de Castro financed publications such as the *Fin de los dias [The End of Days]*, a messianic treatise of Moses Gideon Abudiente. Hamburg at that time was a center for heterodoxy, especially among the powerful Jewish community. There one could find representatives of all the European religious outgrowths, from the wildest to the most serious. De Castro, who in 1629 had published a *Tratado de calumnia*, a defense of Jewish medical practices, was in touch with an atheist, Uriel da Costa (1583/4–1640), who eventually committed suicide. De Castro took an interest in the Arabic and Hebrew sources of the imposture theme.[16] Salvius wrote to him three times in 1635, asking him to obtain for him, at any price, a copy of the *De tribus maximis mundi impostoribus*, as well as other dangerous works, such as the *De fato* of Cremonini, or the *Amphitheatrum aeternae providentiae [Amphitheater of Eternal Providence]* of Lucilio Vanini.

This effort apparently failed, because three years later, Salvius wrote to Johannes Müller, still at Hamburg, to say he was sure that in 1616, when he was traveling in the Low Countries, he had seen a copy of the *De tribus* printed in Dutch. He stated that many people attributed the treatise to Cardano, but that he himself tended to think that it was of Arab origin. It was likely the work of Merula, an apostate Muslim, later known as Joannes Andreae. This man, who had rejected Islam in 1487, had written a work entitled *Confusio sectae mahometanae*.

It appears that Salvius eventually succeeded in obtaining the copy he sought, perhaps at the very end of his life. On 6 July 1652, Bourdelot, who was then at the Swedish court in Stockholm, wrote: "There came here a Jewish doctor from Hamburg." This was probably de Castro, bringing with him the *De tribus*.[17] In any case, Salvius's confessor, Johann Balthasar Schuppe, declared later, in 1674, that the diplomat had the book in his library and that, gnawed by remorse, he had burned it just before his death, 23 August 1652. According to his secretary, his death was due to excessive sexual activity.[18] Later on, rumors began to circulate that Salvius had given a copy of *De tribus* to a Swedish captain, who had sold it in Germany, which contributed to its diffusion; in 1706, a German soldier was said to have recovered a copy while ransacking Munich.

These ulterior developments cannot be verified, but what appears certain is that in the mid-seventeenth century the *De tribus* was a big issue in the Baltic region. On 12 July 1647, Johann Georg Dorsche (1597-1659) wrote from Rostock to Abraham Calow at Wittenberg that "the book *De tribus magnis mundi impostoribus* has been distributed by a great lord" in the region. The historian Gericke sees this as a reference to Salvius, since the title as given corresponds to the wording used by the diplomat in his letter to de Castro. But did Salvius have the treatise in his possession at that time? In any case, there are other candidates, because there were several aristocratic circles in the region where people discussed heterodox ideas, and even atheism: At Königsberg with the syncretic theologians Drejer, Behm, and Laterman; in the circle of the Duke of Mecklenburg; in that of Prince Christian Ludwig of Brunswick-Luneburg; or at Lübeck with the hermetic Joachim Morsius; and at Hamburg with Joachim Jungius, a neighbor of Salvius. Johann Christoph Harenberg has even suggested that the interest in the theory of the three impostors in this region may have been due to the influence of the Teutonic Knights, who brought back with them, on their return from the Crusades, ideas on political imposture influenced by Averroes. This would reinforce the theory of an Arabic origin of the three impostors, which would have blended with a Jewish tradition derived from Maimonides.[19] Queen Christina's collections actually contain a chart of the rules of the Teutonic order. If this were the case, we would have a syncretism of unbelief, coming from the heterodox among three religions, each presenting its own impostor. In any event, Swedish Pomerania, in the mid-seventeenth century, at least had a version of the *De tribus* circulating, and was a center for its diffusion.

Holland and England: Heterodox Contexts

Another region of northern Europe that had close relations with Germany and Sweden was rocked at the same time by similar debates and became a hotbed of heterodoxy: the United Provinces. Born from a desire for liberty and a rejection of absolutism and Catholicism, by the end of the sixteenth century this republic was a place of comparative tolerance that attracted immigrants from all over Europe who had been persecuted for religious or political reasons. By the beginning of the seventeenth century, Amsterdam was celebrated as a place of refuge for the various strains of heterodoxy, Jewish as well as Calvinist. A progressive tradition grew, characterized by intellectual audacity and reinforced by the Thirty Years' War, in which the United Provinces was one of the principal partners of France and Sweden against the Catholic forces of the Holy Roman emperor and the king of Spain. Political life was tense, however, and freedom of expression had its limits. Still, in an absolutist Europe, this country was a liberal exception.

In 1673, a Swiss Protestant officer in the service of Louis XIV of France, one J.-B. Stouppe, expressed his astonishment and disapproval in *La Religion des Hollandais [The Dutch Religion]*. They have three main groups, he wrote: the reformed, the Catholics, and the "sectarians." Among the sectarians he included Mennonites, Quakers, Lutherans, Remonstrants, Collegians, spiritualists, Jews, Socinians, and Spinozans. And they do nothing, he added, to prevent the propagation of these sects.

Stouppe exaggerated. Orthodox Calvinists, under the leadership of Gijsbert Voet, exerted pressure to eliminate both Cartesianism and Socinianism. They accused the Cartesians of crypto-atheism, wrecking the authority of the scriptures by emphasizing their historical context; the Socinians they accused of antitrinitarianism. The latter was a major heresy in the eyes of Christians, because by reducing God to one person, it destroyed the divinity of the Son. Jesus was a great prophet, but he was not God: this was exactly what the Muslims claimed. The Arminians, who were called Remonstrants, were also persecuted for their belief that Jesus had died for all men and not only for the elect, and that he did not wish for sinners to be damned. The synods' fight against these currents of thought intensified from the mid-1650s. But there was also—confirming Stouppe's assessment— a liberal Calvinist current, led by Johannes Koch (Cocceius, 1603–1669), a professor of theology at Leiden and a distinguished philologist, who had a more flexible conception of scripture. In his view, as expressed in his *Summa doctrinae* of 1648, scripture was not to be interpreted literally. He took a more tolerant position with regard to dissident movements, which Voet considered as encouraging atheism. The judgment is extreme, but it is true that the revival of such debates, in a climate of semi-tolerance, contributed to the growth of skepticism with regard to religions.

And then there were the Jews, whose numbers increased through immigration: about six thousand at Amsterdam, and sizable communities at Rotterdam, Middelburg, Amersfoort, Maarssen, The Hague, and Nijkerk. Most were German Jews, but there was a significant minority of Sephardic Jews from Portugal. At the heart of this group existed, if not currents of heterodoxy, at least heterodox personalities, some of whom were as good as atheists. Thus, Uriel da Costa published his *Examination of the Traditions of the Pharisees*, a work that denied the immortality of the soul, in 1624 at Amsterdam. The book was condemned by the Sephardic authorities, and was burned by order of the city magistrates of Amsterdam. Da Costa, thus persecuted, killed himself in 1640. His thought survived him, however, and the publication of his autobiography helped revive his memory. This is the same Uriel da Costa who studied the Hebrew and Arabic sources of the thesis of religious imposture, and who was in contact with Baruch de Castro, who sought a copy of the *De tribus* for Salvius, as we have seen.

The Dutch environment was thus favorable to the reception of the thesis of the three impostors by the mid-seventeenth century. It was here that it would assume its definitive form, toward the end of the century, in the aftermath of two key events with a combined effect: the work of Spinoza and the immigration of French Huguenots after the revocation of the Edict of Nantes in 1685.

Before turning to these major developments of the second half of the seventeenth century, however, we must examine the case of England, where it appears that manuscripts of the *De tribus* circulated during the reign of Elizabeth I. In 1593, Gabriel Harvey complained in a letter about the "monster of iniquity" who had engendered the "hateful *Blackebooke de tribus impostoribus mundi.*"[20] Is this simply an allusion to the phantom book that people had been talking about since the thirteenth century, or had Harvey actually seen a manuscript bearing the title? If so, this would have been its first physical appearance, chronologically. It is impossible to say for sure, but several historians favor the latter hypothesis. One is Jan W. Wojcik, who wrote: "It is possible (and in my opinion likely) that an early manuscript version of *The Three Impostors* was circulating in England in the late 1590s. . . . What is certain, however, is that the specific thesis expressed in *The Three Impostors* was known in England at this early date and that this thesis was associated with a treatise entitled *De tribus impostoribus mundi.*"[21]

And what is this thesis? That "Her Majesty need neither believe nor defend the Scriptures with regard to doctrine, faith, and salvation, but solely for politics and civil government." In March 1594, a commission in Dorset sought out individuals who upheld this point of view—in other words, those who affirmed that religion had a purely political origin, that it was simply an instrument invented in order to better control the minds of subjects.[22] In 1597, the theologian Richard Hooker wrote that, for the atheists of his day, the fear of God was

> nothing els but a kinde of harmeles error, bredd and confirmed in them by the slightes of wiser men. For a politique use of religion they see there is, and by it they would also gather, that religion it selfe is a meere politique devise, forged purposelie to serve for that use. Men fearinge God are thereby a greate deale more effectually then by positive lawes restrayned from doinge evell, in as much as those lawes have no farder power then over our outwarde actions onlie, whereas unto mens inward cogitations, unto the privie intentes and motions of theire hartes religion serveth for a bridle.[23]

This discourse recalls Machiavelli and prefigures Hobbes. It is also typical of the English version of the three impostors: religion is an imposture with a pragmatic goal, an instrument of politics.

The troubled history of religion in England in the sixteenth century abetted this point of view. The country changed religion five times in the course of the century, as sovereigns imposed their personal affiliation upon their subjects by force. With the definitive establishment of Anglicanism under Elizabeth I, religion was intimately linked to the state, to nationalism, and to patriotism, and it appeared to be truly an instrument of government. It required only an external conformity, in the form of attendance at services and use of the official Prayer Book. Beyond that, no official notice was taken; it was the politics of "don't ask, don't tell." Government, having abandoned the notion of proving the truth of one doctrine in relation to another, no longer sought to examine people's hearts; it was up to the individual to set himself straight with God.

The result, if we can believe the lamentations of the clergy, was that the churches filled up with hypocrites. The importance of atheism in England at this time is no doubt obscured by the fact that many unbelievers were now able to hide behind an uncomplicated external practice. But recent studies show that unbelief was in fact widespread by the end of the reign of Henry VIII. British historians agree on the amazing degree of indifference to religion that characterized the reign of Elizabeth I, behind the superficial disputes between Puritans and Anglicans, which concerned only a small minority. One of them calls this period the most indifferent to religion until the twentieth century.[24]

The example came from above. The Earl of Oxford declared that the Bible served only to "hold men in obedience, and [was] man's device"; he himself "could make a better and more orderly Scripture in six days." For him, "the blessed virgin made a fault ... [and] Joseph was a wittol [cuckold]." "After this life, we should be as we had never been and that the rest was devised but to make us afraid like babes and children of our shadows." "More plain reasons and examples may be vouched out of Scripture for defence of bawdry than out of all the books of Aretinus."[25] The Earl of Oxford was at the center of a circle of libertines that included the poet Thomas Watson. Many other courtiers shared this reputation, such as the Earl of Essex, whose unbelief is well known. The famous navigator, explorer, and courtier Sir Walter Raleigh thought that human beings die like beasts, and that when people are gone, nothing of them remains.[26] One of his men, Thomas Harriot, who took part in the administration of Virginia's Roanoke colony, experimented with the use of religion as a means of domination. In his *Brief and True Report of the New*

Found Land of Virginia (1588) he explained how he used Christian beliefs and symbolism to subject the credulous natives, thus doing even better than Moses—a practical use of religious imposture.

The halls of government were widely contaminated. According to the spy Richard Cholmeley, the noblest peers and honorable councilors were atheists who turned scripture to ridicule. According to the Jesuit Robert Persons, who sent an *Advertisement Written to a Secretary of My Lord Treasurer* in 1592, Lord Burghley, the queen's principal councilor, and other councilors were unbelievers who lived as out-and-out atheists, mocking the credulity of others. For Persons, Sir Walter Raleigh kept a veritable "school of atheism," where Moses and Jesus, the Old and the New Testaments, were all turned to ridicule.

Significant testimony about the spread of atheism in England between 1590 and 1610 comes from the philosopher, scientist, statesman, and future chancellor Francis Bacon. A man of enormous learning, he had read a French edition of Montaigne's *Essays*, as well as Charron's *Wisdom*. Like Montaigne, Bacon also wrote a book of *Essays*, published in 1612, in which he devoted a chapter to atheism. He found it hard to understand how someone could be an atheist: "I had rather believe in all the fables in the legend, and the Talmud, and the Alcoran, than that this universal frame is without a mind; and, therefore, God never wrought miracle to convince atheism, because his ordinary works convince it."[27]

In this light, how are we to interpret this passage in his *Religious Meditations?* "Amongst states men and politikes, those which have been of greatest depths, and compasse, and of largest and most universall understanding, have not onely in cunning made their profit in seeming religious to the people, but in truth have been toucht with an inwarde sence of the knowledge of Dyetie."[28] "Not onely"? There is, then, a certain element of calculation in these men's conduct. We are approaching the notion of imposture, which Bacon had addressed in the two preceding chapters, distinguishing several categories, such as those who "doe make and devise all variety of tales, stories, and examples, whereby they may leade mens mindes to a beliefe, from whence did growe the Legendes and infinite fabulous inventions and dreames of the ancient heretikes" or those who "fill mens ears with misteries, high parables, Allegories, and illusions:

which misticall and profound forme many of the hereticks have also made choyce of." Men's minds are "inveigled," "astonished and en-chanted," but at the same time "seduced and abused."[29] Clearly, he is speaking only of heretics, but the element of imposture is there.

Bacon applied the notion openly to Mahomet, recalling the leg-end of his abortive miracle, when the Prophet commanded a moun-tain to come to him, and it failed to move. "If the mountain will not come to Mahomet, then Mahomet will go to the mountain," he supposedly said, and for Bacon, this was evidently the proof of his imposture.[30]

Some years later, in 1621, another Englishman, Robert Burton, treated religious imposture at greater length. This great melan-cholic, born in 1577, spent his life at Oxford, surrounded by books, building up a colossal amount of learning on all subjects and all pe-riods, which allowed him to write an immense treatise of two thou-sand pages, stuffed with citations, called *The Anatomy of Melancholy*. For Burton, one of the causes of the sickness of living that affected society was religion, or rather excess in matters of religion. This in turn led him to consider religious imposture in general. Like a good Anglican, he spared Jesus, but he harshly criticized all other proph-ets and mystics, and made no secret of his belief that religion had always been used to manipulate the common people and hold them in subjection.

The three monotheistic religions were placed at the same level of ridicule, and Burton did not hesitate to produce the arguments by which each religion mocked the others:

> But for the rest I will not justifie that pontificial consubstantiation, that which *Mahometans & Jewes* justly except at, as *Campanella* confes-seth, *Atheismi triumphat. cap. 12. fol. 125.* . . . They hold it impossible, . . . and besides they scoffe at it. . . . But he that shall read the *Turks Al-coran*, the *Jewes Talmud*, and Papists *Golden Legend*, in the meane time will sweare that such grosse fictions, fables, vaine traditions, pro-digious paradoxes and ceremonies, could never proceed from any other spirit, then that of the divell himselfe, which is the Author of confusion and lies, and wonder withall how such wise men as have bin of the Jewes, such learned understanding men as *Averroes*, *Avicenna*, or those heathen Philosophers, could ever be perswaded to

beleeve, or to subscribe to the least part of them: ... but that as *Vani-nus* answeres, ... they durst not speake, for feare of the law.[31]

The use of Lucilio Vanini, cited as an authority, is at the very least ambiguous, given that Vanini had just been burned as a heretic in 1619. In another passage, Burton cited him again, approvingly, in support of the argument that religion in general is a politically motivated imposture. Everything said by the inventors of a creed is only fable. Only the common people, whom it is easy to fool, believed in it (says Vanini in speaking of religion). It was all only fables, "but they were still silent for feare of lawes."[32]

Thus Burton seems close to espousing the thesis of the three impostors. Of course, for him there was a true religion, the Church of England, but after all that he had said, the reader would find it hard not to put Jesus into the same category with Moses and Mahomet, since Catholics, with all their superstitions, laid claim to him. Burton, however, stated that only atheists accepted the thesis: "for their parts they esteeme them as so many Poets tales, Bugbeares, *Lucians Alexander, Moses, Mahomet* and *Christ* are all as one in their creed" (3:396). But aren't the atheists right to do so? the disoriented reader might ask. Isn't that just what you have made us understand? Burton had at least heard talk of the treatise *De tribus impostoribus*, which he condemned categorically as the work of an atheist, all the while maintaining notions that were very close to those of the book's thesis. He did not hesitate to state that the founders of religions all profit by the ignorance and foolishness of the people:

> Their owne feare, folly, stupidity, to be deplored Lethargy, is that which gives occasion to the other, and puylls these miseries on their own heads. For in all these Religions and superstitions, amongst our Idolaters, you shall still finde, that the parties first affected, are silly, rude, ignorant people, old folkes, that are naturally prone to superstition, weake women, or some poore rude illiterate persons, that are apt to be wrought upon, and gulled in this kinde, prone without either examination or due consideration (for they take up religion a trust as at Mercers they doe their wares) to beleeve any thing. And the best meanes they have to broach first, or to maintaine it when they have done, is to keepe them still in ignorance: for *Ignorance is the mother of devotion*, as all the world knows, and these times can amply witnesse.[33]

Would Lucian and Julian have said anything different?

Thus Robert Burton, who called himself a good Christian, unintentionally contributed to discrediting Christianity and accrediting the thesis of the three impostors. How, and in what name, would one distinguish between Moses, Jesus, and Mahomet after the denunciation of religious imposture in general that *The Anatomy of Melancholy* indulged in? The work was either ambiguous or tactless, and in either case it furnished arguments to the atheists and deists whom it claimed to challenge. Burton knew, however, how to maintain the respectable and inoffensive image of an Oxford don, a solitary library rat whose enormous and tiresome work would only reach a very small number of people.

Very different was the case of a man like Christopher Marlowe, whose provocative and blasphemous energy seemed to seek out trouble. His life was short, cut off by murder at the age of twenty-nine, in 1593, and punctuated by dark stories of killings, espionage, counterfeiting, pederasty, and atheism. All of which made this dramatist, a contemporary of Shakespeare, into a sort of *poète maudit*, proclaiming the revolt of the mind and the senses against religious oppression. But while the bard of Avon became a national icon, Marlowe as a disreputable character was discreetly made to disappear from the English collective memory. Recent studies, however, have shown that this creator of the myth of Faust represented an important current of irreligion,[34] daring to say out loud what many people were thinking in private—especially the notion that Moses, Jesus, and Mahomet were a trio of impostors.

Marlowe's unbelief shows through in his works as well as in his life. His first big theatrical success, *Tamburlaine the Great*, performed in 1587 by the troupe of Admiral Charles Howard, takes place in the Islamic world. We see the hero, a Scythian chieftain, burn the Qur'ān and defy Mahomet to do something about it. To be sure, he is struck down shortly thereafter by a bad fever, but the explanation for it is strictly natural, and he recovers. Fear of the gods rests on illusions.

In his *Doctor Faustus*, Christopher Marlowe took up a myth that appeared around the beginning of the Renaissance: that of George, a reincarnation of Simon the Magician, who makes a pact with the devil. Marlowe, however, transformed the myth into an accusation against religion, attacking the Calvinist god, who predestines some people to hell and others to paradise, no matter what they may do:

Ay, we must die an everlasting death.
What doctrine call you this? *Che serà, serà,*
What will be, shall be? Divinity, adieu![35]

But it was mainly Marlowe's conduct and opinions that made his reputation. Unlike the learned libertines in France, he was not a discreet atheist. He proselytized, and was accused of having converted some colleagues at Cambridge. According to Simon Aldrich, Marlowe had a friend whom he converted to atheism and who stated that the soul died with the body, and that just as we remember nothing that happened before our birth, we will remember nothing after our death.[36] Likewise, Marlowe was said to have defended atheism before Sir Walter Raleigh, who was himself more than a little bit suspect.

What we know about Marlowe's private opinions comes mainly from the proceedings of his trial. The playwright's life was quite troubled. In 1589, he was mixed up in a killing; arrested and imprisoned at Newgate, he was quickly freed, which told some people that he had secret links to the government. Two years before, he was said to have been living in Reims at a seminary that trained Catholic priests who were then secretly sent as missionaries to England. Marlowe was suspected of having been sent there as a spy of Queen Elizabeth I's government. But the man was a liability; insistent rumors accused him of murder, of counterfeiting, of atheism. He was arrested. His main accuser was his one-time companion at Reims, another Cambridge product, Richard Baines. According to Baines, Marlowe maintained that the primary goal of religion was to control men through fear; that Christ was a bastard and his mother a whore; that if he were going to create a new religion, he would use a better method; that Saint John the Evangelist lay with Christ and rested on his breast, and that he sodomized him. He spread atheism on the grounds that he did not want men to be frightened by scarecrows and bogeymen. According to another of Marlowe's Cambridge companions, Thomas Kyd, the author was in the habit of mocking divine scriptures and ridiculing prayers. Still another, Richard Cholmeley, stated that Marlowe was capable of giving better reasons in favor of atheism than any priest could give in proof of divinity, and that he had given an atheist lecture before Sir Walter Raleigh and others. He used to say in jest that Jesus Christ was a bastard, Saint Mary a whore, the angel Gabriel a toyboy of the Holy Spirit, that the Jews were right to persecute Christ because of his madness, and that Moses was a mountebank.

These charges, assembled in a note in seventeen articles, included openly accusing Moses and Jesus of imposture, and applying to them the statements of Livy, Polybius, and Machiavelli on the origin of religions. Thus, it was easy for Moses, who had been trained in Egyptian magic, to fool the Jews, a simple and primitive people. Moreover, Moses was only a mountebank, and a certain Harriot, one of Raleigh's men, could do much better. He proved it by subjugating the Indians through his Christian fables. As for Jesus, the Jews did well to condemn him and to pardon Barabbas.

That Marlowe should have been released after all, and then assassinated shortly afterward in a tavern brawl, deepens the mystery surrounding this sulfurous individual. It reinforces the thesis that he was a government agent who became a liability because of his rowdy atheism, and who was eliminated under cover of a quarrel that got out of hand. For the defenders of religion, this miserable death was obviously divine judgment against the blasphemer, the man whom some people accused of being the author of a treatise of the three impostors. Although Marlowe certainly never troubled himself to write such a treatise, his plays and his opinions contained its essential idea.

The idea in question circulated widely in England in the first half of the seventeenth century, where the political-religious context of the civil war served—as always in such cases—to harden religious fanaticism, on the one hand, and, on the other hand, to bring religion into disrepute. As early as 1616 Henry Wright, in a book dedicated to the mayor of London, hinted that all religions have a political origin. He did so in posing a series of rhetorical questions: Why do the wisest lawgivers place religion under the power of a prince? Is it because they consider that it is a subject that should depend only on our betters? Or because they believe that those who fear God will be more subservient? Or because they think that God will favor princes whose subjects serve him? "Or to conclude, was it for the generall good of a Common-wealth, as a certaine Diuine plainely protested, who held that *Religion*, and the *Feare of God*, were the surest bands for conseruing of Humane Society?"[37]

During the civil war and under Cromwell, numerous pamphlets developed this theme, such as those of Gerrard Winstanley, who stated that the clergy had first used the threat of punishment in this life—that is, a sort of immanent justice—to subject the people, and that when the people found out their "hypocrisy," they cast the threat of punishment into a future life. Thus, the "sly big brother" cheated his "naive little brother" out of all the freedoms of this life.[38] It is the whole story of the impostors.

The French Trail: Learned Libertines and Religious Imposture

The same pattern can be found in France, where the first half of the seventeenth century was the time of "learned libertines" who discreetly developed the themes that we find in the three impostors. The term *learned libertines* was coined by René Pintard, who in 1943 published a well-known study focusing on this particular milieu.[39] More recently, Françoise Charles-Daubert presented a broader view of the subject, which is now relatively well known.[40]

The learned libertines were libertines in the sense of free spirits and learned insofar as they were authentic intellectuals, teachers, and librarians to princes. Mastering a wide culture, they referred to themselves as "wisened up" or "illuminated," in the sense of having been enlightened and cured of the errors of the people. As great lords, wealthy, and enjoying the protection of the powerful, they inhabited the corridors of power and profoundly despised a credulous people and their religious beliefs. They themselves were skeptics, agnostics, deists, or frank atheists. Their reading and their proximity to the powerful convinced them that power, whether religious or political, was based on imposture. In spite of the protection they enjoyed, they were unable to proclaim their ideas openly, and agreed in believing that a conformist façade was necessary for the maintenance of public order. They were men of discretion, who spoke their thoughts only in private, in the cloistered atmosphere of certain salons and libraries. Their writings were necessarily deceptive, since to fool the censors they resorted to contradictory dialogues, jest, derision, or false interrogation, all of which left unwary readers in a state of confusion.

Their adversaries, the guardians of orthodoxy, were not deceived, and reacted strongly, beginning in 1623. In that year appeared two enormously long antiskeptical works: the *Quaestiones celeberrimae in Genesim [Famous Questions on Genesis]* of Father Marin Mersenne, and the thousand-page *La Doctrine curieuse des beaux esprits de ce temps [The Curious Doctrine of the Wits of the Day]* by the Jesuit Francis Garasse. These works marked the beginning of a fusillade of apologetic works that reveal the discomfort of the religious authorities faced with a rising tide of unbelief. Mersenne came back for a second round as early as 1624 with his *L'Impiété des déistes, athées et libertins du temps [The Impiety of the Deists, Atheists, and Freethinkers of the Day]*; an additional thirty-one titles followed in the years leading up to 1640.

Among recent authors, the learned libertines owed a special debt to Charron and Vanini. A lawyer turned theologian, Pierre Charron (1541–1603) was acquainted with Montaigne. Charron was the very type of the ambiguous writer just described: one whose writings claimed to defend religion, all the while providing weapons to its adversaries. This was why his book *De la sagesse [On Wisdom,* 1601] was attacked by Jesuits, the university, and the Parlement of Bordeaux. In his *Trois veritez [Three Truths]* of 1594, he began by deploring the progress that had been made by "atheists and the irreligious," to whom he quickly paid homage supported with arguments: these were men who had to have "an extremely strong and hardy spirit" in order to maintain their atheism in a hostile world. The atheist, "alone and without support," faced with "weariness and despair," had a tragic grandeur. If many men lost their faith, said Charron as he wept a crocodile tear, they had good excuses; taking account of the multitude of religions that vied with each other, they concluded that they were all impostures. "First of all, it is a terrifying thing to consider the great diversity of religions that have existed and still exist in the world, and even more to ponder the strangeness of some of them, so fantastic and excessive that it is a marvel that human understanding could have become so dulled and so intoxicated with impostures, for it seems that there is nothing in the upper or lower world that has not been deified somewhere and has not found a place to be worshipped."[41]

For these strong minds, "all religions share the characteristic of being strange and offending common sense. They all mutually condemn and reject each other, and the newer one always builds on the older one, which it gradually destroys, enriching itself with the spoils, as the Judaic religion did to the Gentile and Egyptian, Christianity to Judaism, and Islam to Judaism and Christianity together."[42]

Who could fail to draw the conclusion that Moses, Jesus, and Mahomet were three impostors?

Charron defended himself well against such a view, but his skepticism is obvious. The reasonable man simply had to conform to outward respect for the cult: "One must not in any case despise or disdain the outward and public service, which one ought to attend and participate in with others . . . and always in the recognition that God wishes to be served with the mind, and that what happens outwardly is more for ourselves than for God, more for human unity and edification than for divine truth." What Garasse saw as hypocrisy, Charron called wisdom.

Charron was one of the writers most read and cited by the learned libertines. They found in his work numerous arguments against religion and in favor of the thesis of imposture. With Vanini, they found a still more direct and aggressive expression of such views, and an explicit formulation of the idea of the three impostors. Lucilio Vanini (1584–1619) was a wandering monk, a teacher and philosopher who was executed at Toulouse for atheism. Like Giordano Bruno, he was one of the emblematic characters of freethinking. His "philosopher's death" made him a martyr: after he refused to recant, his tongue was torn out and he was burned alive, which gained him a place in the pantheon of freethinkers.

He is a baffling character, someone who throughout his life cultivated paradox and contradiction. Thus, in *The Amphitheater of Eternal Providence* (1615), he announced that he was going to defend divine providence against "ancient philosophers, atheists, Epicureans, Peripatetics, and Stoics." A curious defense, in which he expounded clearly and in detail the arguments of atheists against creation, and gave as his entire refutation this statement: "Let us leave to one side the innumerable objections that we might bring against a system so entirely opposed to reason."[43] Elsewhere, he reported the opinions of Machiavelli ("certainly the prince of atheists") and those of an anonymous "German atheist" against miracles, and confined himself to mentioning that he had already refuted all that in his works, something that one might search for in vain. Seeking to prove the reality of providence through oracles and miracles, he showed, to the contrary, that oracles are "tales" and that "miracles were invented and created by the rulers to tame their subjects, and by priests in order to gain honors and respect."[44] As for arguments drawn from the

Bible, why bother mentioning them, since "atheists place as much stock in Holy Scripture as I do in Aesop's Fables"?[45]

Vanini's *Dialogues* explicitly contain the thesis of the three impostors. We see Moses, a cruel and wily military man, who once put to death eighty thousand idolators at one time, who used Egyptian magic to establish his laws, and—the supreme imposture—threw himself alive into a chasm, so that the crowd, no longer seeing him, would believe him to have been carried up to heaven. (We must, in all fairness, point out that this last item was Vanini's own vision; the biblical text and the rabbinic tradition maintain Moses' strictly human character and emphasize that his death far from human sight was solely so that his tomb would not become a place of worship.) Next, we see Jesus, an admirable sophist, answering questions with questions, making use of obscure parables, and, in a remarkable example of deceit, declaring the everlastingness of his religion and announcing in advance that those who oppose it are themselves part of his plan: they are Antichrists, persecutors of the Christians, heralding the final victory. Moses is the magician impostor, Jesus the philosophical impostor, and Mahomet the military impostor who wipes out the infidel and takes his inspiration from the other two. He has a disciple put at the bottom of a well and has him cry out: "I am God, and I swear to you that I have designated Mahomet to be my great prophet!" He then has the disciple buried alive by covering the well with stones. In one way, Vanini might be called the author of the three impostors, even if he never wrote the famous treatise.

The learned libertines took their inspiration from these authors. And as in England, the idea of religious imposture was favored by the political context. Not that France suffered the kind of revolutionary upheavals occasioned by the English Civil War—the French Fronde of the mid-seventeenth century was only a shadow—but the realpolitik of the cardinal-ministers Richelieu and Mazarin in many respects served as an illustration of this imposture, with the triumph of reasons of state. The security of the state, as the supreme value, justified the manipulation of individual conscience by means of religion and the unscrupulous use of assassination.

The great defender of realpolitik was one of the most representative learned libertines, Gabriel Naudé (1600-1653). A doctor by training, and a passionate bibliophile who collected thousands of books in the course of his travels in Europe, Naudé became librarian to Cardinal Mazarin. He corresponded with Peiresc and with the Dupuy brothers, and was a friend of the physician Guy Patin. In his works, especially his *Considérations politiques sur les coups d'état [Political Considerations on Regime Change]*, he developed a realist, even cynical, conception of reasons of state. Political power was based on an imposture that involved the use of religion as a means of control of the populace, and this was a good thing: this was the gist of his message, which was unquestionably an apology for imposture.

All political power, to the extent that it is the government of the majority by a minority, necessarily supposes institutionalization of inequality and exclusive use of "legitimate" violence. The use of physical force, which inspires fear of earthly punishment, is a good match, in Naudé's view, for the use of religion, which inspires fear of future punishment. Like a good disciple of Machiavelli, Naudé shows how monarchy succeeded in establishing itself by making use of obvious tricks aimed at subjugating the people, that stupid wild animal—"a beast with many heads, unstable, mad, stupefied, lacking conduct, spirit, or judgment"—tricks like the sacrament of coronation at Reims, the holy ampoule miraculously brought by an angel, the healing power of kings, or the mission of Joan of Arc. "He who does not know how to lie does not know how to rule"—and thanks to the cooperation of the priests, royal power was able to establish itself, assisted by popular superstition. If Peter the Hermit preaches the Crusade to the populace, he will bring with him relics consisting of hairs from his donkey, writes Naudé. If superstition alone does not suffice, they complete the work by means of repression, which must be pitiless: if the St. Bartholomew's Day Massacre[46] was a mistake and a failure, in Naudé's view, it was because it failed to wipe out *all* the Protestants.

The use of religious imposture by political imposture was necessary to avoid the chaos of civil war. This type of proposition was clearly not intended for the wider public. Naudé's *Political Considerations* was a confidential work, intended only for those in charge; Naudé himself printed only twelve copies.

Another of the "enlightened" was François de La Mothe Le Vayer (1588-1672), who shared Naudé's analysis of politico-religious imposture but drew an opposite conclusion from it. Far from approving of subterfuge, he despised it and made it the cause of his retirement from public affairs. Finding that the world turned on the axis of trickery, this philosopher saw himself as a spectator of the human comedy. A royal prosecutor and friend of Pierre Gassendi, Naudé, and Giovanni Diodati, La Mothe Le Vayer nonetheless placed his pen at the service of Cardinal Richelieu and took up the post of tutor to the young Duke of Anjou and the dauphin. He was the author of a pious *Petit discours chrétien de l'immortalité de l'âme* [*Short Christian Discourse on the Immortality of the Soul*, 1637] and a treatise *De la vertu des payens* [*On the Virtue of Pagans*, 1642]. He also wrote *Soliloques sceptiques* [*Skeptical Soliloquies*, 1670] and *Quatre dialogues faits à l'imitation des Anciens* [*Four Dialogues in Imitation of the Ancients*, 1606], a work inspired by Pyrrhonian skepticism. All this tells us that we have here a Janus whose public face was that of a believer and his private face that of an unbeliever.

The atheism or the skepticism of the learned libertines had a philosophical and psychological basis. They saw in the unbelief of some the proof of their intellectual superiority, and in the credulity of others, the manifest sign of their ignorance. In his *Apologie pour tous les grands personnages qui ont esté faussement soupçonnez de magie* [*Apology for Those Great Men Who Have Been Falsely Suspected of Magic*, 1625], Naudé showed that those great men were in fact learned men, philosophers or mathematicians, who had been seen as magicians by the common people, who were incapable of understanding the true powers of reason. "I pray you to reflect but a little, not only on the errors, stupidities, and impertinence of vulgar opinion . . . but also on the tyrannical authority of the times and customs that gave rise to them, and on the invincible stubbornness with which they were so blindly upheld. I am sure you will be forced to admit that an honest and truth-loving man would not know how to distance himself far enough from all this."[47] These are the words of La Mothe Le Vayer, who added that any idea taken up by the people was guaranteed to be false: "The word *plebiscite* makes me take three steps back." In Naudé's words: "The common herd can be compared to a sea subject to all sorts of winds and storms. . . . In brief, everything they think is only vanity, everything they say is false and absurd, what they disapprove is good, what they approve is bad, what they praise is infamous, and everything that they do and undertake is pure folly."

CHAPTER FOUR

Debates on the Origin of Religions
(Second Half of the Seventeenth Century)

One could say that the *Treatise of the Three Impostors* was the late fruit of the "European crisis of conscience" (to use Paul Hazard's phrase) that characterized the years from 1680 to 1720. It was appropriate for this period, which saw the birth of the modern critical spirit, to focus on this manifesto of the demystification of religions. The most elaborate version of the *Treatise of the Three Impostors* basically took up the complementary arguments of the two great destroyers of religion in the mid-seventeenth century: Hobbes and Spinoza.

Hobbes and Spinoza

Thomas Hobbes (1588–1679) was without doubt one of the most powerful intellects of the seventeenth century. The son of an unpretentious Anglican vicar from the neighborhood of Malmesbury, he studied at Magdalen Hall, Oxford, and became tutor to the son of the Duke of Devonshire, William Cavendish. He accompanied his young charge on the Grand Tour of the Continent. Between 1621 and 1626, he was in close contact with Francis Bacon, who imparted to Hobbes his own passion for the sciences. Hobbes's obsession can be described in two words: certainty and security. Throughout his long life of ninety-one years, he sought serenity within and without, through intellectual knowledge and civil peace. He sought knowledge by means of a type of mathematical logic; for him, geometry was the queen of sciences because of its reassuring rigor. As for civil peace, he envisaged it in the form of an authoritarian state, directing the activities of individuals who, ruled by their appetites for power and pleasure, are all wolves who devour each other. A liberal political system can only give rise to civil war. Hobbes's convictions were reinforced by the vagaries of his personal life, which included his friendship with Bacon; a second and then a third trip to France in the years between 1634 and 1637, in the course of which he frequented the scientific circle of Marin Mersenne and made an excursion to Florence to meet Galileo during his house arrest; and a return to England from 1637 to 1640, followed by a voluntary eleven-year exile in Paris, from 1640 to 1651, to escape the civil war that was ravaging his country. It was in France that he wrote his major work, *Leviathan*, published in London in 1651, the same year he returned to England at the age of sixty-three. For the next twenty-eight years, he lived discreetly in a country that regained civil peace, first under the Puritan dictatorship of Cromwell, then under the Restoration of Charles II.

Historical opinion about Hobbes is divided, as it is for all the suspect authors of the period. Was Hobbes an atheist? He himself claimed to be a good Anglican, for obvious reasons of prudence. But his philosophy is undeniably materialist: the soul is as material as the breath, and thought is aroused by the physical movements of the body. The body is affected by sensations that arise through the action of the environment upon it, and these sensations produce in the brain "phantasms" or "idols of the brain." Memory is the physical preservation of the traces of these phantasms, which the imagination makes use of. As for language, it is the means invented by men to preserve and communicate memories, obeying a certain number of rules. Thus, discursive thought is nothing more than an assemblage of words, which depend on the imagination, which itself comes from the body. This is also why mankind's existence is determined; freedom is an illusion that comes from the greater or lesser absence of obstacles to the realization of our desires. Man is moved solely by his anarchic, egoistic instincts, and social life thus requires a strong state capable of reining in these instincts.

As for religion, its origin is purely psychological, something that Hobbes explains in chapter 12 of the first part of *Leviathan*. For him, religious belief has four sources, starting with man's need or desire to know the causes of what happens to him; the need to know the origins of events; the fact that everything has a reason. Thus, "when he cannot assure himselfe of the true causes of things, . . . he supposes causes of them, either such as his own fancy suggesteth; or trusteth to the Authority of other men, such as he thinks to be his friends, and wiser than himself."

Ignorance of the true causes of events creates anxiety about the future. This fear is the most important of the four sources of religious belief, because

> that man, which looks too far before him, in the care of future time, hath his heart all the day long, gnawed on by feare of death, poverty, or other calamity; and has no repose, nor pause of his anxiety, but in sleep.
>
> This perpetuall feare, alwayes accompanying mankind in the ignorance of causes, as it were in the Dark, must needs have for object something. And therefore when there is nothing to be seen, there is nothing to accuse, either of their good, or evil fortune, but some *Power*, or Agent *Invisible*.

They suppose that this agent is incorporeal, of the same substance as dreams. "Men not knowing that such apparitions are nothing else but creatures of the Fancy, think to be reall, and externall Substances," and because they do not understand them, they suppose them to be all-powerful and eternal, and set themselves to worshiping them, serving their cult.

This is where the founders of religions come in. They are of two sorts:

> One sort have been they, that have nourished, and ordered them, according to their own invention. The other, have done it, by Gods commandement and direction: but both sorts have done it, with a purpose to make those men that relyed on them, the more apt to Obedience, Lawes, Peace, Charity, and civill Society. So that the Religion of the former sort, is a part of humane Politiques; and teacheth part of the duty which Earthly Kings require of their Subjects. And the Religion of the later sort is Divine Politiques; and containeth Precepts to those that have yeelded thyemselves subjects in the Kingdome of God. Of the former sort, were all the founders of Commonwealths, and the Law-givers of the Gentiles: Of the later sort, were *Abraham, Moses*, and our *Blessed Saviour*.

Here we see a face-saving device: only the first kind are impostors, like Numa Pompilius or Mahomet, who "to set up his new Religion, pretended to have conferences with the Holy Ghost, in forme of a Dove." The distinction seems ambiguous, since all base their religion on the will to ensure the obedience of believers. Admittedly, the second type act on orders from God, but after what Hobbes has said about the imaginary origin of the gods, we may indeed feel perplexed.

Equally ambiguous are the criteria he proposes to distinguish good and bad religions: a bad and false religion is one that requires its adherents to believe impossible things, a religion whose clergymen conduct themselves in ways that violate its own precepts, or one that fails to produce miracles and true prophecies. This reference to a miracle as a criterion, from the pen of an advocate of determinism, is astounding. In chapter 37 of the third part of *Leviathan*, Hobbes reveals his thoughts on miracles. They are natural phenomena that amaze the ignorant, or else they are tricks of entertainers or ventriloquists: "For example; if a man pretend, that after certain words spoken over a peece of bread, that presently God hath made it not bread, but a God, or a man, or both, and neverthelesse it looketh still as like bread as ever it did; there is no reason for any man to think it really done."[1] But this was exactly what those superstitious Catholics believed. Hobbes was careful to safeguard Anglicanism in his words, but his formal precautions didn't fool many, especially given that, if there ever was a religion expressly created from political motives, this was it. Thus, Hobbes was clearly undermining the foundations of all religion, and not just those of one religion or another.

A similar and even more daring project is that of Hobbes's Dutch contemporary, Baruch Spinoza (1632-1677), whose life was much shorter than that of Hobbes. Spinoza played a central role in the theme of the three impostors, as it was under his name that there appeared in 1719 the first printed version of the treatise in French: *La Vie et l'Esprit de Spinoza [The Life and Thought of Spinoza]*. Thus, we shall need to spend a bit more time with him.

Born in Amsterdam in 1632, to Portuguese Jewish parents, Baruch Spinoza studied at a Jewish religious school. He soon discovered an interest in the sciences and in the philosophy of Descartes, learned Latin, and quickly distanced himself from Jewish orthodoxy. For reasons that scholars are still trying to penetrate, but which no doubt were linked to his denial that Moses had written down the Pentateuch (as dictated by God), he was excommunicated by the Jewish community and exiled from Amsterdam in 1656, at the age of twenty-four. He ended up in The Hague, where he lived a modest and orderly life as a lens grinder. Over the course of twenty years, in addition to thousands of glass lenses, he produced such works as a

Short Treatise, Treatise on the Improvement of Understanding, Principles of Cartesian Philosophy, Metaphysical Thoughts, Ethica [Ethics], Tractatus theologico-politicus, and a *Treatise on Political Authority.* In these works he developed an austere, complex system of thought, in which God and nature were considered as two aspects of a single, unique reality, something that immediately gained him a reputation for atheism and the undying hatred of Christian intellectuals who saw in him the incarnation of two supreme moral taints: he was a Jewish atheist.

It was not even necessary to read his books to know that they were bad, wrote Antoine Arnauld. "I have not read Spinoza's books, but I know that they are wicked works. He is an avowed atheist, who believes in no other god than nature." The Swiss writer Jean-Baptiste Stouppe, in his *Dutch Religion,* wrote that Spinoza was "a wicked Jew, and no better as a Christian." Nicolas Malebranche rose up against "this impious man of our day who made the universe his god." The theologian Musaeus, a professor at the university of Jena, stated that "the devil has seduced many men; . . . among them, no one worked so hard and so effectively to ruin all human and divine law as this impostor, who had nothing else in view than the fall of the state and of all religion." After all, was he not the devil himself? "He was small, yellowish, with something black in his physiognomy, he wore on his face an unsavory character," we may read in the 1695 edition of the *Menagiana.*

In the mid-seventeenth century, the Portuguese Jewish community of Amsterdam was roiled by strident debates and scandals revolving around the character of Moses. In 1658, one of its members, Daniel Ribeira, was accused of having denied the existence of providence, and of having said that Moses was a magician who, in establishing his laws, had acted in his own interest and in that of his brother Aaron.[2] In fact, what Ribeira upheld was no more nor less than the thesis of the three impostors. This became clear from the deposition of Abraham Franco de Silvera, who told how one day, when he entered Ribeira's room, Ribeira spoke so frankly as to state that what Moses said was as false as the speeches of Mahomet and Christ, and that everything they said was deceitful or expedient.[3] Ribeira was not the only Portuguese Jew in Amsterdam to hold these views. Juan de Prado, who arrived in 1655, posed the question of why anyone should believe Moses more than the teachings of other sects.

There ought to be a reason, he maintained, for choosing to believe Moses over Mahomet, "but that is pure imagination."⁴ The idea of the imposture of the founders of revealed religions became such an important preoccupation that the great rabbi Saul Levi Morteira felt it necessary to publish an apologetic work to defend Moses, the *Tratado da verdade da Lei de Moisès [Treatise on the Truth of Moses' Law]*. Not long after Spinoza's excommunication, Juan de Prado was excommunicated. He had been in contact with Henry Oldenburg, who, from England, asked Adam Borel in Amsterdam to write a refutation of the thesis of the three impostors, a work that he finished in 1661, as we shall see. The idea of the triple imposture clearly was an essential preoccupation of the Jews of Amsterdam; historian Richard Popkin has even suggested that the *Tractatus theologico-politicus* was a response to the *Treatise of the Three Impostors*.⁵ An unlikely hypothesis, to be sure, but it is certain that Spinoza was surrounded by the controversy over this theme, which filled the Jewish community.

Spinoza's *Tractatus* dates from 1670. It was preceded by several bold works that also discussed the relations between politics and religion. In 1665, Franciscus Van den Enden, an ex-Jesuit from Anvers who took refuge in Amsterdam, and who incidentally had been Spinoza's Latin teacher, had published a republican treatise written in Dutch, the *Vrije politijke stellingen [Free Political Proposals]* as a plea for democracy, religious freedom, and the rights of atheism. The ex-Jesuit would be hanged in 1674 at the Bastille for his participation in a plot against Louis XIV. In 1666, a friend of Spinoza's, Lodewijk Meijer, published a Latin work, the *Philosophia S. Scripturae interpres [Philosophy as Interpreter of Holy Scripture]*, which caused a scandal by applying the Cartesian method to biblical study. Putting aside any idea of divine revelation, it examined the text of the Bible in the sole light of reason in order to retain only clear and evident ideas. With contradictions, errors, and absurdities eliminated, not much remained of the sacred text. How could anyone claim that such a tissue of foolishness could be the word of God? Such was the implicit lesson of the book, which instantly came under attack by conservative Calvinists of Voet's faction, and was sporadically banned in Holland. Two years later, another friend of Spinoza's, Adriaan Koerbagh, went even further by publishing, under his own name and in Dutch, the *Bloemhof van allerley lieflijkheid [The Flower Garden of All Sorts of Delights]*, accusing the Bible of being a purely human source of confusion. He demanded that the people should be informed of this, in order to put an end to the imposture of the ministers of the cult. The people needed to hear the truth: that the Bible is only a pile of myths and old folktales. He demanded that theology be subjected to the philosophical method, and openly took on the idea of the Trinity. Even in the United Provinces, there were limits that could not be transgressed: denial of the Trinity, the divinity of Christ, original sin, the immortality of the soul, or the divine authority of scripture. Koerbagh set off all the alarms. He was arrested and sentenced to pay a heavy fine and serve ten years in prison. He died in his prison cell in October 1669.

At the same time a major anti-Socinian campaign was taking place in Holland, orchestrated by Voet and his supporters. The Socinians were accused of being antitrinitarian, denying the divinity of Christ, and denying original sin, positions that in Voet's view were completely incompatible with a Christian society. In September 1653 the States-General of Holland had prohibited Socinianism. In Amsterdam and Rotterdam, communities had been dispersed, but their former members regrouped in small private associations. The persecution went on into the 1670s and touched all the philosophical currents of an "atheistic" tendency. The famous reputation for tolerance enjoyed by the United Provinces in the seventeenth century had significant limits.

It was in this climate and in the midst of these debates that Spinoza composed his *Tractatus theologico-politicus*. In the 1660s, the philosopher/lens grinder seemed above all to be a Cartesian. In 1663, he published an explanation of the philosophy of Descartes. But he had other ambitions. Let us not imagine him as a humble craftsman alone in his shop. He was already at the center of a circle of intellectuals with advanced ideas, who sought to liberate the work of philosophy from the tutelage of the theologians. Spinoza wanted to show that the alliance of religious power and theological zeal, already responsible for the fall of the liberal regime of Oldenbarnevelt, similarly endangered the regime of De Witt. Only tolerance and individual freedom could guarantee a legitimate government. On the other hand, he was aware that the thesis of his book was controversial. "I do not separate God from Nature," he wrote to Henry Oldenburg. "I do not have any definite plan regarding publication.... I fear, of course, that the theologians of our time may be offended and with their usual hatred attack me, who loathes quarrels."[6] To which Oldenburg replied that he ought not to fear "arousing the pygmies of our age."

This was not Spinoza's opinion, however. Instead, with a truly Cartesian prudence, he equivocated until 1670, perhaps shocked by the punishment suffered by Koerbagh. He wanted his book to be a resounding success, and yet not cause trouble for him, which was a great deal to ask. He thus decided to publish it anonymously and in Latin, so as to avoid a condemnation that would ruin his reputation. When he learned in February 1671 that an unauthorized Dutch translation was in the works, he put a stop to it. Nonetheless, there was a scandal. The consistories of Leiden and Haarlem protested loudly; the burgermeisters, when consulted, agreed that the book could not be tolerated and had it withdrawn from bookshops; the synod of Southern Holland, at Schiedam, declared that the book was the worst of the recent wave of "execrable and blasphemous books." Even a liberal such as the regent Van Velthuysen wrote that it "destroys and absolutely ruins every cult and every religion, and introduces atheism by the back door." Stouppe opined that the *Tractatus* "had as its main goal the destruction of all religions, especially Judaism, and the introduction of atheism, free thought, and freedom for all religions." In 1674, the *Tractatus* was banned in Holland, at the same times as Hobbes's *Leviathan*: the association of the two works in the same condemnation is revealing. In 1675, Spinoza, whom everyone had known from the start was the author of the accursed work, had to give up the idea of publishing his *Ethics*, which came out ten months after his death, in 1677, thanks to the efforts of Meijer. The book was banned by the Dutch States-General in 1678 as containing "very many profane, blasphemous, and atheistic propositions."[7]

Looking at the entirety of Spinoza's works, we see that what he calls God is the wholeness of being, of existing, of the all; in philosophical language, God is the unique substance, endowed with an infinite number of attributes, of which we can know only two: thought and extension. God is thus not a pure spirit, he is also the entirety of the material world, which is one of his manifestations, one of his attributes. He is not transcendent, he is nature, but nature is only one of his manifestations. This God is a creator, but he does not create freely. Instead, he creates through the necessity of his own nature, because to create by free choice would be to renounce other possibilities, and thus to limit himself. The universe is a necessary manifestation of God, under his attribute of materiality. Nature is not to be confused with God, of whom it is only a manifestation. Spinozism is thus more than a type of pantheism: it is, according to the universal reading of his contemporaries, a form of atheism, even if it is a spiritual and not a materialist atheism. Although Spinoza denied free will, providence, divine reward, and punishment, he did not rule out the possibility for the soul to gain immortality by acquiring true ideas.

In the appendix to the first part of the *Ethics,* Spinoza develops the consequences of these principles, a development that is especially important for the history of the three impostors. "All men are born ignorant of the causes of things; . . . all have the desire to seek for what is useful to them, and that they are conscious of such desire" (R. H. M. Elwes, ed. and trans., *The Chief Works of Benedict de Spinoza* [London: George Bell & Sons, 1909], 2:75). They believe themselves to be free, acting always with a goal in mind, and they think that God does the same, that he has made the universe with such and such a goal. They imagine that all sorts of natural phenomena are intended either to reward them or to punish them. This view of a final cause is the consequence of human ignorance; since we do not know the true causes of events, we attribute them to a superior will. The complexity of the human body or the beauty of the universe can only be the work of an infinite intelligence acting with a deliberate intent. This is the common illusion of men, who cannot resign themselves either to chance or to necessity. "They necessarily judge other natures by their own," and when they are ignorant of the causes, they say that it is the will of God, "the sanctuary of ignorance" (ibid., 78).

The principal factor in the origin of established religions is ignorance, and the second is fear, as Spinoza explains in the *Tractatus theologico-politicus.*

[Men] (especially when they are in danger, and cannot help themselves) are wont with prayers and womanish tears to implore help from God: upbraiding Reason as blind, because she cannot show a sure path to the shadows they pursue, and rejecting human wisdom as vain; but believing the phantoms of imagination, dreams, and other childish absurdities, to be the very oracles of Heaven. As though God had turned away from the wise, and written His decrees, not in the mind of man but in the entrails of beasts, or left them to be proclaimed by the inspiration and instinct of fools, madmen, and birds. Such is the unreason to which terror can drive mankind![8]

Thus, religions are "the vestiges of an ancient servility of the spirit." They are perpetuated by the imposture of priests, so that "faith has become a mere compound of credulity and prejudices—aye, prejudices too, which degrade man from rational being to beast, which completely stifle the power of judgment between true and false, which seem, in fact, carefully fostered for the purpose of extinguishing the last spark of reason! Piety, great God! and religion are become a tissue of ridiculous mysteries; men, who flatly despise reason, who reject and turn away from understanding as naturally corrupt, these, I say, these of all men, are thought, O lie most horrible! to possess light from on High."[9] Governments, especially monarchies, make use of the imposture of the priests: "In despotic statecraft, the supreme and essential mystery [is] to hoodwink the subjects, and to mask the fear, which keeps them down, with the specious garb of religion."[10]

They endow religion with ceremonies and rites aimed at impressing men and curbing reason—"a system which has been brought to great perfection by the Turks, for they consider even controversy impious, and so clog men's minds with dogmatic formulas, that they leave no room for sound reason, not even enough to doubt with."[11] Christians and Jews are not spared.

> I have often wondered that persons who make a boast of professing the Christian religion, namely, love, joy, peace, temperance, and charity to all men, should quarrel with such rancorous animosity, and display daily toward one another such bitter hatred, that this, rather than the virtues they claim, is the readiest criterion of their faith. Matters have long since come to such a pass, that one can only pronounce a man Christian, Turk, Jew, or Heathen, by his general appearance and attire, by his frequenting this or that place of worship, or by his employing the phraseology of a particular sect—as for manner of life, it is in all cases the same.[12]

Judaism, Christianity, Islam: three impostures responsible, according to Spinoza, for innumerable ills, and which men practice by venerating texts that claim to be revealed and sacred, which they can interpret as they please, which allows them to avoid having to present any proof. Priests, rabbis, pastors, imams, and others "[lay] down beforehand, as a foundation for the study and true interpretation of scripture, the principle that it is in every passage true and divine. Such a doctrine should be reached only after strict scrutiny and thorough comprehension of the Sacred Books . . . and not be set up on the threshold, as it were, of inquiry." These texts need to be analyzed using the tools of philology, grammar, history, and archaeology, to make a serious study. Instead, "we see most people endeavouring to hawk about their own commentaries as the word of God, and giving their best efforts, under the guise of religion, to compelling others to think as they do."[13]

Religious imposture and political imposture mutually support each other. Only a democratic government, ensuring freedom of thought and expression as well as tolerance, would permit men to free themselves from these illusions, thought Spinoza, no doubt with an overdose of optimism. At the time, his thoughts commit a sort of crime of *lèse-religion*. "Not content with undermining the bases of religion and a healthy theology, he goes so far as to overturn the political order and the notions of common sense," wrote Huet in his *Demonstratio evangelica* of 1679. This was "systematic atheism," with which even strong minds were afraid to compromise themselves. Those who adopted his ideas did so under cover of criticizing them, such as Boulainvillier, who made the first French translation of the *Ethics*, which remained unpublished. His *Essai de métaphysique dans les principes de B. de Spinoza [Metaphysical Essay on Spinoza's Principles]* did not appear until 1731, in a collection entitled *Refutation of Spinoza*. Similarly, F. Kuyper portrayed Spinozism sympathetically in the *Arcana atheismi revelata [Atheism's Secrets Revealed]* of 1676, as did Jarrig Jelles in his *Profession de foi universelle et chrétienne [Profession of Universal and Christian Faith]*. Overt apologies were rare, and were either clandestine or condemned. The *Vie de Spinoza* by the physician Lucas of The Hague was not published until 1719 with the *Esprit de Spinoza*, a French version of the *Three Impostors*. In December 1697, a materialist disciple of Spinoza, Johannes Duijkerius, published anonymously at Amsterdam 1,500 copies of a sequel to a philosophical novel, *Het leven van Philopater*, in which he popularized Spinozism. The books were seized and burned in Holland and in Zeeland, and the publisher was sentenced to eight years in prison, followed by banishment and payment of a heavy fine.

It was a holy union of Protestants, Catholics, and Jews against impiety. Even Bayle, in his *Dictionnaire historique et critique* of 1696, felt obliged to howl with the wolves, writing that the *Tractatus* was "a pernicious and hateful book where [Spinoza] slipped in all the seeds of the atheism that showed itself openly in his *Opera posthuma*." Merely showing an interest in Spinoza was enough to make someone suspect. The famous physician Hermann Boerhaave told how, as a passenger on a barge in 1693, while he was a student, he overheard a discussion about the philosopher, in the course of which the participants criticized Spinoza vehemently. He asked them if they had read him. Immediately, someone asked him his name and made a note of it; he thereby became suspected of Spinozism and his hopes for a clerical career were dashed. Spinoza became the scapegoat, the author of all intellectual evil, at once materialist, pantheist, atheist, and libertine. This was true especially after the publication of Stouppe's *Dutch Religion* in 1673, which held that, for Spinoza, "God is not a being endowed with intelligence, infinitely perfect and happy, as we imagine [a revealing choice of term!] him, but is nothing other than this virtue of nature that is distributed among all creatures." He was further accused of ruining the authority of scripture. For Leibniz, who knew him personally, corresponded with him, and met him in 1676, he was above all a Cartesian, an affiliation that was rejected with horror by the disciples of that French philosopher, including Malebranche, Fénelon, and Lamy, in his 1696 *Athéisme renversé [Atheism Overturned]*. In short, he was an untouchable; his admirers hid themselves, especially if they belonged to the official church, such as the pastor in the Lower Palatinate, J. C. Laukhard, who only after his death was discovered to have been a fervent Spinozan.

Holland and the Birth of the Radical Enlightenment

In the arrival in Holland of the radical Enlightenment,[14] which gave rise to the French text of the *Three Impostors*, one event played an essential role: the immigration of Huguenot refugees after the revocation of the Edict of Nantes in 1685. Of course, there was a French presence before then, composed of heterodox elements who had come there in order to enjoy the relative freedom of expression and of publication in the Dutch Republic. After 1685, an estimated thirty-five thousand new arrivals established themselves. They formed communities and developed French-speaking networks. Among them were many artisans, but also intellectuals, publishers, and authors, many of whom did not speak Dutch and took little interest in local issues. The most famous of these, Pierre Bayle (1647-1706), lived in Rotterdam for twenty-five years without ever learning to speak Dutch; Prosper Marchand, who arrived in 1709, made no effort to learn Dutch in all his fifty years there. We might also mention Jacques Basnage (1653-1725); Jean Le Clerc (1657-1736), a Swiss Calvinist; Jean-Frédéric Bernard (1683-1744), author of a monumental treatise entitled *Cérémonies et coutumes religieuses de tous les peuples du monde [Religious Ceremonies and Customs of All the Peoples of the World]*, which relativized religions; Jean Rousset de Missy (1686-1762), a former soldier who became a journalist at The Hague and Amsterdam; Jean-Maximilien Lucas (1646-1697), who was personally acquainted with Spinoza and who wrote a biography of him in French that was published anonymously in 1719. These circles of exiles were especially influenced by Spinozism, though their relationship to it was ambiguous.

The case of Pierre Bayle offers a good illustration. A Huguenot trained as a Cartesian, he expressed his own intimate thoughts in a contorted and kaleidoscopic manner, so that even today they remain mysterious. He is known for his paradox of the virtuous atheist, showing that the atheist is capable of distinguishing good from evil and that a republic of atheists could indeed exist. But does this mean that he himself was an atheist, behind his believer's façade? He always maintained the contrary, and expressed his hatred of materialism: "Do we conceive of laws that were not established by an intelligent cause? Do we conceive of such that could be regularly executed by a cause that does not know them and does not even know that it itself exists in the world? You have there, metaphysically speaking, the weakest point of atheism. It is a rock upon which it cannot help but run aground; it is an insoluble objection,"[15] he wrote in his *Continuation des Pensées diverses sur la comète [Continuation of Various Thoughts on the Comet.]* According to Bayle, this was the great weakness of ancient pagan thought, especially Epicureanism, of which he admired the physical aspect (the theory of atoms) but deplored the metaphysical aspect, which delivered up these atoms to chance. This, he said, was an "error." At the same time, he proclaimed the "right to error," the basis of tolerance: if this right is not recognized, the world "becomes a cutthroat." All of ancient thought leads to atheism, including skepticism. Bayle was the inventor of the "skeptical atheist," as Gianni Paganini has shown.[16] To suspend one's judgment with respect to the existence of God is in fact to deny his existence: in order to be an atheist, it is not necessary "to affirm that theism is false; it suffices to regard it as a problem."[17]

From Spinoza, Bayle retained the principles of biblical exegesis. He admitted, somewhat artificially, that scripture is an inspired text, but one whose study requires a method that respects the principles of historical criticism. In this he followed Richard Simon, but he did not accept the systematic rationalism of the Arminian Jean Le Clerc, whose *Traité sur l'inspiration [Treatise on Inspiration]* seemed to him to destroy the divine origin of the text. He wrote to him: "Your entire Treatise on the inspiration of the prophets and apostles can only sow a thousand doubts and a thousand seeds of atheism in people's minds."[18] With regard to Moses, for example, he did not go as far as Simon; he accepted him as the author of Genesis, but admitted that his narrative did not conform to the rules of historical science, and he made this the sign of inspiration: if the Bible expresses itself in such an imprecise fashion when it could have done so in a more appropriate way, this is precisely the proof that it is God who speaks through the intermediary of Moses.

> We must admit that the narrative of Moses, however perfect it may be in relation to the degree of understanding that God has granted us, is not exact with respect to the method that our masters prescribe for a good historian. . . . That alone must convince any reasonable person that Moses' pen was guided by the Holy Spirit. If Moses had been the master of his expressions and his own thoughts, he would never have covered up such a story in such a way; he would have spoken of it in a more human style and one more appropriate to teach posterity; but a stronger force, an infinite wisdom guided him, so that he wrote not according to his own views, but according to the hidden workings of Providence.[19]

Moses, thus inspired, is no impostor. No such restraint marked Bayle's discussion of Mahomet, whom one could accuse of all the evils of Christian society. He devoted a very long article in his *Dictionnaire historique et critique [Historical and Critical Dictionary]* to this "impostor," this "false prophet," this "idol." But read closely, this article slings mud over *all* the founders of religions. The most honest, in the end, are the ancient pagans, whose beliefs were not deliberately forged with the goal of deception, but were only "intellectual games of certain poets who did not dream of canonizing their fictions and made them up only to amuse themselves." Later these "games" were taken seriously; philosophers even attempted to explain them allegorically. But, in all of this, there was no deliberate imposture.

Mahomet, on the other hand, is the archetype of the impostor. "Since he was subject to the falling sickness, and wanted to hide this weakness from his wife, he convinced her that he only fell into these fits because he could not stand up to the sight of the angel Gabriel, who used to come tell him on God's behalf many things concerning religion." Later he bribed people to spread the rumor that he was a prophet. Did he himself genuinely believe this? Bayle treated the question seriously. Many people, he said, believe that Mahomet was deceived by the devil in the form of the angel Gabriel, while others see him simply as a madman or a sick person. Thus, "the famous Gijsbert Voet had no doubt that Mahomet was an enthusiast and even a fanatic." "As for me," Bayle continued, "I prefer to believe, as is commonly said, that Mahomet was an impostor; because ... his sly manner and his skill at manipulating his friends testify that he only made use of religion as an expedient for his own benefit."

How was Islam able to spread so fast? In brief, because it made use of armed force. "How to resist conquering armies that require signatures? Ask the French dragoons, who played this role in the year 1685, and they will tell you that they would undertake to make the whole world sign up for the Qur'ān, provided that you give them the time to make the most of the maxim *compelle intrare, force them to enter.*" Christians have done the same thing: look at Constantine, look at Charlemagne and the conversion of the Saxons. Their case is even worse than that of the Muslims: "Muslims, following the principles of their faith, are obligated to use force to destroy other religions, and yet they have tolerated them for several centuries. The Christians are ordered only to preach and teach, and yet from time immemorial they have exterminated by fire and sword those who were not of their religion."

Somehow the "impostor" Mahomet ends up appearing almost respectable. He led an austere life, based on a strict morality and fasting. He was not responsible for all the stories that circulated about him: "It is not permissible to build an argument against Mahomet on the basis of the tales that his sectarians tell about him." It was his own faithful who passed on these fables: "I must say in favor of the Christian authors that it was the sectarians of this impostor who told the most ridiculous fables about him," which Bayle takes pleasure in obligingly reporting.

It is the common fate of all the founders of religions, Bayle concluded, to see extraordinary powers and actions attributed to them, and also to give rise to false prophets. "For the rest, the religion of this impostor was subject to the same problem that we noted at the birth of Christianity and at that of Luther's Reformation, because no sooner was it prophesied than false prophets came along, and the faithful quickly divided themselves into camps." All this is not exactly innocent. Bayle was not obligated to repeat these bits of gossip; in dismissing them as tittle-tattle, he helped disseminate them and provided grist for the mill of the enemies of religion. The authors of the *Traité des trois imposteurs* would make good use of this material.

The idea of composing such a treatise gradually took root in the mingled French and Dutch environment of the late seventeenth century. With the thought of the learned libertines and the philosophies of Hobbes and Spinoza, there was sufficient material to construct and illustrate a theory of religious imposture, using—for reasons both commercial and ideological—the old and incendiary title *De tribus impostoribus*. The French immigrants were not the only ones to work at this. The Dutch, on their own initiative, also contributed.

Between 1680 and 1700, the debate over tolerance and freedom of expression raged in the United Provinces. Valckenier, Ericus Walten, Gregorio Leti, Gerard Noodt, and Van Limborch all upheld the freedom of the written word. Van Limborch demonstrated this by publishing in 1687, in Latin, the autobiography of a heterodox Jew, Uriel da Costa (1583/4–1640), whose book had been burned by the magistrates of Amsterdam. In the eyes of the foreigners who came from absolute monarchies, the Dutch enjoyed a degree of freedom that was extraordinary if not scandalous. But everything is relative. Bayle noted in 1701 that those who denied the Trinity ran a great risk of imprisonment. The most fertile aspect of this atmosphere of relative freedom was the birth, in the United Provinces, of literary magazines, which surveyed European publications and provided reviews in French, a handy practice in a period when the knowledge of living foreign languages was as yet quite limited. These magazines created a powerful intellectual ferment, contributing to the dawn of the European Enlightenment. The pioneer in this project was Bayle, with the *Nouvelles de la République des Lettres [News of the Republic of Letters]*, begun in 1684. Then came the *Journal littéraire [Literary Journal]*, the *Bibliothèque anglaise [English Library]*, the *Bibliothèque germanique [German Library]*. The *Journal littéraire*, published at The Hague, revealed the dominance of the United Provinces in publishing at the start of the eighteenth century: 55 percent of books were issued by Dutch presses, 25 percent came from France, 8 percent from England, 7 percent from Germany. Dutch publications gave an important place to the sciences, and contributed to the spread of the model of a mechanistic universe, thus providing nourishment for the development of an atheistic explanation of the world. Christiaan Huygens (1629-1695), with his telescopes, microscopes, and clocks, decisively improved knowledge of time and space; he collaborated with Spinoza on scientific matters and proposed a mathematical model of the universe, in accordance with his deistic views. Leeuwenhoek, Swammerdam, Ruysch, and Vincent made progress in biology and medicine. The universities of Leiden, Utrecht, and Franeker were livelier than their counterparts elsewhere in Europe and attracted many German Protestant students. However, scientific progress was also a tool in the hands of the defenders of established religion: Bernard Nieuwentyt (1654-1718), for example, developed an anti-Spinozan physical theology that foreshadowed Fénelon's *Démonstration de l'existence de Dieu par les merveilles de la nature [Demonstration of God's Existence through Marvels of Nature]* (1712).

In parallel to scientific progress, Dutch intellectual circles vibrated with controversies that were not only theological, but demonological, such as the one that broke out in 1691 over a book written in Dutch by Balthasar Bekker, *De Betoverde weereld [The World Bewitched]*, denying the existence of Satan and his demons. This also became one of the themes discussed in the *Three Impostors*. For Bekker, demons were originally ancient fables, then biblical allegories, ratified by a superstitious imagination. Even though he was an anti-Spinozan, Bekker was accused of favoring atheism. There was a public scandal, and the country divided into opposing camps. Two editions (in 1691) of *De Betoverde weereld*, totaling 5,000 copies, sold out in Amsterdam in a matter of weeks, as did the 750 copies printed in Frisia. Among the ardent supporters of Bekker was Anton Van Dale (1638–1708) who, in his Latin work *De oraculis [On Oracles]* of 1683, had affirmed that all oracles were based on the superstitious credulity of the people, exploited by the priests, who had spread belief in demons and magical beings in order to solidify their own power. His book was translated into Dutch and French in 1687, and in 1696 he repeated its arguments in his *De origine et progressu idolatriae et superstitionis [On the Origin and Progress of Idolatry and Superstition]*. The affair of the devil took on a political dimension when another great partisan of tolerance, Ericus Walten, appealed to the Stathouder William of Orange, who was also king of England. But he was arrested in March 1694 and tried for blasphemy, as an enemy of the church and a proponent of atheism, for having declared that the episode in the gospels of the temptation of Christ by the devil was only a trifle. He died in prison at The Hague in 1697. Under pressure from the synod, the municipal authorities in Amsterdam suspended Bekker, but refused to ban his book. The affair of the devil divided Dutch society for several years and gave rise to a flood of writings; 170 works for or against Bekker appeared in three years. The controversy reached Germany, where a defender of religion, Friedrich Ernst Kettner, published at Leipzig in 1694 a work entitled *De duobus impostoribus, Benedicto Spinoza et Balthasare Bekkero dissertatio [Treatise on the Two Impostors, Benedict Spinoza and Balthasar Bekker]*, a hostile wink at the *De tribus impostoribus*.

These debates show the extent to which the religious question was discussed in Holland in the second half of the seventeenth century. It is not surprising that the *Treatise of the Three Impostors* should have issued from this environment. It was to some extent the end result of the controversies around Spinozism, in which all the people we have just discussed took part, such as Jan Vroesen (1672–1725), the son of a burgermeister of Rotterdam, who mastered French to perfection.

Rumors of the De tribus in England

In April 1656 Henry Oldenburg, of Oxford, wrote to Adam Borel in Amsterdam asking him to compose a treatise proving the certainty of divine revelation, in response to the theory of the three impostors. This letter has caused large quantities of ink to flow,[20] because its reference to the three impostors provides a firm point of reference in an extraordinarily complex history.

Henry Oldenburg, born in Bremen, established himself in England in Cromwell's day, attended Oxford University, and made his living from tutoring posts in the O'Bryen and Cavendish families. At the time he wrote this letter, he was preparing to leave on a European tour with his pupil, the son of Lady Ranelagh. Deeply religious, Oldenburg was in touch with reformist circles such as those of Dury and Hartlib. In 1664 he became secretary of the Royal Society in London. He died in 1677 at Charlton, near Greenwich. His correspondent, Adam Borel, was a Dutch Arminian who, in the mid-1640s, founded a community around a college in Amsterdam, whence the name "Collegiants." He was in close contact with the Portuguese Jewish community and made a Latin translation of the Mishnah, the second-century rabbinic code that formed the basis for Talmud. He made several trips to England, notably in 1655, where he met Oldenburg. His major work up to that time was the *Ad legem et testimonium [On Law and Testament]* of 1645, in which he showed that Christ had established the church by authority of the Holy Spirit, and that it had lost its legitimacy little by little through the admixture of secular goals. He advocated the creation of a small community to recover the original spirit—the Church of Tolerance, which he founded in 1646.

For Oldenburg, Borel was the man who seemed most capable, thanks to his biblical learning and his knowledge of Hebrew, to respond to the increasingly fierce attacks that treated the mere idea of divine inspiration as an imposture. It appears that Moses was the primary target: according to Oldenburg, some people said that Moses had invented the story of the creation of the world in seven days, with the goal of institutionalizing the Sabbath; once people had accepted that, they could next be persuaded that all the liberator's demands were revealed to him directly from God. On the other hand, wrote Oldenburg,

> Moses certainly encouraged and excited his people to obey him and to be brave in war by hopes and promises of acquiring rich booty and ample possessions, and the man Christ, being more prudent

than Moses, enticed his people by the hope of eternal life and happiness though aware that the soul seriously contemplating eternity would scarcely savor what is vile and low. But Mohammed, cunning in all things, enlisted all men with the good things of this world as well as of the next, and so became their master, and extended the limits of his empire much more widely than did any legislator before or after him.[21]

This is precisely the thesis of the three impostors. Where had Oldenburg encountered this argument? According to him, he found it in a heretical work that was poisoned by "the love of reasoning" and that destroyed "the certainty of divine revelation." He said nothing more about it. Some scholars have deduced, perhaps too hastily, that he was referring to *De tribus impostoribus*. But if this were the case, would not Oldenburg have explicitly cited the title? It seems more likely that he was referring to a theme then current in many antireligious works, and not to the notorious treatise itself, which remained a myth. The theme of the triple imposture was circulating widely in England at that time. In 1672, a person of the London parish of Saint-Giles-in-the-Fields was tried for "impious, blasphemous, and heretical words" for having declared that "Jesus Christ, Moses, and Mahomet were three great scoundrels."[22]

More troubling is the testimony of the bibliophile Richard Smith, who, in the 1660s, wrote his "observations" on the report of "a blasphemous treatise on the three great impostors that some say was recently printed."[23] Smith stated that the treatise was "a rumor" spread not only by illiterate common folk but also by their betters. According to him, it was a question of the Latin work written by Simon of Tournai, recopied and recently printed. There is nothing to prove that he had seen it, but evidently the subject was fashionable in England in the context of the religious troubles of the interregnum and the Restoration.

For the radical element, the great founders of the monotheistic religions were in fact purely politicians and legislators. This position was defended notably by Henry Stubbs (1632–1676), a close friend of Thomas Hobbes, linked to the republicans and independents. Stubbs was an underlibrarian at the Bodleian Library at Oxford and a man of great learning, historical, political, and religious. According to one of Oldenburg's friends, John Beale, he formed part of an atheist sect, a group of "Hobbesians, Stubbians, atheists, mockers, blasphemers." Oldenburg himself was somewhat wary of him, and after the publication in 1659 of his pamphlet on "Light Out of Shadows," he spoke of "an unstable and dissolute mind, tending more to libertinage and profane things than to the serious and conscientious search for truth." In 1671 Stubbs wrote an "Account of the Rise and Progress of Mahometanism," which remained in manuscript form for a long time.

If Mahomet was the main subject, the book also had implications concerning Jesus. The founder of Islam was more than ever viewed as an impostor, on both sides of the Channel. In France, Jacques Bénigne Bossuet made Mahomet the instrument of that impostor of impostors, the devil. Islam was a "monstrous religion": "O Lord, how credulous humankind is regarding the impostures of Satan! ... this monstrous religion, which belies itself, has ignorance as its reason; violence and tyranny for persuasion; and for its miracles, armies, terrifying and victorious armies that cause the world to tremble and that reestablish by force the empire of Satan over the universe."[24] In England, Francis Osborne, in his *Political Reflections upon the Government of the Turks* (1656) and Sir Paul Rycaut, in his *Present State of the Ottoman Empire* (1668), were no more gentle in their treatment. Only the Socinians, by reason of their rejection of the Trinity, were more indulgent. Stubbs took a different approach: for him, Mahomet should be seen as a legislator who succeeded in uniting the Arabs, who until then had been divided into rival sects. He proposed to them a new religion based on monotheism, but divine inspiration had nothing to do with the story. Rather, it was a purely political question, and Mahomet, far from being a "vile impostor," was "the wisest legislator who ever lived." The "impostures" of Mahomet, such as the story of the pigeon that he passed off as the Holy Spirit, or that of the believer buried in the well, were Christian inventions. Christian theologians themselves were in the habit; Stubbs gave a whole list of impostures of the church fathers intended to blacken their enemies. He wrote that Mahomet is undoubtedly considered an impostor by Christians, but why? Not on the basis of his own testimony, or that of his friends, but on that of his enemies.[25]

Certainly, the Qur'ān is not the divine word, but nor is the Bible. If we are so strenuously critical of the words of the Qur'ān, then we ought to show the same critical severity with regard to the writings of Moses and the others. "I have often reflected upon the exceptions made by the Christians against the Alcoran, and find them to be no other than what may be urged with the same strength against our Bible; and what the Christians say for themselves will fully justify the Alcoran."[26] The Qur'ān and the Bible should be treated in the same manner. Mahomet and Moses are two legislators, no more and no less. And Jesus enters into the same category: he is someone who perceived the messianic tendencies of his people and skillfully slid into the role. Miraculous accidents, improbable effusions with the Holy Spirit, and all the rest are illusions. Christ was a simple man, who adapted Mosaic law to the needs of his own time; it was later, after the destruction of the temple, that Christians, in order to definitively distinguish themselves from Jews, made him into a god. Jesus assured his own secular power by using religion. And here again, he drew the parallel between the New Testament and the Qur'ān: "[I] do think that our Notions of the Torments of the Wicked in a lake of fire and brimstone somewhere underground, hath as much of folly and absurdity in it as is in any fable of Mahometans." Besides, according to Stubbs, the prophecy of the Paraclete in John 16:7 is seen by the Muslims as the announcement of the coming of Mahomet.[27]

Moses, Jesus, Mahomet: three skillful legislators, all purely human. This thesis comes as close as possible to that of the three impostors, and it was this menace that Oldenburg was reacting to. It was an urgent matter to prove divine inspiration with regard to Jesus. The writings of Stubbs, who died in 1676, circulated fairly widely after his death. They were taken up and developed by Charles Blount, a radical and a member of the Green Ribbon Club. Blount translated into English passages of Spinoza's *Tractatus* and Philostratus' *Life of Apollonius* (1680). In 1693 he wrote *Oracles of Reason*, a precursor of English freethinking. He wrote that "supposing that there were but three laws, viz. that of Moses, that of Christ, and that of Mahomet: either all are false, and so the whole world is deceived; or only two of them, and so the greater part is deceived." The three founders are exclusively legislators, for "we must know, as Plato and Aristotle well observe, that a Politician is a physician of minds, and that his aim is rather to make men good than knowing: wherefore, according to the diversities of men, he must make himself agreeable to the diversity of humours, for the attainment of his end."[28] Continuity and solidarity between the three persons and the three religions was also upheld by the Unitarians.

It was to save Jesus that Humphrey Prideaux in 1697 published his *True Nature of Imposture*, affirming that Christ had never presented himself as a Jewish messiah, promising a temporal kingdom, but that he had always spoken of a spiritual kingdom; his message had none of the "marks, characteristics, and properties" of imposture, while Mahomet was the very type of the impostor.

In his 1656 letter to Borel, Oldenburg likewise pressed him to definitively establish the truth of Christianity by clearing Jesus of the slightest suspicion of imposture and by proving that he was indeed inspired by God. Several times he urged him, as if Borel were the only man capable of achieving this goal. In November 1657, from Saumur, he asked him to produce "powerful arguments" in favor of "revealed truth," and "to finally bring into the light of day these things that I know you have thought about, concerning the necessity for religion in general, truth, and the excellence of the Christian religion and above all, of the legislator of the world."[29] At Paris, in 1659, Oldenburg took notice of the *Colloquium* of Jean Bodin, and he wrote to John Worthington that Borel ought to refute that work as well. But Borel had other things to do besides. He translated the Mishnah; he debated with the Quakers of Amsterdam. He was also getting older, approaching his sixtieth year, and his health suffered in the Dutch climate. In 1660 he fell ill. His friends felt that the great work was not advancing as quickly as they wished. In January 1660, Hartlib told Worthington that Borel "hath written a large Tr.[eatise] about the Divinity of the N. Testament, as likewise a larger Work against all sorts of Atheists. He is very much pressed to publish it, but I cannot tell yet, how soon it will be done."[30] In the spring, Dury encountered Borel, and assured Oldenburg that he was still working on the great project. In August, Oldenburg recommended to Borel that he emphasize "the three great principles of the religion: the existence of a god, his providence, and the divine origin of the revelation made in Holy Scripture." In December, he wrote once more to Borel that the good Christians in England were impatient to see his work finished. The Restoration of Charles II had just taken place, and the heterodox "do not hesitate to return to their vomit." It was necessary to prove to the Muslims that "the New Testament, as we profess it, is authentic, unaltered, and free of all addition or reduction."

The great work would never see the light of day. Or we might say that Borel gave birth to an abortive text. As Rob Iliffe noted in his study of this affair, the unfinished work was a jumble, but the machinations of Oldenburg and others show how highly Borel's abilities were valued.[31] In June 1665, Borel was dying. Time was up, and Oldenburg asked him to have the work copied in the state it was in. He agreed to pay six pounds for it, which he thought was a bit high, even for a work touted as clearing Jesus of any accusation of imposture. The manuscript, which was never published, is now in the library of the Royal Society. It is quite a disappointment: titles of chapters, notes, biblical citations, all grouped under the title *Jesus Nazarenus legislator*. Borel's intention was to compose a great work of apologetics aimed at three types of reader—what we might call the general public, nonspecialist intellectuals, and specialists—adapting the type of proof to each. This was an ambitious project that ended in a muddle and had no hope of dissipating the rumors of imposture. Jesus was presented as a legislator supported by divine inspiration. No new argument was advanced.

This affair offers an additional illustration of the spread of the theme of the three impostors in Holland and England in the second half of the seventeenth century. It does not allow us to confirm that Oldenburg had seen the notorious treatise, and even less, as Richard Popkin suggested, that Spinoza wrote his *Tractatus* as a response to it. Françoise Charles-Daubert made short work of that hypothesis.[32] In the England of the Restoration, between 1660 and 1671, the interpretation of the work of Moses, Jesus, and Mahomet as that of inspired legislators was exploited by three Anglican theologians: Edward Stillingfleet (1635-1699), John Tillotson (1630-1694), and Sir Charles Wolseley (c. 1630-1714). Their point of view was that of the Erastians—that is, those who believed that religious matters belong to the state and not the church, an understandable position for dignitaries of a state church like the Anglican. Their thesis ran like this: yes, Moses, Jesus, and Mahomet were legislators, using religion in the service of politics, and that was part of the divine plan. God wanted religion to help maintain order. Thus, they were not impostors.

Like any other apologetic work, the books of Stillingfleet, Tillotson, and Wolseley were two-edged weapons: in order to effectively attack the atheists' arguments, they had first to present them and thereby contribute to spreading them. Of course, we find the arguments of Celsus in Origen, and those of Julian in Cyril of Alexandria. Similarly, Wolseley, forgetting that silence is the best weapon to suppress a case, thought it helpful to add to his book an "atheist's catechism," in twenty-two questions and answers, which clearly exposes the thesis of imposture:

—What is that men call religion?
—A politick cheat put upon the world.
—Who were the first contrivers of this cheat?
—Some cunning men that designed to keep the world in subjection and awe.
—What was the first ground of it?
—Men were frightened, with Tales, that were told them, about invisible nothings.
—When did this fright first seize men?
—'Tis very long ago: and (for ought we can find) 'tis as old as the world it self.
—Has this fright upon men been general?
—Yes: the whole world, in all ages of it, have been possessed with a fear of nothing.[33]

Stillingfleet, Tillotson, and Wolseley differ from Bayle in their belief that it is impossible for an atheist to be virtuous. In this respect, they are closer to Hobbes: for a state, there must be religion or else chaos. The state ought to make use of religion; this is not an imposture but rather a political necessity willed by God himself.

The theme of religious imposture was more than ever at the center of debates in the second half of the seventeenth century, especially in Holland and England, where politico-religious confrontations and a relative freedom of expression permitted the controversy to develop. It was based both on historical examples, such as Apollonius of Tyana as exploited by Charles Blount, and on contemporary cases that illustrated the theory, such as that of the English Quaker James Nayler, who claimed to be Christ.

Confusion was ensured by a proliferation of works entitled *Three Impostors*, connected to various individuals. In 1654, in a case of "the world turned upside down," the astrologer Jean-Baptiste Morin published a *De tribus impostoribus* targeting the trio of Gassendi, Neuré,

and Bernier, who refused to accept his horoscopic calculations. Guy
Patin mentioned a *De tribus nebulonibus* attacking Cromwell, Mazarin, and the Neopolitan Anicello; he himself would have preferred,
he said, the trio of Cromwell, Mazarin, and the general of the Society
of Jesus. In 1667 there appeared at London a book called *History of
the Three Late Famous Impostors*, featuring Shabbetai Ẓevi (a famous
false messiah who mobilized Jewish communities worldwide before converting to Islam), Mahomet Bei, and Padre Ottomano. This
work was published at Hamburg in 1669, and at Paris in 1673, and
the three individuals reappeared in *Imposteurs insignes [Famous Im-
postors]*, printed at Amsterdam in 1683. A famous *De tribus magnis
impostoribus* by Christian Kortholt was published at Kiel in 1680,
then at Hamburg in 1693. This work reversed the roles: the three impostors in question were Hobbes, Spinoza, and Edward Herbert of
Cherbury (the "father of English deism"). Jean Dekker in turn gath-
ered under this rubric Hobbes, Spinoza, and Tommaso Campanella
(a Dominican friar condemned for heresy for having denied the authority of Aristotle, and who later upheld Galileo). Jean Henri Ursin,
in 1661, grouped Zoroaster, Hermes Trismegistus (mythical author
of esoteric texts in the Greco-Egyptian tradition), and Sanchoniatus
Phaenicius. A Parisian engraver grouped Confucius, Mahomet, and
Arius (an early medieval bishop who rejected the doctrine of the divinity of Jesus). Adrian Beverland used the label *tribus impostoribus*
for three English bishops who disapproved of his writings. A French
minister at London "united under the same title of three impostors,
the three persons of Mahomet, Ignatius of Loyola [founder of the
Jesuit Order], and George Fox [founder of Quakerism]." Prosper
Marchand wrote of Loyola that

it seems to me that this did him an injury; that he deserved infinitely more to be put in the number of idiots and crazy people than
among sharps and impostors.... Someone who today holds the first
rank in one of the major Protestant churches associated him a bit
more appropriately with a madman and a lunatic, because he shared
these two characteristics about equally. Saint Dominic, said this famous figure, bragged of being invulnerable; Saint Francis claimed
to have been nourished on the bread of the angels; and Saint Ignatius claimed to have been granted spiritual gifts much greater and
more admirable than those of all the other saints combined.[34]

Marchand also cited *L'Espion turc dans les cours des princes chrétiens* [*A Turkish Spy in the Courts of Christian Princes*], which associated Mahomet, Judas, and Luther, "calling them the most wicked, evil, and detestable men who ever lived." He concluded his overview:

> Finally, one could make a new work under this same title of *Three Impostors*, on infinitely better foundations than any of its predecessors, by grouping the Ismaelite Mahomet, the Jew Abdulla, and the Christian Sergius, if it is true that they united to compose this bizarre rhapsody of paganism, Judaism, and Christianity, entitled the Qur'ān, and which holds the place of a divine revelation for all the members of the Mahometan sect. Jews and Christians have affirmed it for several centuries as a certain and incontestable truth, and the publisher of the letters of *L'Espion turc* was so far convinced of it that he found no difficulty in representing them as such at the start of the last volume of the work and in calling them "three impostors."

The world was full of impostors, who often went in threes. There was nothing more common than this idea in the second half of the seventeenth century. And there was nothing surprising in the fact that rumors concerning the notorious blasphemous treatise *De tribus impostoribus* became more insistent than ever. Debates around the idea of religious imposture, nourished by the decisive support of Hobbes and Spinoza, increased public interest in this mysterious work. Was it merely by chance, then, that in the course of this "European crisis of conscience," they finally "discovered" the devilish work? They even discovered two versions of it at once, one Latin and one French!

From the *De tribus* to the *Trois imposteurs*: Discovery or Invention of the Treatise? (1680–1721)

Born in the thirteenth century, the myth of the *Treatise of the Three Impostors* circulated for centuries in Europe as a rumor before becoming a reality at the start of the eighteenth century. The text appeared suddenly—or rather the texts, since there exist a great variety, in diverse languages, with multiple variations. This proliferating presence poses as many problems as the absence over the five previous centuries. Where did they come from, all these copies, in manuscript and print, that seemed to sprout up everywhere by a sort of spontaneous generation? Scholars and historians of ideas have brooded for a long time over this mystery, which is all the more difficult to unravel as the treatise belongs to clandestine literature, a genre whose defining characteristic is to cherish secrets—of origins, of authors, of circulation. The historian's task is thus especially difficult, and the results are extraordinarily complex. In the absence of official sources, the researcher is reduced to exploring signs, sometimes enigmatic, of doubtful reliability, and sometimes contradictory. Even the contemporary authors, publishers, and collectors of the eighteenth century disagreed among themselves on the origin of the texts; added to their debates are those of the historians who, especially since the 1970s, have attempted to untangle the skein. Hypotheses clash and only serve to deepen the mystery. We make no claim to bring new light to bear; rather, we shall sketch the outlines of the question. Out of concern for clarity, we shall limit ourselves to a simplified presentation of the main facts, as attested, while attempting to avoid caricature. But to simplify such a confusing history seems like an impossible challenge, and we ask our readers' forgiveness in advance if clarity is not always apparent.

The fundamental problem is that we are dealing with the origin of both a Latin text, *De tribus impostoribus*, and a French text, the *Traité des trois imposteurs.* There are important differences between the two, but also distinct interrelations. Since the Latin text is chronologically the older, we shall begin with it.

Sources of the De tribus: *Kiel, 1688*

The trail begins in 1662. In a letter of 3 February addressed to Huet, Jean Chapelain told how Claude Hardy, a mathematician and friend of Descartes, had told him, in the presence of Huygens and Thévenot, "that a foreigner had shown him this printed book," that "the printing resembled books printed at Vregovia [*sic*]in Silesia," but that he had not read it.[1] Attention then turns to Germany, where the following year, 1663, Théophile Spitzel, the first historian of atheism, in his *Scrutinium atheismi historico-aetiologicum [Historical-Aetiological Investigation of Atheism]*, mentioned "tractatus ille horrendus de Tribus impostoribus [that horrifying treatise on the three impostors]," which he deemed worthy of the eternal flames for its treatment of Moses, Jesus, and Mahomet as impostors.[2] In 1680, Christian Kortholt declared that he also had seen the *De tribus*, at a bookseller's in Basel; in 1681, Jean Dekker wrote that "the detestable book is openly sold in France";[3] in 1682 a scholar, Martin Lipenius, affirmed that "the *De tribus impostoribus* had been printed in 1669 in octavo."[4]

However, all this was still rather vague. Matters began to get serious with the entrance onto the stage, still in the 1680s, of famous individuals: Prince Eugen and his librarian Baron von Hohendorf, the philosopher Leibniz, the preacher Johan Friedrich Mayer, and some others. These developments also occurred in Germany.

On 3 April 1688 a *disputatio* took place at the University of Kiel, in which Johan Friedrich Mayer presented a communication entitled *Comitia taboritica a Christo, Mose et Elia celebrata*, in which he discussed the episode of the transfiguration of Jesus, with the apparition of Moses and Elijah. Mayer (1650–1712), a Protestant minister and councilor to the Swedish King Charles XII, was obsessed with imposture. Active on the southern shores of the Baltic Sea, in Swedish Pomerania, he published several works at Hamburg, and forced the false prophet Olger Paulli to leave Hamburg for Amsterdam. At the end of the session on 3 April, an assistant, Johann Joachim Müller, asked him questions, and several days later brought him a copy of a manuscript, to which he had added a personal appendix containing antibiblical criticism borrowed from Spinoza and the German atheist Matthias Knuttel. Müller, born in Hamburg in 1661, was the grandson of the Hamburg theologian Johannes Müller (1598-1672), author of *Atheismus devictus [Atheism Vanquished]*. As a law student at Leipzig and then at Altdorf, Müller apparently gave Mayer a copy of the notorious *De tribus*, augmented with a personal commentary. This is according to a colleague of Mayer's at the Swedish University of Greifswald, J. H. V. Balthasar. Where did Müller's manuscript come from? What connection did it have to the one that Salvius alluded to in his letters to de Castro in 1635? Or to the one at Wittenberg, said to date from 1645? What was Müller's role in its composition? These are all questions that remain unanswered.[5] The known presence of forty-one manuscripts of the *De tribus* in the Baltic region, as listed by historian Wolfgang Gericke, underlines the importance of this region in the birth of the treatise. Gericke studied these texts minutely and divided them into three groups, based on their differences. According to him, the common ancestor actually came from Switzerland, around the middle of the sixteenth century, in the circles opposed to Calvin. But he advanced no decisive argument.[6]

It is still true—and here we come back to firmer ground—that from 1688 Johan Friedrich Mayer had in his library a copy of *De tribus impostoribus*, whatever its origin. The manuscript excited envy and aroused curiosity. Many people asked to see it. Some privileged ones were even allowed to copy it: Christen Worm (1672-1737) had one of these copies by 1695,[7] through Palthenius as intermediary. One of Worm's friends, Peter Friedrich Arpe, also had one made. This man is an important link in the history of the *Three Impostors*. Raised in Schleswig-Holstein, a personal possession of the king of Denmark, he studied at Kiel, then moved to Copenhagen, where he rubbed shoulders with historians and scholars such as Worm, all of whom took an interest in heterodox literature. There, he attached himself to the diplomat Gerhard Ernst Franck von Frankenau (1676-1749), whose library he frequented and to whom he dedicated an *Apologia pro Vanino*, a brief for Vanini, composed around 1705. Frankenau, of Heidelberg, had been the secretary of the Danish embassy in Spain. He took a great interest in the *De tribus*, having seen Worm's copy, which he said had come from the one in Mayer's library.[8]

Arpe had his own copy, which he attributed—according to a pastor of Hamburg, Nikolaus Staphorst—to Johann Joachim Müller. He did not believe in the antiquity of this text, as he himself wrote: "Johann Müller having mentioned in his *Atheismus devictus* that infamous book on the three impostors in terms implying that he had read it and had access to a copy, Johan Friedrich Mayer, Th.D., a thorough polymath, enquired after that abominable but very rare production of the human mind from Müller's grandson, who did not utterly refuse a request from a man of renown who at that time had power in the city." He procured for him a text "received . . . under the title *De tribus impostoribus*."[9]

In 1712, Arpe accompanied the Danish diplomat Johann Heinrich von Ahlefeld to the United Provinces, where he was to participate in the negotiations for the Treaty of Utrecht. He settled in The Hague, bringing with him his copy of *De tribus*. While there, he associated with many diplomats, intellectuals, exiled Huguenots, booksellers, and publishers. He took advantage of these contacts to publish his *Apologia pro Vanino* at Rotterdam, with the publishers Fritsch & Böhm, to whom the Calvinist pastor Jacques Basnage had introduced him. At Rotterdam, he was in contact with the circle of the Chevaliers de la Jubilation, a group to which Prosper Marchard belonged, as well as Levier, Fritsch, and Böhm. This group was preparing to publish *L'Esprit de Spinoza*—that is to say, a French version of the *Three Impostors*, of which we shall speak later. They took an interest in Arpe's Latin manuscript, which had nothing to do with their own text. But Arpe remained quite discreet about his Latin copy. He spoke a little about the *De tribus* in his *Apologia*, but in terms so vague that the *Journal des savants*, in commenting on the work, felt safe in affirming: "There are many indications that the book of the three impostors is purely a chimera."[10]

The Intervention of Leibniz and of Baron von Hohendorf

In the United Provinces, Arpe, a good networker, also made the acquaintance of other interesting individuals, such as Pieter Neef (Naevius) (1667-1731), a Dutchman who had married the niece of Adrian Beverland. The latter was the author of a *De tribus impostoribus*, something that caught Arpe's attention. He obtained a copy for himself, but the work turned out to be no more than a diatribe against three bishops. Much more interesting was the presence at The Hague of Baron von Hohendorf.

Hohendorf had formed part of the inner circle of Prince Eugen of Savoy (1663–1736), a brilliant general and a great-nephew of Cardinal Mazarin, who had recently distinguished himself by his victories in the War of the Spanish Succession. Beyond his military talents, Eugen of Savoy was a knowledgeable bibliophile, and Hohendorf, who had many qualities, was at the same time his aide-de-camp and his supplier of rare books. He was also a diplomat, "more of a spy than a minister," as Torcy wrote; "a knave more skilled than most," according to Saint-Simon.[11] A connoisseur of men and manuscripts, he furnished the court at Vienna with valuable works, all the while keeping the best for himself, especially proscribed works. He collected "unexpurgated editions, works that had been suppressed or proscribed and of which most copies had been burned," according to Albert-Henri de Sallengre in 1715.[12] His library was one of the richest in Europe. It held all the clandestine literature, invaluable and often unique works, such as the *Theophrastus redivivus* of 1659 (an anthology of ancient materialism), the works of Giordano Bruno, and those of Bonaventure Des Périers. Such a man owed it to himself to possess a copy of the *De tribus*.[13] He had the financial means and the connections necessary to obtain it. The negotiations at Utrecht in 1712–1713, like the earlier negotiations at Westphalia, offered the opportunity to encounter the cream of diplomats—collectors of forbidden works. He was also in touch with all the notable freethinkers, such as the Englishman John Toland; he knew the publisher Prosper Marchand. Did Arpe actually meet him? There is no evidence to say so, but Hohendorf had in his library the *Apologia pro Vanino*.

The baron was looking for the *De tribus impostoribus*, which became a kind of grail for freethinkers. Undeniably, copies existed, but the fortunate possessors did not proclaim their ownership from the rooftops, and even in their private correspondence they affected great revulsion with regard to it: it was always a "pernicious," "detestable," "damned," "abominable" book. To possess it, unless you were a great lord effectively above the law, was dangerous. The *De tribus* was sought by all the police forces of Europe. Thus in Saxony in 1716, all the bookstores were ransacked, and all the books that had the words "three impostors" in their title were confiscated. Publishers were arrested, such as Johann Gottlieb Krause, who had mentioned the forbidden book in his *Bücher-Historie*.[14] Prudence and dissimulation were necessary.

Arpe was all the more aware of this because his own name began
to circulate, both as the owner of a copy of the *De tribus* and as the
author of a *Réponse à la dissertation de Monsieur de La Monnoye sur le
Traité des trois imposteurs [Response to the Discussion of Monsieur de La
Monnoye on the Treatise of the Three Impostors]*, an anonymous work
published at Rotterdam in 1716 which affirmed that such a treatise
existed. This *Response* aroused the curiosity of someone else who
took a close interest in the *De tribus*, the philosopher Gottfried Wilhelm Leibniz, famous all over Europe, who was then seventy years
old. At the time, Leibniz had just consulted the copy from Mayer's
library. This was a rare privilege, because Johan Friedrich Mayer kept
a close eye on his treasure. He showed it only to friends he could
trust, but would not permit even them to read it. In January 1709, a
Leipzig journalist wrote:

> While in Saxony, I saw the book of the *Three Impostors* in the study of
> M.... It is an octavo volume in Latin, with no mark, no publisher's
> name, no publication date, but to judge by its appearance, it seems
> to have been produced in Germany. In vain did I make use of all
> imaginable ploys to obtain permission to read it in its entirety, but
> the owner, a man of delicate piety, would never give his permission,
> and I even knew that a famous professor of Wittenberg had offered
> him a large sum.[15]

After Johan Friedrich Mayer died in 1712, his son, Doctor Mayer,
decided to sell his books. Hohendorf was interested, and it was probably at his request that Leibniz, whom he knew personally, sought
to see the notorious book. Despite his fame, the philosopher found
it difficult to obtain permission. Under close watch, he was able to
read the book in Mayer's room, which did not take long, because it
numbered only twenty-eight pages. On 13 March 1716, Leibniz wrote
to Baron von Hohendorf:

> Doctor Mayer finally permitted me to read, in his room and in his
> presence, the manuscript treatise *De imposturis religionum.* I will give
> you the most exact information possible. This work consisted of
> 14 leaves and 28 pages in a small folio, each page containing about
> 25 lines. The first period, which I shall report shortly, consists of
> four and half lines, the last of six lines. The work appears to have
> been written more than sixty years ago by a very legible German

hand. . . . One could read nothing more execrable, more impious, or even more dangerous. . . . The style is full . . . of affected gallicisms. The fourth page of the work has been almost entirely effaced with a pen, apparently because of the blasphemies it contains.[16]

The manuscript, which thus was entitled *De impostoribus religionum breve compendium*, was immediately purchased and became part of Prince Eugen's library.

Leibniz's attention was next attracted by the *Réponse*, which public rumor attributed to Arpe. We shall return to these texts in the context of the French copy of the three impostors. La Monnoye (or La Monnoie) had written that the *Treatise of the Three Impostors* had never existed, neither in Latin nor in French. In 1716 he drew an anonymous response that declared the contrary. At first the author was thought to be Arpe. Leibniz, who knew that the treatise existed, since he had just read it, wrote on 31 March 1716 to a librarian of Berlin, Mathurin Veyssière de La Croze: "I must thank you for the information that you give me concerning the book *De imposturis*. You know that Monsieur de La Monnoye had added to the *Menagiana* a discussion of the book *De tribus*. A certain Mr. Arpe, to be found in Leiden, a German I believe, wanted to refute this dissertation by a letter that he had printed, where he appeals to experience, saying that he had held the book in his hand, and reporting details."[17] La Croze had never heard of Arpe. He asked for information about him, on 7 April, from his friend the theologian Johann Christoph Wolf, who responded on the 24th: "I know this Arpe about whom Leibniz wrote you. He lives in Kiel. . . . He did not miss the opportunity, elsewhere and above all at Copenhagen, to acquire an excellent knowledge of literary questions; but he seemed to me to be drawn by a sort of impulse toward forbidden books, as one calls them, so much so that I was not surprised that he might have confidential information on the *Liber de tribus impostoribus*."[18] On 1 May, in another letter to La Croze, Wolf wrote further about Arpe's bad reputation:

> I have more than once lamented the fate of this Arpe, a cultivated and refined man, who seems to me to waste his energy and his intelligence. I was told that, in a certain society that gathers in Kiel on fixed days each week to discuss recent publications, his contributions betrayed a mind that took the greatest interest in things that others considered of the least value. He told me to my face, about ten

years ago, that he had read the notorious *Colloquium heptaplomeres* of Jean Bodin, in which I myself found no trace, several years later, of I know not what knowledge and understanding that he claimed to have found there.[19]

On 19 May, Leibniz wrote to La Croze that Arpe "is a man who appears not to worry himself about 'what will people say,' nor about the articles of faith," but he did not believe him to be the author of the *Réponse*. After Leibniz's death in 1716, La Croze continued to take an interest in Arpe and in the three impostors in his correspondence with Johann Lorenz von Mosheim. He expressed his discomfort at seeing how Arpe defended Vanini, and his friend Krause got himself arrested for having had in his shop, among other things, the notorious *Réponse*. La Croze wrote to Mosheim: "If you please, tell me if it is true that a certain good and wise man [Leibniz] once said that Arpe was the author of this work published in French, on the subject of this wicked book, of which rumor reports the existence, on the three impostors. You know that the reprinting of this French pamphlet at Leipzig irremediably damaged the reputation and the fortune of an excellent man, my great friend Johann Gottlieb Krause."[20] Mosheim responded:

> I can assure you on my word that he is absolutely not the author of this pamphlet that has caused so much harm to my very honorable friend, as well as yours, Krause, whose misfortune I sincerely regret. It is true that he had in his possession, with many other things of the same type, the wicked book [the *De tribus*] described in the pamphlet [the *Réponse*] by this phantom author, whoever he may be.... However, I don't wish to hide from you either that he had the intention of relating the content of this book [*De tribus*] at greater length than he actually did, if that other Frenchman had not intervened and the affair had not made so much noise.[21]

La Croze was not entirely convinced. On 16 August 1718 he returned to the subject that Arpe had a copy of the *De tribus*—where did it come from? He was not alone in posing the question.

> I shall not prevent this opinion, already so widespread, from sticking in the minds of practically all those learned men. This conjecture or judgment of men is supported by your statement that Arpe possesses this little book. Some ask themselves how the author of

the French pamphlet published by Krause knew it? Where do all the copies come from of this book until now unknown to the learned world? Moreover, suspicion is increased by the fact that, for all those who understand French, it is evident on reading the pamphlet that it was written by a German and not by a Frenchman. But this should remain *entre nous* [in French in the original text].[22]

Arpe was not the author of the *Réponse*. He defended himself again in a text of critical importance for our subject: a note that he composed for the second edition of his *Apologia pro Vanino*, after 1717. He stated:

> I publicly deny being the author of that letter, as some people would like to believe, even if I possess two copies of two works that exist under this title [*The Three Impostors*]. One, from the library of Johan Friedrich Mayer, is in Latin, the other in French, whose recension in the *Umbständliche Bücher-Historie* caused so much trouble for Krause. Concerning the leaves that came from Mayer's museum, I can only add the report of a man worthy of trust: it was a recent concoction by Johann Joachim Müller, who wrote it to defend his intellectual position in a dispute; his grandfather had mentioned the book, and had not denied that he owned it; in consequence, Mayer, his close friend, demanded it from him repeatedly. . . . I admit readily and concede that it exists and that unfortunate papers of that nature circulate, but I am firmly persuaded that it is not as old as people say, nor of those authors, and that it has never been printed.[23]

Arpe thus rejected any medieval origin of the *De tribus*, any attribution to Frederick II and des Vignes. For him, it was the work of Müller. Moreover, he added, the title exerted such a fascination that it was taken up by many, in order to attract attention and stimulate sales: "Any book of an irreligious nature is generally sold under this name."

Arpe also admitted that he had a copy in French, which today resides in the Staatsbibliothek of Berlin. It is a treatise in eight chapters, in which Arpe wrote an important note, naming the authors; Jean Rousset de Missy and Vroesen: "P. M. [Prosper Marchand] reported that M. Rousset, at The Hague, had taken upon himself to defend the fable of the three impostors against M. de La Monnoye. This was the occasion for M. Vroesen, councilor at the court of Brabant, to print the work there, augmented under the above-mentioned title [*L'Esprit de Spinoza*] with the inclusion of some chapters from *De la sagesse* of Charron and some from the *Coups d'État* of Naudé."[24] Prosper Marchand later confirmed this.

Arpe thus had in his possession both versions, the Latin and the French, the latter under the title of *L'Esprit de Spinoza*. These were only two flowers from his "remarkable collection of rare and forbidden books," as H. Schröder noted.[25] Also to be found there were works of Bruno, Beverland, Toland, Servetus, Knützen, and Lau. The last-named, Theodor Ludwig Lau, born at Königsberg, had studied philosophy and theology there. He then studied under Christian Thomasius at the University of Halle before traveling around Europe—Holland in 1685, England in 1697, France in 1700—and establishing himself as a jurist at Frankfurt-am-Main. In 1717 he published *Meditationes philosophicae de Deo, mundo, homine* [*Philosophical Meditations on God, the World, and Man*], which was immediately condemned, confiscated, and burned. This should not have surprised him, since he himself had written in the preface: "They will call me a heretic, an atheist, a Spinozist, and will revile me with even worse names and titles." However, he found the sanction too hard to take, and declared that even if his book was worse than the *De tribus impostoribus*, it deserved confiscation at most. He appealed in vain to the University of Halle and to his old teacher Thomasius. His *Meditationes* took up once again the idea that religion is the invention of priests and politicians, and his list of impostors included—besides Moses, Jesus, and Mahomet—Confucius, the Pope, Luther, and Calvin. Later, an unknown person commercialized his book under the title *De tribus impostoribus*, thereby illustrating Arpe's point: the notorious treatise exerted such a strong fascination that people made use of the title to sell more copies at higher prices of all sorts of antireligious works. In this particular case, there was fraud concerning the merchandise: Lau's book, full of hermetic reflections, was not worth much.

The De tribus: A German Affair

Arpe's case illustrates perfectly the intellectual atmosphere of northern Germany at the start of the Enlightenment, in the opening years of the eighteenth century. It was an ambiguous atmosphere, where dissimulation and distrust ruled, and where interest in religious criticism was evident but hidden under a pious, or even pietistic, exterior. The fascination with the *De tribus impostoribus* shows this quite well. People claimed to see the book everywhere; they confused it with other books; they fabricated fakes, which others bought at the price of gold; and they did all this while cursing the work. Thus, in a letter of 12 August 1700, an anonymous correspondent of W. E. Tentzel, author of the *Curieuse Bibliothec*, wrote to him:

> As far as the manuscript of *De tribus impostoribus* is concerned, I hereby announce to you that I shall soon receive the same book translated from the Italian. Thus, the content of the latter [is] written like W., whose title [would have been] snatched in Holland by the author (or rather the translator), because he did not want to have problems because of it. The entire book consists of eight notebooks, and the author discusses in the first chapter the general ignorance of men, who are full of prejudices. In the following chapter, he deduces at length the causes that have pushed men to imagine an invisible being, whom they call God; from there, he goes on to the Bible and speaks of it in a disorderly manner. In the third chapter, he proves exactly what religion is and that it was created by ambitious men. From there, he takes the occasion to focus on Moses and Christ, of whom he speaks great blasphemies that I recoil from transcribing; and after that he goes on to Mahomet. Finally, he speaks in a very subtle manner of Hell, the Devil, and other things.[26]

Tentzel immediately made the connection to a copy of the *De tribus* that he thought he could pinpoint to the library of Wolfenbüttel. In January 1689, another of his friends apparently said, "I remember having read in an evangelical theologian whose name escapes me at present, that the book *De tribus impostoribus* had been obtained by the library of Wolfenbüttel, at great expense, by its noble founder. I almost regret not having asked for it at that time, when I was there. But I was so taken up with pious thoughts that it never crossed my mind to dream of these wicked deviltries. Let us leave that research to someone else."[27]

Thus, there is alleged to have been a copy of the *De tribus* in Italian, translated from Latin at latest in 1688. Tentzel's correspondent apparently testified to having the work in his possession. His friend B. G. Struve evidently tried in vain to see it, writing: "I myself can testify about this friend, who claimed to possess the book in Italian, which I did not succeed in seeing in spite of my urgent solicitations."[28] Tentzel's luck was no better. In a loan exchange for another rare book, his correspondent promised to send him a translation of the Italian copy of *De tribus*, but he postponed the date repeatedly, writing to Tentzel on 10 January 1701: "I would also have sent you, as promised, the book *De tribus impostoribus*, but the friend of W. has not yet sent it to me, and relates with many details that it truly exists *in rerum natura*, but that he hesitates to publish it or to pass it to someone by reason of its great impiety, but he is quite willing to show it off."[29]

Miguel Benitez, who has studied this episode, concluded that the Italian text never existed, and that Tentzel's correspondent "was the victim of a regrettable misunderstanding."[30]

> Everything leads us to believe that he must have received a letter from his friend, probably in Latin, containing the description of a work on the three impostors, and that he confined himself to transcribing this passage in his first letter to Tentzel. But he never saw this work, and even less the supposed Italian original, because if that had been the case, it would be difficult to understand both his interest in the translation and the attitude of his friend, who not only hesitates to send him a copy, but feels obliged to protest that the work really does exist. This friend surely would have alerted him that the treatise on the three impostors was—or claimed to be—a translation of the *De tribus impostoribus* whose existence had long been debated. He must have thought that this translation had been made from the Italian—no doubt because, like Tentzel, he believed the original to have been the work of Aretino.[31]

As for the Wolfenbüttel copy, it would simply be a copy of the one belonging to Mayer, who never went to Wolfenbüttel. The librarian of the Herzog August Bibliothek wrote on 25 July 1721 to Professor Cornelius Koch: "I can tell you squarely that the book you seek does not exist in the August library, although Tentzel affirms this on the report of his friend."[32]

Mystery, jealousy, curiosity, and the coyness of collectors all combine to muddy the waters and create a sort of psychosis of the three impostors; the spirit of the work seems to bleed into these scholars, who vie with one another to commit imposture, to the point that no one knows any longer who is deceiving whom. Add to this the fact that many of these individuals had a double life: respectable, orthodox believers and conformists on the one side, working in official institutions, and skeptical freethinkers or atheists on the other, with no one knowing clearly which of these two faces was the cover-up for the other. Professors like Thomasius at Halle or Reimarus at Hamburg are examples. They all revered Vanini, while at the same time vilifying him. Johann Lorenz von Mosheim, Arpe's friend, had a good career as an academic theologian, all the while interesting himself in anti-Christian clandestine literature. He admired John Toland, and wrote against him; as part of a small group that included Arpe, the law professor Heubel, and the jurist and historian Westphalen, he projected writing a "history of burned books," which never saw the light of day. Frontal attacks were a rare event, like that of Matthias Knützen, the son of an organist of Oldenmouth in Holstein, who became an atheist thanks to his theological studies at Königsberg, then enrolled at the University of Copenhagen. He wrote incendiary pieces, which caused him to be pursued across Germany and Denmark in the 1670s. He was the self-proclaimed founder of an atheist group, the Conscientiaries, and wrote in his pamphlet *Amicus, Amicis, Amica*: "We deny God and we throw him down from his heights, rejecting the Temple with all its priests. What suffices for us Conscientiaries is the knowledge not of one but the greatest number . . . , this conscience that nature, the benevolent mother of the meek, has granted to all men, in place of Bibles."

Another finding comes out of the research on the confused origins of the *De tribus*: the localization of the controversies in northeast Germany and Denmark. Certain locations come up over and over again, such as Saxony, Brandenburg, Pomerania, Schleswig-Holstein, Berlin, Halle, Königsberg, Kiel, Hamburg, Leipzig, and Copenhagen. Everything points to a Germanic origin of the text. The present-day locations of the known copies, both manuscript and print, show a heavy concentration in German territory and its borders: Berlin, Celle, Constance, Krakow, Dresden, Gotha, Danzig, Göttingen, Halle, Hamburg, Hanover, Kiel, Lübeck, Oldenburg, Tübingen, Weimar, Wittenberg, and Wolfenbüttel. In 1990 Miguel Benitez, who has published a list of known copies, sketched the variants of these texts, starting from what he called a "common trunk," that is, the "theological, moral, and political dissertations on the three notorious impostors."[33] The existing copies bear different titles, in French or Latin:

- *Livre des trois imposteurs*
- *Traité des trois imposteurs*
- *Les trois imposteurs*
- *De trois imposteurs*
- *Traité des trois réformateurs c'est-à-dire Moïse, Messie et Mahomet*
- *De tribus impostoribus*
- *Liber de tribus impostoribus*
- *Manuscriptum de tribus impostoribus gallico sermone*
- *Manuscriptum de tribus impostoribus*
- *De tribus impostoribus Moyse, Jésus-Christ et Mahomet*
- *Damnatus liber de tribus impostoribus*
- *Liber famosissimus de tribus impostoribus*

Among these copies of copies, there are variants, additions, and omissions. Since the treatise gained its status from its supposed dating to the thirteenth century, some anonymous contributor even saw fit to add, between 1712 and 1716, a forged letter from Frederick II to Otto of Bavaria, and to relate, in a *Dissertation sur le livre des trois imposteurs*, the circumstances in which he had learned of the book. He claimed that a soldier had lifted it in the course of pillaging the library of the Prince Elector of Bavaria, at Munich, after the battle of Höchstädt in 1704. He added details, such as that the writing was so tiny, full of abbreviations, and lacking in punctuation that it was almost illegible. According to him, the hand was that of Pierre des Vignes, while the letter came from the hand of Frederick II himself. This improbable *Dissertation* immediately raised suspicions. Leibniz wrote on 30 April 1716: "The city of Munich was not taken in disorder, but given up in a manner that kept the Elector's belongings sheltered from pillage by the soldiers, and I doubt that an officer in the troops could have penetrated unseen into the library of His Highness. His Great Library is not in his residence; one must be speaking of a small personal library. Whatever, the thing deserves more precise research."[34] Caspar Fritsch was much more blunt: "It is all a complete fabrication. I made inquiries about it once in Frankfurt.... Everyone was in complete ignorance of it," he wrote in 1737 (letter to Prosper Marchand, 7 September 1737; the letter is given in English translation in Margaret C. Jacob, *The Radical Enlightenment: Pantheists, Freemasons and Republicans,* Early Modern Europe Today [London: George Allen & Unwin, 1981], 277–79).

Can we still speak of an authentic original text of the *De tribus impostoribus?* Such a notion scarcely makes sense in view of the proliferation of copies, the multiplication of variants, and the anonymity of the scribes. All the copies are in some sense "authentic" in their originality—they are all authentic impostures. That said, the general sense can be traced across all the versions, and the variants rest on differences in inspiration and emphasis. If one of the texts can be chosen as a reference, the "standard" text, the vulgate of the *De tribus,* that text is without doubt the one from Mayer's library, purchased in 1716 by Eugen of Savoy, which bears the title *De imposturis religionum breve compendium.* In 1753, the manuscript was published by Straub, a bookseller of Vienna, with the made-up date of 1598—a mysterious choice, perhaps pure chance, perhaps recalling the birth date of Johannes Müller, grandfather of the "discoverer," Johann Joachim Müller? Or was it an allusion to Frederick, whose name encoded numerologically is 1599? No one knows. The only certainty is that the Mayer copy is now held by the National Library of Vienna.[35] It bears all the distinctive traits described by Leibniz in his letter to Hohendorf: octavo, twenty-eight pages, German-style writing, quite legible, page 4 effaced. There is a copy in the University Library of Strasbourg.[36] We shall rely on this version, a translation of which was published in 2002 by Raoul Vaneigem, to analyze the contents.[37]

Preliminary Polemic: Does the Trois imposteurs Exist? (1715–1716)

But first, we need to investigate the origin of the French treatise of the *Trois imposteurs,* whose text and context are quite different from those of the *De tribus,* even if there was often interrelation and confusion between the two. The first, imprecise trace of such a text comes from the 1670s. A lawyer at Reims, Marc Antoine Oudinet, in a memoir written around 1672, spoke of a *Traité des trois imposteurs,* which he claimed to have seen and read. He gave a summary of it that corresponds to the content of chapter 3 of the definitive version. We find there the argument of Philo against Moses, that of

Celsus against Jesus, and the history of the "oracle pit" in connection with Mahomet, a story that Naudé had published in 1667 in his *Considérations politiques*.[38]

Then we move to 1694, with the publication of a book entitled *Menagiana, ou Les bons mots et remarques critiques, historiques, morales et d'érudition de Monsieur Ménage, recueillies par ses amis [Menagiana, or The Wit and the Critical, Historical, Moral, and Learned Observations of Mr. Ménage, Collected by His Friends].* On page 332, we read:

> They say that the poor man who was put to death some time ago had in his pocket an extract of a book of the *Three Impostors*. It was a small piece of paper containing insults against J.-C. and against the Holy Virgin. M. Baudelot, who saw this paper, claimed that it was not an extract from the book of the *Three Impostors*; he said that it was only a collection of the worst calumnies against our religion that could be found in certain wicked works composed by Jews and printed in Germany under the title *Tela ignea Satanae [The Fiery Weapons of Satan]* together with refutations. . . . We must ask of M. l'abbé Drouyn if he has discovered anything concerning the book of the *Three Impostors*.

This short passage shows at least one thing: the treatise was already so well known that the slightest examples of blasphemy were presumed to be extracts from it.

In reaction to this psychosis, in 1712 the learned Bernard de La Monnoye of Dijon, a friend of Bayle, wrote a *Lettre à Monsieur Bouhier, Président au parlement de Dijon, sur le prétendu livre des trois imposteurs [Letter to M. Bouhier, President of the Parlement of Dijon, on the So-called Book of the Three Impostors].* The letter was published in a greatly expanded edition of the *Menagiana* (1715). In the letter, La Monnoye was formal: the *Traité des trois imposteurs* was a purely legendary work, a fiction, a fable invented by the libertines "because they wanted it to be true." If this book "whose mere title evoked fear" existed, it would have been placed on the *Index*, condemned, burned, refuted; people would have quoted from it. But nothing! Not a trace, not a copy. It stank of imposture. "Some years ago," said La Monnoye, "one of my friends read me a letter from Bayle, in which he spoke of a German scholar's intention to publish a dissertation proving that there was indeed a printed book entitled *De tribus impostoribus*. I responded in a letter proving the contrary, a copy of which was sent to Bayle. M. de Beauval quoted it in his *Histoire des ouvrages des savants [History of Learned Works]*, in February 1694. At the request of President Bouhier, I shall redo the proof here." There followed long sections recapitulating the rumors that for centuries had attributed the mythical treatise to all the heterodox writers, without the slightest proof: "Stupid compilers, lacking any concept of what we call criticism, fixed on the first likely prospect they could find—whether Étienne Dolet of Orléans, or Francesco Pucci of Florence, John Milton of London, or someone named Merula, a false Muslim—and entangled them all in the net of the same accusation."[39] "And I am by no means the only one to deny the existence of this treatise," wrote La Monnoye. "Struvius has done so in his *De doctis impostoribus*, Kortholt in his *De tribus impostoribus*, Placius in his *De anonymis et pseudonymis*."

Bourdelot, who was occupied with the editions of the *Menagiana*, had written to the Abbé Nicaise: "I believe that M. de La Monnoye's treatise will be very interesting, and that it will determine once and for all what we should think of the notorious treatise *De tribus impostoribus*."[40] On the contrary! La Monnoye's *Dissertation* ignited a blaze. For in Germany and Holland, some knew quite well that the *De tribus* existed; they had a copy, as we have seen, even if it was not very old. In 1715 there appeared an anonymous *Réponse à la Dissertation de Monsieur de La Monnoye*, published in 1716 at The Hague by Henri Scheurleer; Albert-Henri de Sallengre reproduced extracts in his *Mémoires de littérature* (1716). The message of the *Réponse* was as blunt as that of the *Dissertation*: the treatise exists, I have seen and read it, I have translated it, and here is a summary.

This mysterious *Réponse* caused a lot of ink to flow—first of all, concerning its author. We have seen that Arpe was wrongly suspected at first, but then consensus settled on Jean Rousset de Missy (1686–1763), as we learn from a letter of 7 November 1737, from Fritsch to Marchand: "I am relieved to know that Sieur Rousset is the author of the *Réponse*."[41] Some were still skeptical on the subject, like B. E. Schwarzbach and A. W. Fairbairn, who recalled that the thirty-year-old schoolmaster had always shown an altogether conventional piety.[42] But in an era when playing a double game was practically the rule, this scarcely constituted a major objection. All indications seem, on the contrary, to point to Rousset de Missy as the author of this *Réponse*. Beyond Fritsch's letter, the elaborate circumstances invented to explain how he came in contact with the *Traité* remind us that this radical journalist, a great enemy of France, fought in the army of Prince Eugen. He wrote Prince Eugen's biography and also a description of the battle of Höchstädt. In the preface of his *Réponse*, he told how at Frankfurt-am-Main in 1706, in the company of a theology student named Frecht, he made the acquaintance of a German officer, Trawsendorff, who was looking to sell books and manuscripts that he had stolen during the pillage of the library of Munich following the battle of Höchstädt. Among these manuscripts was the *De tribus impostoribus*, whose history here crosses that of the French *Traité*. Therefore, we must take a closer look at this episode to which we have already briefly alluded.

The officer refused to share his copy, for which he hoped to get a good price. Eventually, after having emptied several bottles, he agreed, but he made Rousset de Missy and his companion promise not to copy it. They promised, but with mental reservations: if they didn't exactly copy it, they nonetheless quickly made a French translation of the work before giving it back to its owner, who not long afterward sold his bundle of manuscripts for 50 thalers to a Frankfurt library that the Prince Elector of Bavaria had charged with recovering the valuable stolen volumes.

I thus have in my study the French translation of the notorious *De tribus*, wrote the author of the *Réponse*. Trawsendorff's manuscript was the original, unique, authentic, never-before-published version. The proof: it was preceded by a manuscript letter from Emperor Frederick II to Otto, duke of Bavaria. Here is the text of the letter:

Frederick, emperor, to the very illustrious Otto, my very faithful friend.

I took care to have a copy made of the *Traité*, which has been composed about the three notorious impostors, by this learned man with whom you yourself conversed on this subject in my study. Although you may not have asked me for it, I am sending you shortly the manuscript, whose purity of style equals the truth of its content. For I know how eagerly you are hoping to read it. Also I am persuaded that nothing can give you more pleasure, unless it might be the news that I had squashed my cruel enemies and that I had my foot on the neck of the hierarchy of Rome, whose skin is not yet red enough from the blood of so many thousands of men, whom

its madness has sacrificed to its abominable pride. Please believe
that you will one day hear that I have triumphed over them, or else
I shall die of the effort. For, whatever reverses may happen to me,
never will they see me, like my predecessors, go bend my knee before her. I place my hope in my arms, and in the faithfulness of the
members of the Empire; and your good wishes and help will contribute no small amount. But nothing would contribute more than
if one could persuade all Germany of the sentiments of the learned
author of this book. This is much to be desired. But where are those
who would be able to carry through such a project? I recommend to
you our common interests. Live in happiness. I shall always be your
friend. F.I.[43]

Then Rousset de Missy gave a resume of his translation of the
De tribus. It was composed, he said, of six chapters. The first spoke
of God, or rather of the false image that men make for themselves;
the second, "of the reasons that have led men to imagine a God";
the third, of "what the word *religion* means, and how it slid into the
world," giving the examples of Numa Pompilius, Moses, Jesus, and
Mahomet; the fourth, of the "sensible and evident truths"; the fifth,
"of the soul"; and the sixth, "of the spirits who are called demons."

What are we to make of this *Réponse?* According to Françoise
Charles-Daubert, one need only replace the names of Trawsendorff
and Frecht, in this unbelievable story, with those of Hohendorf and
Fritsch in order to understand what happened: Hohendorf loaned to
Rousset de Missy and Fritsch the copy of the *De tribus* in the library
of Prince Eugen, along with two other clandestine books, the *Theo-
phrastus redivivus* and the *Spaccio della Bestia trionfante* of Giordano
Bruno, and Rousset de Missy did the French translation. Perhaps.

A word now on the article called "Dissertation sur le livre des *Trois
imposteurs* et Réponse à M. de La Monnoie," also published in 1716 by
Albert-Henri de Sallengre (1694-1723) at The Hague, in the *Mémoires
de littérature.* This young man, a precocious scholar, was a collaborator on the *Journal littéraire* of The Hague. The editorial team of this
periodical formed a closed, even secret, circle, with links to freema-
sonry and a taste for radical ideas. It included men like Wilhem Jacob's Gravesande, Prosper Marchand, Thémiseul de Saint-Hyacinthe,
and Justus van Effen, who directed the effort from 1712 to 1723. The
group's specialty appeared to be muddying the waters, in the style of

van Effen, who could write equally that "our religion is not of a kind to require us to sacrifice our good sense," and that the enemies of religion "make a show of two of the most monstrous opinions that have ever emerged from the bizarre recesses of the human imagination": those of Epicurus and Spinoza.[44] In his article, Sallengre is true to this spirit of confusion. He takes up all the cases of the authors cited by La Monnoye and dismissed by him as possible authors of the *De tribus*, and he puts them forward, declaring that the *De tribus* exists, and that La Monnoye is in agreement, that he only wrote his *Dissertation* in order to disguise his own heterodoxy. Sallengre profits by this to say that Ménage himself had a very ambiguous attitude and that "the same thing can be said of La Monnoye, except that La Monnoye was more open to the accusation of atheism than Ménage himself." La Monnoye, one might say, participated in the tradition and in the intellectual and moral games of the learned libertines.[45]

What was Sallengre trying to do? His object is not clear. Up to this point, all the protagonists in this affair seemed to be playing a double game, unless quite simply they were participating in a sort of anachronistic public relations campaign, with the goal of building public interest in the *Traité des trois imposteurs* just ahead of its publication. Three years later, in 1719, it appeared in French under a double title: *La Vie et l'Esprit de Spinoza*.

The Reference Edition: The Hague, 1719

This edition is the first one of which copies survive, four in all: one in Los Angeles,[46] one in Brussels,[47] one in Florence,[48] and one in Frankfurt.[49] It is possible that it may have been preceded by an earlier edition, in 1712, of which there is no known surviving example, but whose existence is mentioned in a manuscript notation at the front of the copy in Los Angeles. An owner of the book wrote: "No one yet knows the author of this infamous production, which ought never to have seen the light of day and copies of which are already becoming scarce. It is attributed, but with no certainty, to a medical doctor of The Hague, called Lucas, who was a Spinozan. Bure Bibl. vol. 1, p. 494, no. 868, which cites an octavo edition of 1712." The note alludes to the work of G.-F. De Bure, *Bibliographie instructive, ou Traité de la connaissance des livres rares et singuliers [Instructive Bibliography, or Treatise on the Knowledge of Rare and Unique Books]* (Paris,

1763), which does indeed mention that *La Vie et l'Esprit de Spinoza* was "printed (in Holland) in 1712." Silvia Berti, who has made a thorough study of all the existing copies, supplies two more indications, but nonetheless remains a skeptic: "We cannot exclude the possibility that Levier or some other of his publisher friends might have released a 'pre-edition' in 1712 with a very limited print run. This hypothesis receives support from the fact that the chapters drawn from Charron and Naudé seem to have been added by Levier in 1712, according to what we learn from a manuscript of the *Esprit* preserved at Munich. . . . Further research should confirm or invalidate this hypothesis."[50]

In the absence of new discoveries, we must consider the edition of 1719 as the first. So let us examine this work. Its exact title is *La Vie et l'Esprit de Mr Benoît de Spinoza*, a title that makes no allusion to the three impostors. It is followed by a quatrain:

> *Si faute d'un pinceau fidèle*
> *Du fameux Spinoza l'on n'a pas peint les traits,*
> *La sagesse étant immortelle,*
> *Ses écrits ne mourront jamais.*

> If for lack of a faithful brush
> No one painted Spinoza's face
> Wisdom being immortal
> His writings will never die.

The content is dual: a very laudatory biography of Spinoza, the *Vie*, which everyone agrees in attributing to Jean-Maximilien Lucas, a Huguenot who emigrated to Holland and who would have composed it around 1678; and *L'Esprit*, which is in reality the text that would be republished many times under the title of the *Traité des trois imposteurs*. Why not use this title, which had attained the status of myth and was the object of so much research and controversy in that era—a title that would certainly be more evocative and more appealing than *L'Esprit de Spinoza*? No doubt because the authors, having borrowed liberally and in an easily identifiable way from the scandalous philosopher, could scarcely present their text under a title that would suggest an ancient origin. Later editions, after 1721, were less scrupulous and took the classic title of *Traité des trois imposteurs*.

The work of 1719 bears no indication of the place of publication, nor the name of the publisher, nor, of course, that of the author. If the two first mysteries are now resolved—the book was published at The Hague by Charles Levier in collaboration with Thomas Johnson— the third continues to give rise to hypotheses. Only the Los Angeles copy includes a portrait, possibly that of Spinoza (which would be logical), but which, in the absence of the slightest resemblance, could also be that of Charron or of Naudé, since the work is based on a skillful collage of passages from these authors, with the addition of borrowings from Hobbes and Vanini. From Spinoza, the author took the appendix of book 1 of the *Ethics*, of which this constitutes the first French translation.

The book is preceded by an ironic "Advertisement," very much in the spirit of the times, specifying that the "monstrous work" that follows is only being published to give good Christians the opportunity to refute it, because

> there is perhaps nothing that gives strong minds a more plausible pretext for insulting religion, than the manner of behavior of its defenders. On the one hand, they treat their objections with contempt, and on the other hand, they zealously demand the suppression of books that contain these objections that they find so despicable.... It is to intelligent folk, capable of refuting it, that we shall take care to distribute this small number of copies. There is no doubt that they will keep the author of this monstrous work on the run, and that they will upset from top to bottom the impious system of Spinoza, upon which are founded the sophisms of his disciple.

This is a good reason to sell dear. "So few copies of this work were printed that the work will scarcely be less rare than if it had remained in manuscript." There follows a "Copyist's Preface," which hammers home the point: "The work is sufficiently rare to be worth examining by intelligent people." It reports the ideas of Spinoza, who "gained such a dishonorable reputation because of his doctrine." But "the author is unknown, in truth, although he who composed it was one of his disciples."

Scholars embarked on a search to discover the identity of this bold writer. The publisher must of necessity have used a manuscript as the basis for his edition: where did it come from? The text being a veritable puzzle, the study of the origin of the different components has made it possible to piece together the complex history of this book. Even if some points are still disputed, the explanation given as early as 1756 by Prosper Marchand in his *Dictionnaire historique* is generally accepted as the most probable.

Marchand was well positioned to have inside knowledge of this publication. Born in 1675 at Guise, he belonged to a dynasty of well-known musicians. From 1698 to 1711, he was a bookseller-publisher at Paris, in the rue Saint-Jacques. As a Protestant, he chose exile in Holland in 1711, at Amsterdam and at The Hague. A bookseller-publisher at first, he went on to devote himself to learned works, with a special interest in heterodox works. We owe to him a republication of the *Cymbalum mundi*. He collaborated on the *Nouvelles de la République des Lettres*, annotated the *Satire Ménipée*, and published the work of Brantôme and Villon. His lifetime achievement was the *Dictionnaire historique*, or *Mémoires critiques et littéraires, concernant la vie et les ouvrages de divers personnages distingués, particulièrement dans la République des Lettres* [*Historical Dictionary*, or *Critical and Literary Memoirs, concerning the Life and Works of Various Distinguished Persons, Particularly in the Republic of Letters*]. He lacked the time to finish it; it was his collaborator and successor Johannes Nicolaas Sebastiaan Allamand who would publish it in 1758 at The Hague. Voltaire himself complained of being ill-treated in the work, as he noted in a letter to Allamand of 1 June 1758: "They tell me that this Prosper Marchand whom you have condescended to publish was formerly a bookseller who wrote worse than he printed. I have never heard tell of this man except on the occasion of the crude insults they say he clothes me with in his posthumous works."[51] The great man, who could not stand criticism, sounded off against "these vile impostures that today are so despised, and scarcely read by lackeys in antechambers."[52] Prosper Marchand dared to scratch King Voltaire—clearly a crime of lèse-majesté and one that illustrates the independent spirit of Marchand. This remarkable scholar pretended, like everyone else, to be scandalized by the story of the three impostors. But he frequented all the social and publishing circles of Holland, including the most radical, and was personally acquainted with the writers and printers who surrounded the publication of *La Vie et l'Esprit de Spinoza*: Jean Rousset de Missy, whom we have already met; Jean Aymon (1661–1734), a Piedmontese who had been a priest, then converted to Protestantism at Geneva, before becoming an author at The Hague;

the publisher Johnson, and above all his colleague Charles Levier, a French Huguenot who settled in Rotterdam in 1716 and was a member of the society of the Chevaliers de la Jubilation, along with the bookseller-publishers Caspar Fritsch and Michael Böhm. Levier published some important works, such as those of Jacques Basnage and Rapin de Thoyras. He was above all an ardent Spinozan, "a man extremely infatuated with the system of Spinoza, although he was in no condition to read him in the original, and had not a jot of the abstract knowledge required," in the polite words of his friend Marchand.[53]

Marchand himself knew, better than anyone else, the circle of French immigrants in Amsterdam and The Hague, where the memory of Spinoza mixed with speculations on the three impostors.[54] In his *Dictionnaire historique*, he devoted a long article to the question of the "Impostoribus (Liber de tribus)." His opinion was categorical: the *De tribus impostoribus* never existed. It was a

chimerical work, one of which everybody spoke but that nobody had actually seen, and which probably owed its existence—or, better, the noise that its title had made for so long—only to the libertine and impious thought of Simon of Tournai, a doctor of philosophy and theology at the University of Paris in the thirteenth century.... I do not believe that all those who brag boldly of having seen and read this work have seen and read anything other than some evil rhapsody, answering more or less well to a title so well suited to dazzle the curious with its supposed rarity, and cobbled together in secret by some one of those miserable compilers who hardly care what they put in a book; and who, seeking only to astonish fools with the seductive appeal of an impressive and deceptive title, get them to buy as dearly as possible not only the loss of their time and trouble but also often the corruption of their mind and heart.

The Birth of L'Esprit de Spinoza *and of the* Trois imposteurs (1700–1721)

That said, there were many *De tribus* and *Trois imposteurs* treatises in circulation. But they were all recent. Marchand undertook to retrace the history of the composition of *La Vie et l'Esprit de Spinoza* (1719). The base text would be a dissertation on the Spinozan conception of religion, which would necessarily date the text after 1677, the year of publication of the *Ethics* in the philosopher's *Posthumous Works*. Chapter 2 of *L'Esprit* was a quasi translation into French of the appendix of chapter 1 of that book. The date of composition of the original text of *L'Esprit* can be narrowed to between 1700 and 1710 on the basis of a statement by Marchand, writing in 1752: this work, he said, "which we saw making the rounds in manuscript for the past forty or fifty years ..." As for the author, said Marchand, it was "a Mr. Vroese, councilor of the court of Brabant at The Hague"; this was what was written at the end of a manuscript copy of the *Traité*. There was indeed a Jan Vroese, or Vroesen, born at Rotterdam on 4 October 1672, son of a burgermeister of Rotterdam named Adrian Vroesen. Jan studied law at Utrecht, carried out diplomatic duties in France in 1701 and 1702, became a member of the court of Brabant, and died in 1725. The man did indeed exist, and a document discovered by Silvia Berti has confirmed in a decisive manner that he was the author of the original treatise. It is an anonymous remark from 1737 concerning a copy of the *Traité des trois imposteurs*:

> The author of these last remarks (quite lengthy, on a thesis where the M.C. religion and M. are attributed to three impostors), Mr. Aymon, well known by his rare knowledge and his change of religion, could not be ignorant of the true author of the manuscript, known under the title of the three notorious impostors, and of which he published an edition under the title *On the Thought and the Life of Spinoza*, because Mr. Aymon himself and Mr. Rousset were those who corrected the original of Mr. Vroesen, councilor of the Council of Brabant at The Hague, the true author of the above-mentioned manuscript. Mr. Rousset, to make his friend's manuscript more valuable and sought-after and to amuse the public at the same time, added to it a dissertation on the three impostors which he had printed afterward by Sr. Scheurleer, bookseller at The Hague.[55]

There are other indications as well. Arpe, who also had a copy of *L'Esprit*, attributed its paternity to Vroesen. And we should not be surprised if, being a Dutchman, he wrote in French: his private journal was in French, and he belonged to the Walloon Church, which used French as its main language.

The next stage: *L'Esprit* was recopied in 1711 by the printer and publisher Charles Levier, an enthusiast for everything relating to

Spinoza, as we have seen. He made his copy from a manuscript of Benjamin Furly, according to a letter from Fritsch to Marchand dated 7 November 1737: "La Vie de Spinoza was copied stroke for stroke from the copy that Levier made from the MS of Mr. Furly: there is nothing new except some notes, the little advertisement, and the catalog of works: but L'Esprit de Spinoza was reworked and expanded. Are we permitted to know by whom? . . . Levier copied it in 1711; this type of book was his hobby. If, since that time, he had dealings with Rousset, all the doubts about it turn into evidence."[56] Fritsch even specifies later that "Levier copied it in a hurry."

And who is this Furly, who possessed the original or a copy of Vroesen? He was an Englishman of Essex, a Quaker, who emigrated to Holland. Born in 1636, he was quite old (he died just a few years later, in 1714) and was the owner of an impressive library of some five thousand volumes. He was close to Vroesen, and knew many English deists.

So there is L'Esprit, in Levier's hands. Fritsch's letter suggests that it was Rousset de Missy who made the project possible. He was already thinking about affirming, contrary to La Monnoye, the existence of a Traité des trois imposteurs, and Vroesen's text interested him for this reason. Together with Jean Aymon, they "reworked the language," as Marchand wrote in his article. Nothing surprising in that: Vroesen's French was somewhat rough.

Vroesen's text was to undergo more than grammatical changes. Charles Levier and his associate Johnson added entire paragraphs borrowed from Charron and Naudé. Here is Marchand's description of the process:

> Two other booksellers, men even more filled with irreligion than he of Rotterdam was with stupidity, having recovered one of these copies, revised and corrected it in numerous places; they made many additions, both impious and historical—one major one among others dealing with Numa Pompilius, whose imposture they discussed at greater length—expanded it here and there with some notes of the same character, divided up the chapters differently, and added six new ones, composed of shreds torn from the Trois véritez and the Sagesse de Pierre Charron and the Considérations de Gabriel Naudé sur les coups d'État, and placed between chapters 3 and 4 of their manuscript. Finally, having placed their own Advertisement at the head of

the compilation, they had it printed under this title: *La Vie et l'Esprit de Mr Benoît de Spinoza.*

What are the precise extent and tenor of the modifications made by Levier and Johnson? Thomas Johnson was a publisher and bookseller of The Hague, who maintained contacts with English freethinkers. In 1709, he published a Latin work of John Toland, *Adeïsidaemon,* and in 1719 he was associated with Levier. Both men took an interest in the works of the learned libertines of the first half of the seventeenth century. Their contribution to *L'Esprit* consisted of expanding the episode of Numa Pompilius, as found in Machiavelli, and the theme of political imposture, with reliance on Naudé. They deliberately accentuated the political side of the manipulation of religion by rulers, and borrowed from Charron some thoughts on superstition. They also drew on Vanini. The borrowings were not innocuous: taken out of context, they were used in a clearly anti-Christian sense. Thus, the borrowings from Charron were drawn from the first edition (1601), the most extreme, and not from the expurgated editions of 1604 and 1607; all the passages making Christianity a noble exception were suppressed. For example, in chapter 13, where they cited Charron's diatribe against the cruelty of religions, they left out the end of the paragraph, which read: "but all that was abolished by Christianity." Similarly, when Charron posed the question of what is the "true" religion and wrote, "We have no doubt or difficulty in knowing which is true, with Christianity having so many advantages and such high and authentic privileges above the others," that sentence disappeared. In short, Levier and Johnson took a harder stance: *all* religions are impostures. All the ambiguity of the libertines disappeared.

L'Esprit, thus reworked and expanded with six new chapters, now contained twenty-one chapters in all. It is this edition that will serve as the basis for our study of the text. Later editions may be carved up differently, but the content is practically identical. As for *La Vie,* which precedes *L'Esprit,* it was unanimously attributed to Dr. Lucas. The two texts, joined, were then published in 1719 by Levier and Johnson at The Hague as *La Vie et l'Esprit de Mr Benoît de Spinoza.*

The story would be too simple if it stopped there. In fact, an anonymous letter of 1714, published in 1731 in the catalogue of the library of Jacob Friedrich Reimmann, already referred to a manuscript of

L'Esprit de Spinoza, in eight chapters, whose titles correspond to those of the classic version,[57] and the letter writer implied that the treatise was due to Dr. Lucas. And when, in 1719, *La Vie de Mr Benoît de Spinoza* was published in the *Nouvelles littéraires*, it was accompanied by the following commentary: "However, we do not believe that we need to be mysterious about the fact that we copied this writing after the original, whose first part treats the life of this person, and the second gives an idea of his mind. . . . You might say, perhaps with certainty, that the entire work is in fact that of the late Sr. Lucas, so well known in these provinces for his *Quintessentes* but even more by his habits and manner of living."[58] Was Lucas, rather than Vroesen, the author of the *L'Esprit*? Certain similarities between the style and content of *La Vie* and *L'Esprit*, disclosed by Françoise Charles-Daubert, might make us think so. But the history of Vroesen as set out by Rousset de Missy and Jean Aymon rests all the same on the solid base of Marchand's testimony. Therefore, it seems more plausible to think that Levier and Johnson worked from two manuscripts—that of Vroesen and that of Lucas, blended into one with the additions of the editors.

The edition of 1719 was very limited, as stated in the preface: "So few copies of this work were printed that the work will scarcely be less rare than if it had remained in manuscript." Marchand confirmed this, adding that the few copies printed sold poorly because of the exorbitant price being asked for them. When Levier died, there remained three hundred copies, which his heirs had burned. The rare copies that escaped were worth a fortune:

> It was Charles Le Vier, bookseller/publisher in this city, who had the work printed; he sold only a few copies because he demanded a *pistole* apiece; when dying he ordered that the rest be burned; and after that, they sold for as much as 50 florins. What is certain is that after the death of one of these booksellers, his heirs sent me 300 copies of this edition, which, according to their wishes, were all put to the flames; reserving nonetheless the *Vie de Spinoza*, which could be kept, and to which a bookseller that we dealt with found it good to have a new title added: *La Vie de Spinoza, par un de ses disciples; nouvelle édition non tronquée, augmentée de quelques notes, et du catalogue de ses écrits, par un autre de ses disciples. À Hambourg, chez Henry Kunrath, M.DCC.XXXV. [The Life of Spinoza, by One of His Disciples: New Edition,*

Unabridged, Augmented with Some Notes and a Catalogue of His Works, by Another of His Disciples. At Hamburg, by Henry Kunrath, 1735].[59]

The decision by Levier and his heirs to destroy the stock was probably due to a bad conscience. In any case, *La Vie* and *L'Esprit* thereafter led separate lives. *La Vie,* the more respectable, was reprinted at Hamburg in 1735. As for *L'Esprit,* it became the *Traité des trois imposteurs* and was reprinted as early as 1721 under this title, in an edition of only one hundred copies, of which none has survived. This is how Marchand presents matters: one copy of *L'Esprit de Spinoza,*

> having landed in Rotterdam in the hands of a crook, a German named Ferber, a self-described doctor by profession, a man extremely suspect and discredited, together with a bookseller/publisher of that city, named Michel Böhm, a man as disorderly as himself, but very stupid and thus very ready to allow himself to be seduced by a skillful and experienced rogue, they had it printed under the following title: *De tribus impostoribus, des trois imposteurs. À Francfort sur le Main, aux dépens du traducteur, M.DCC.XXI.* It was a small quarto of about seven and a half leaves, or sixty pages; but they did not include the *Préface historique et analytique* which I have summarized here. This bookseller died shortly afterward, and the so-called doctor was so bold as to demand from his widow 200 ducats that he claimed to have loaned on the 100 copies that were printed of this edition, and of which he had command, as well as of the copy and proofs. Some people thought they would take their complaints about this to the magistrate, but one of the ministers of the Walloon Church of that city, considering the annoying consequences that might follow on this, said that it would be much better to suppress such an affair, and this advice was followed. However, out of fear that they might rethink that decision, this miserable man retreated at once from Rotterdam, with all his copies, of which we have heard no more since.[60]

A Franco-Dutch Commercial Imposture?

For Marchand, it was a question of a purely commercial operation. The text of *L'Esprit,* reworked to reduce it to six chapters, and with a new title, circulated from this point on under the catchy name of *Traité des trois imposteurs.*

People imagined that this was actually the notorious treatise *De tribus impostoribus*. However, it was not like that at all, for it was only a question of a fairly new work, since this printed work was nothing other than *L'Esprit de Spinoza*, a writing that people had seen circulating in manuscript for some forty or fifty years, preceded by the *Life* of this philosopher—a work of which several copies exist in the studies of several interested parties, and of which some impostor, after having reduced chapters 3, 4, and 5 into a single chapter, and thus reduced the whole work to six chapters instead of eight, had decided to change the title, in order to sell it under more than one face and thus fool the same people more than once.[61]

The circumstances surrounding the birth of the French *Traité des trois imposteurs* were troubled, to say the least. It was basically, as we have seen, a collage of texts borrowed from Spinoza, Naudé, Charron, Vanini, and La Mothe Le Vayer. The borrowers were a small group of scholars, libertines, journalists, and booksellers, with aims that were at once commercial and ideological, under the façade of piety. The role of Marchand himself is not terribly clear. What goal was he pursuing in devoting such a long discussion to this little "red book," as the 1719 edition was familiarly referred to? He displayed in his article his distaste for the purely commercial methods of the booksellers-publishers, whose practices he trashed in a letter of 1711, citing Guy Patin: "There is nobody more crooked than the booksellers."[62] Marchand himself was a scholar and a good Christian, which did not prevent him from publishing the *Cymbalum mundi*. But he defended freedom of expression and intellectual honesty, as was noted by the Calvinist scholar Jean Alphonse Turretini, who wrote to him in 1730: "The third way of which you speak, which is to use equivocal terms, is very bad; . . . let us leave to each man the freedom to think what he wishes on particular questions."[63] Marchand, in developing the notes for his article "Impostoribus," wanted to denounce the commercial practices that surrounded the release of the *Traité*. The fact that he burned, apparently without emotion, the three hundred copies that had been confided to him, and which could have brought in a considerable sum, is a serious indication of his sincerity.

The people who collaborated in the publication of the three impostors included journalists, or, as they were called, *gazetiers, nouvel-*

listes, publicistes. This profession was then in its beginning stages, if we except the official press as Renaudot had practiced it under Richelieu. The magazines, mostly literary, that grew up at the start of the eighteenth century in the climate of relative freedom that then existed in Holland, were at the origin of this new profession, which was still finding itself and was already confronted with problems of professional ethics. It is interesting to note that Marchand had among his papers an *Essay on the Journalist's Profession*,[64] in which he emphasized the inevitable temptation of journalism: to create the event, if necessary by twisting it, by deceiving, by exaggerating, by publishing articles that were genuine impostures: "What is a gazette? . . . a writing based on the relations that cheating, imposture, and interest dictate. Is it thus the master of these events? or will it create them to feed the curiosity of the public?" The journalist had to "examine the nature of the news, the number, the good faith, and the sincerity of his correspondents." The *Traité des trois imposteurs* appeared to scoff at all these rules: it was a fake that passed for a medieval work while it was only a jumble of borrowings from recent texts whose paternity was not always recognized. It was an imposture on top of an imposture, which Marchand denounced.

Of course, among those who took part in the preparation of the *Traité*, some were sincere: freethinkers, libertines, radical thinkers such as Rousset de Missy. But for Marchand it was the commercial aspect that was paramount in its publication. For him, the bookseller-publishers were the principal parties responsible. The *Dissertation* of La Monnoye and the *Réponse* of Rousset de Missy created suspense and aroused the interest of a specialized public. The attraction of the scandalous, the forbidden, the hidden, fanned by a provocative title, increased the passion of the curious, of collectors, as well as of sincere atheists, and the very limited size of the edition raised the stakes. We might suspect, as John Christian Laursen suggests, that Levier had kept the three hundred copies in order to create an artificial shortage to make prices go up.[65] After the destruction of the stock, said Marchand, copies were selling for as much as 50 florins, for a small book of barely a hundred pages, or nearly one month's salary for a Calvinist minister. In comparison, the four enormous volumes of Bayle's *Dictionnaire* were selling for 60 florins, and ordinary books for less than one florin.

Françoise Charles-Daubert has shown that the publication of *La Vie et l'Esprit*, as well as that of the *Traité*, came about through commercial rivalry between Fritsch, Böhm, and Levier. She concluded:

> Fraud and imposture seem at every level to preside over the publication of the two works, and it appears that commercial profit played a nonnegligible role in the enterprise, more important no doubt than the hypothetical desire to spread the thought of Spinoza. . . . This conclusion, less satisfying to the mind than the supposition of an ideal of spreading Spinozism, seems closer to the preoccupation of the publishers, who thus made double use of *L'Esprit de Spinoza* by publishing it, two years apart, under different titles and in different versions. The two texts appeared with the same aura of scandal and, in the end, the same lack of profit, due to commercial greed that was at once awkward and excessive, and, if we can believe their contemporaries, to the lack of judgment of those who presided over such enterprises.[66]

Still, whatever the motivations of the artisans of the *Trois imposteurs*, the content is indeed there: aggressive, provocative, defying religions in the persons of their founders. And for the history of ideas, that is the essential thing. For if the publishers took the risk to launch such a work—a risk that was not only financial—they did so because it fit the spirit of a period and an environment; it responded to a demand, which the journalists only increased. The mystery that surrounded the publication gave rise to speculation concerning the possible author or authors. Among them, two names stand out, those of Boulainvillier and of John Toland.

Erroneous Attributions: Henri de Boulainvillier (1658–1722) and John Toland (1670–1722)

Henri de Boulainvillier (or de Boulainviller, as he signed his name), comte de Saint-Saire, in Normandy, born in 1658, is a curious and confusing figure. A student of the Oratorians at Juilly from 1669 to 1674, he studied exegesis with Richard Simon, who awakened his critical intelligence concerning the Bible. His father's premature death caused him to give up plans for a military career in order to devote himself to restoring the family fortunes. His appetite for knowledge was insatiable: politics, history, religion, philosophy, science, ethics, and also, unfortunately, astrology. Everything excited him. Studying was his favorite occupation: "He gave it all his free time; he read thoughtfully, and often he put his remarks and his thoughts into writing."[67] The memoirist Mathieu Marais said of him: "He is an excellent genealogist, an exact chronologist, a great historian, a sublime metaphysician, and he took up for his own amusement the science of astrology, which is popular at court . . . and which does less honor to him than all the other, admirable talents which he has brought to the highest degree of enlightenment."[68] His friend Saint-Simon agreed: Boulainvillier "was the sweetest, most easygoing, and most agreeable man in the world, self-confident, and so modest that he seemed to know nothing, yet with the broadest and most extensive knowledge of history, and a great deal of depth. . . . His great fault was to work on too many things at once, and to leave off or interrupt a work that he had begun, often at an advanced stage, in order to apply himself to a different project. . . . Without ever seeking to teach others, he had the talent, when sought out, to do so with simplicity, clarity, and grace that gave enormous pleasure."[69] Sadly, he practiced astrology: "It was a shame that such a learned man should have been infatuated with these forbidden curiosities" and with such irrational foolishness.

In addition, he had a strong interest in the work of Spinoza. But it was an ambiguous interest, as it was for most of the critical minds of his day: he proclaimed his repulsion, yet set forth Spinozan philosophy in detail under the pretext of permitting someone more qualified to refute it. But his presentation was so convincing that many contemporaries and some historians seriously thought that he could be the author of *L'Esprit*.[70]

It was between 1704 and 1712 that Boulainvillier, after having read the *Opera posthuma* of Spinoza, wrote his *Essai de métaphysique* and his *Extrait du traité théologico-politique*, which were in fact formal attacks against all revealed religion: "People commonly rely on revelation as a solid and unvarying foundation, without paying attention to the fact that in the principles of all religions, even Christianity, revelation is only credible in consequence of common opinion. I would not believe in Scripture, said Saint Augustine, if the Church had not ordained it," wrote Boulainvillier, adding that "there is no more absurd proposition than the one they make use of to persuade us that we must believe provisionally everything that is said of the other life."[71]

Boulainvillier, heir of the learned libertines and of Spinoza, placed himself among the deists, which earned him the homage of Voltaire, who made him the principal character of his *Dîner du comte de Boulainvilliers*. His *Essai de métaphysique* became one of the reference works of the Enlightenment philosophers, and in 1788 Pierre-Sylvain Maréchal inscribed his name with those of Bruno, Spinoza, Collins, and Toland as liberators of humankind. In many manuscripts of the *Trois imposteurs*, he appears as the author.[72] That he was not, we have already seen, but this mistaken attribution illustrates in a certain fashion the prestige of the *Traité*, which, or so people thought, had to be the work of a celebrity.

It was much the same for John Toland, but with greater plausibility. If he did not participate directly in the enterprise, the English freethinker frequented the Franco-Dutch heterodox circles from which the book emerged, and it is not out of the question that his own works, notably concerning Moses, may have had a certain influence on them. Toland, who was born in 1670 and died in 1722, lived precisely at the time of the religious crisis in England around 1700. The internal conflicts of Anglicanism, the zeal deployed to get oneself noticed by the religious authorities by demolishing real or supposed unbelievers, the disputes over Socinianism, the relaxation of censorship with the nonrenewal of the Licensing Act in 1695: everything combined to create a context for antireligious controversies. The debates descended into the streets—Atheists Lane, near the London Stock Exchange, was the meeting place of the unbelievers, who hung out at the King's Head tavern.

Some prominent thinkers enriched the deist and antireligious literature. Even if John Locke (1632-1704) was a good Anglican, his philosophy opened the door to materialism by affirming that all our knowledge comes from experience and sensation, and that reason cannot reach the essence of things. The Earl of Shaftesbury (1671-1713), a deist, was a sunny optimist who thought that ridicule was the best test of truth. Anthony Collins (1676-1729) can be considered the real founder of freethinking. This gentleman of the best society, educated at Eton and Cambridge, a man of irreproachable morals, published *A Discourse of Free Thinking* in 1713, which was translated into French the following year under a longer title, *Discours sur la liberté de penser, écrit a l'occasion d'une nouvelle secte d'esprits forts ou de gens qui pensent librement [Discourse on Free Thinking, Written on the Occasion of a New Sect of "Strong Minds" or Men Who Think Freely]*. He established that freedom is the essence of thought and is thus indispensable to it; it is even a kind of religious obligation and necessary for the perfection of society.

John Toland was without doubt the boldest of these intellectuals. He was a link between the English deists and the Franco-Dutch heterodox circles. He appeared in Holland as early as 1692, the date when he enrolled in the University of Leiden. We find him there again in 1699, and then he circulated constantly between France and Germany, sometimes accompanied by Anthony Collins, as was the case in 1707. From 1708 to 1711, he lived in the United Provinces, with a stay in Vienna; most often, he was at The Hague or Rotterdam. There, he knew all those who participated directly or indirectly in the birth of the *Trois imposteurs*: Benjamin Furly, who possessed one of the manuscripts, and at whose home he met John Locke and Jean Le Clerc; Jean Aymon, whom he helped to dispose of manuscripts "borrowed" from the royal library; Charles Levier, the publisher; Baron von Hohendorf and his master Prince Eugen, whose library he visited at Vienna; the journalist Desmaizeaux; the publisher Henri du Sauzet, who published the *Vie de Spinoza* in his *Nouvelles Littéraires* of 1719; the Scottish publisher Thomas Johnson, an associate of Levier, who published in 1706, in French, his *Relation des cours de Prusse et de Hanovre*, and in 1709, in Latin, his *Adeïsidaemon*. Johnson also published the work of Collins, of Shaftesbury, of Buckingham, and the *Vie de Spinoza* of Colerus; it was through him as an intermediary that Toland corresponded with Leibniz in 1709. Toland also frequented the groups, clubs, and semi-clandestine associations such as the Chevaliers de la Jubilation, forums of heterodox thought in which many clandestine pamphlets were composed. These bookseller-publishers took a great interest in the English deists, whose works they published. In 1714, Henri Scheurleer, at The Hague, published the *Discours sur la liberté de penser* of Collins, the French translation of which was partly due to Rousset de Missy. Levier would have liked to publish this work. In 1721, he published an adaptation of the *Tale of a Tub* of Jonathan Swift, under the title *Les trois justaucorps*, which recalled the story of the three rings of Boccaccio, and of which Prosper Marchand wrote that it was almost as pernicious as the *Trois im-posteurs*. In 1710, Scheurleer also published the *Sensus communis: Es-sai sur l'usage de la raillerie* of Shaftesbury, translated into French by Pierre Coste and dedicated to Jan Vroesen, one of the presumed authors of *L'Esprit de Spinoza*. The same year an anonymous work, which contained a reference to the *Tetradymus* of Toland, appeared at The Hague. It was the *Voyages et aventures de Jacques Massé*, whose theme resembled that of the *Histoire des Sévarambes* of Veiras (or Vairasse): the hero travels around the world, encountering representatives of different religions, has discussions with them, and recognizes that they are all impostures; he attempts to defend Christianity but his arguments are ridiculously weak. In the country of Butroh, the king claims to be a descendant of the Sun; he rules by religious deception; when the bees rebel, he sends his only son, who turns himself into a bee, is tortured and put to death, comes back to life, mounts up next to his father, and intercedes with him: his sufferings have redeemed the sins of the bees.[73]

How can we think that John Toland, who frequented all these people, their libraries, their meetings, would not have been aware of the development of the *Trois imposteurs*? The Huguenot journalist Pierre Desmaizeaux, who in 1726 published Toland's work and his biography, portrayed him as very active, not hesitating to intervene in the debates, with an aplomb that was not to everyone's taste.[74]

In his writings, John Toland developed a line of thought that evoked *L'Esprit de Spinoza*. Religious imposture had a large place in his thought. As early as 1696, in his *Christianity Not Mysterious*, he attacked the idea of mystery and challenged the notion of revelation. All the articles of faith can and should be interpreted by reason. In 1704, Toland went even further, in his *Letters to Serena*, explaining that the immortality of the soul was an ancient Egyptian invention, and that matter, endowed with "force" or "action," was at the origin of movement and of thought. Religions and superstitions were once linked to funerary rites and developed through their exploitation by the clergy and theologians, "holy impostors of all religions, taking the trouble to lead the people by the nose while sharing the spoils." Tyrants profited from it to control the masses and to claim divine powers. They then took up the habit of interpreting events through the manifestation of the divine will. On the contrary, science shows that there is no place in the universe for a god, a hell, or a paradise. In

1710, in his *Origines judaïcae*, Toland drew a parallel between Moses and Spinoza, declaring that the latter was as inspired as the former. In his *Nazarenus* of 1718, he denied the divinity of Christ; and in the *Pantheistikon* of 1720, he went to the limit of his atomist materialism: the world is a mechanical apparatus; thought is a movement of the brain; we are dependent on natural laws, which ought to free us from all disquiet, death and birth being the same thing.[75]

One of Toland's major themes was that all the great revealed religions were created in response to specific needs. In the *Nazarenus*, he suggested that the three monotheistic religions were adaptations of the same base to different political contexts. He did not deduce from this that it was necessary to do away with religion, but rather that it had to be transformed into a civil religion, based on reason. Religions were impostures that were necessary to upholding the social order. This desacralization of faith brought down on him the lightning bolts of the religious authorities, who accused him of being "Mahomet's lawyer," of passing off the Qurʾān as a Christian book, and of making people believe that the teachings of an impostor or an enthusiast were good Christian doctrine.[76]

More relevant to our argument is that, through his conversation and his writings, Toland may have contributed to the development of one of the versions of the *Trois imposteurs*. Françoise Charles-Daubert called attention to the fact that "the sections devoted to Moses vary considerably from one copy to another, and constitute the mobile part of the treatise."[77] The version that emerged from the circle of Prince Eugen and Hohendorf has the most fully developed Mosaic section, and it is in this circle that Toland's involvement was most notable. Moreover, he had always shown a special interest in the case of Moses. At the National Library in Vienna, there is a packet of "Diverse Dissertations" dedicated to Eugen and copied for Hohendorf, in which Toland discusses religious imposture and Moses.[78]

The case of Moses was a frequent topic of discussion at the beginning of the eighteenth century. Reacting against the interpretation of Machiavelli, who saw in him only a skilled legislator, the defenders of the providentialist vision of history produced treatises reestablishing the divine aspect of his mission. This was the case, for example, of the *Histoire des juifs* of Jacques Basnage in 1706. Toland, who considered Moses purely as a legislator, the prototype for Solon, Lycurgus, Numa, or Confucius, wrote to Prince Eugen: "You know that I have already promised to the public *La République de Moyse*, which of all forms of government I deem to have been the most excellent and perfect. . . . I shall give a new face and a new twist (though sincere and natural) not only to the political system as a whole and to the majority of the particular laws of this incomparable legislator, but also to many historical circumstances and incidents that are found in the very defective and very abridged narrative of the Pentateuch." The work was never completed, but fragments have been discovered, such as "Projet d'une dissertation sur la colonne de feu et de nuée des Israélites" ["Outline of a dissertation on the column of fire and cloud of the Israelites"], explaining the miracle by means of a natural phenomenon. Another passage was incorporated into the *Origines judicae*, published in 1709 at The Hague. In this book, Toland emphasized that Strabo considered Moses to be "a pantheist or, as we would say in our day, a Spinozist; and he presents him as maintaining that no divinity exists outside the universal order of nature, and the universe is the supreme and unique god, whose parts can be called creatures, he himself being the perfect creator of all things."[79]

In *Le Fameux Livre des trois imposteurs*, we find similar passages that are strongly reminiscent of Toland:

> There are more proofs and reasons than are needed to demonstrate that the most amazing actions of Moses, and all those things that he passed off as great miracles and signs of divine power, as the works of the Lord, were no more than pure impostures, which opened the door to other tricks and deceits, such as that of the cloud that placed itself at the door of the tabernacle, that by which the sanctuary of the First Temple of Jerusalem was perpetually filled, to the great astonishment of those who believed in a manifest sign of the All-Powerful residing in that place, and which made a saint of Moses, because of this phenomenon, although it is evident that it was only a false proof, a fake miracle. However, it is upon these impostures that men have since established the greatest mysteries of Christianity.

Rumors circulated, attributing the *Trois imposteurs* to Toland. The bibliophile and antiquary John Bagford alluded to it in a letter written at Amsterdam in 1709. He did not believe it, but he noted that Toland, for his part, thought that the *Spaccio* of Giordano Bruno was none other than the notorious *De tribus*.[80] This was also what M. de

La Croze wrote in 1711, reporting a conversation he had had with Toland in 1702: "M. Toland, who has his reasons for making much of this work [*Spaccio*], believes that it is the one that is so notorious in the world, under the title of *Traité des trois imposteurs*."[81]

Thus, between 1688 and 1719, the *De tribus impostoribus* and the *Traité des trois imposteurs* were both born in obscure circumstances. They were collective works, developed mainly between northern Germany and Holland in cosmopolitan heterodox circles, motivated by antireligious beliefs and by commercial motives. Manuscript copies were made from these two basic works, constituting so many variants. But the basic contents remained stable, and that is what we must now examine.

CHAPTER SIX

The *Treatise of the Three Impostors*:
The Contents of a Blasphemy

In opening up a treatise with such an explosive title, a believer no doubt expected to find within it outrages against what he held sacred, as if a crowd of demons were to rise up and trample his idols. From this point of view, he risked being deceived. By the time the treatise appeared and became semi-public, its contents had already lost their explosive charge. Its arguments were known, even trivialized, in heterodox circles. It contained no shattering revelations or new ammunition against the three personages. Rather, it offered a recapitulation of antireligious arguments that had been developed from Celsus and Julian all the way to modern atheists, linked more or less coherently to form a sort of handbook for the perfect villain, the Bible of the unbeliever, the "little red book" of irreligion.

Admittedly, the direct and aggressive arguments, the polemical and deliberately blasphemous tone, gave it a considerable force of impact at a time when such writings were absolutely forbidden. But it held nothing radically new. We might wonder why such a book was not immediately put on the *Index of Prohibited Books*, since the works of Nicolas Malebranche were already placed there as early as 1689 (*Traité de la nature et de la grâce*), 1707 (*De la recherche de la vérité*), and 1712 (*Traité de morale*). The Latin *De tribus* never received the honors of the *Index*, and the *Traité des trois imposteurs* was not listed until 28 August 1783—more than sixty years after the appearance of *La Vie et l'Esprit de Spinoza*. Everyone talked about the book, but without having seen it. Its rarity no doubt protected it for a long time. Its listing in the *Index* crowned its success.

The De tribus: *A Slapdash Work?*

That the *Traité des trois imposteurs*, as we have seen, comprised many versions is impossible to examine here. And in any case the variants involved questions of nuance. Still, it is important to distinguish between the Latin treatise and the French, which differ in significant ways. The *De tribus*, the older of the two, basically exploits the arguments of Celsus against Moses and Jesus. It emphasizes the philosophical aspect, while the French treatise also makes political and social arguments. The *De tribus*, as it was published in 1753 in French translation, with the false date of 1598, was a small work, wordy and confused, which operated on the level of religions in general, showing the extent to which they are all uncertain.[1]

The *De tribus* begins with one central notion—God. All religions speak of God, without knowing what they mean by this; they give contradictory definitions, which display their ignorance. So "why not say right off that we do not understand God, thus there is no God"?[2] The pagans invented an array of intermediate gods, mocked by people today, but the Jews, the Christians, and the Muslims are no less foolish. Their clergy are more at fault than the founders of these religions, and accuse each other of idolatry.

Their God, they say, is love. And at the same time they attribute to him a greater degree of perversity than that of men, for "who, knowing perfectly the weakness of human nature, would have placed human beings before this famous tree by which he would have been charged with the sin, as he knew, for their loss and (as certain people would have it) that of all their descendants? And yet, they are to owe a debt of veneration and gratitude for a sublime blessing?"[3] It amounts to placing a gun in the hands of a small child, while asking that he not make use of it, and knowing all the while that he is going to commit a massacre.

> Take up, I say, a sword, you who are a father or a friend, and give it to your friend or your children, if you are a true father or a faithful friend, warning them and telling them that they are not to fall upon it, even though you foresee that that is exactly what is going to happen or that it is going to lead to a terrible bloodbath among those closest to them, innocents above all! Reflect! Could you, who are a father, act in such a way? What sort of games would you forbid, if not

this one? And yet it was necessary that God prescribe it. . . . What is this love that inflicts a sin without limit on innocent descendants, all because of the sin of a single man, which could certainly have been foreseen and thus also predetermined?[4]

Even better: to redeem man from the harmless sin of the apple, God finds nothing better than to have his own son tortured, thus obligating men to commit a sin even worse than the first one. "The father subjects his son to the most extreme suffering in order to subject another to equally extreme torments in order to save the first. This is something that not even barbarians would have done. Why then is God to be loved? Why is he to be honored? Because he created us. With what goal? In order for us to succumb to sin. For he surely foresaw that they would fall, and placed the forbidden apple there as a means without which they would not have fallen."[5]

Why should we honor such a God? Would a perfect God need to be honored? Would he need a cult? No. "It is above all in the interest of the powerful and the rich that men should observe religion in order to weaken the resistance of the people. . . . These men who hold the rudder of the state gain for themselves, on the back of a credulous people, revenues that meet or exceed their luxury, while wielding the threat of supreme power and punishment drawn from invisible powers, and feigning, from time to time, to have a relationship or spiritual links with these powers."[6]

If there is a God, he probably contented himself with giving the initial flick of the finger. "No one would believe that he would be incessantly examining all the fundamental matter and parts of the universe, as a doctor examines a patient."[7]

What about the argument of the moral conscience inside every man? Is this not proof that God placed in everyone some idea of good and evil? This again, according to the *De tribus*, is a subterfuge of the priests, in order to keep the people under their thumb. "Should we, just because little old ladies honor Saint Francis, Ignatius, Dominick, and others, should we really believe that it is a precept of reason that it is necessary to honor at least one of these saints and that these women realized it, through the grace of an invisible supreme being? While all the time it is only an invention of our luxury-loving priests who do it in order to richly embellish their lifestyle."[8]

Definitively, is there a God? According to *De tribus*, no one can answer this question. We are asked to believe in God even while admitting that he is unknowable. But some people, all the same, claim to have had an intimate acquaintance with him. This is where the founders of religions come in. For the *De tribus*, it is all "deception." The deception of Moses, who, trained in the arts of the Egyptians, that is to say astrology and magic, later through force of arms drove out the kings of Palestine and finally, under the pretext of a discussion—after the example of Pompilius—won the troops over to his project and led them to resent what belonged to peaceful folk. All this, in order to become himself a great commander and to make his brother a great priest, to become himself prince and dictator of a great people."[9] Deception of Mahomet, who "won over to his cause, by showing off miracles, the warlike and savage peoples of Asia who had been badly treated by Christian emperors, and by promising a great number of blessings and victories, he gained the obedience of princes who were either disunited or ready to make peace, and assured the success of his religion by the sword."[10]

As for Jesus, he is relatively spared. The author contents himself with saying that each impostor made use of the previous religion as his jumping-off point. Thus, "Moses and paganism, the Messiah and Judaism, Mahomet and Christianity." The name of Jesus is not even used, while the Christian religion is the object of critiques drawn from Celsus and Julian. "If we held to the general reputation of the Christian religion, and to the simple mention of its name, it would be for good reason a thunderbolt for some and for others a subject of mockery."

To know if the founder of a religion is an impostor, we would need to have direct knowledge, which is impossible, or else have recourse to testimony, where there is always a need for caution, or else turn to the writings of these founders themselves. But "one might have doubt about what has come down to us from Moses." Jesus wrote nothing, and as for the Qur'ān, "the friends and disciples of Mahomet" were the real authors. "For this reason, the firsthand testimony of any of them is too uncertain to be genuinely credible." The author devotes long passages to the Bible, and in particular to Genesis, whose "fables" he sees as a tissue of implausibilities and contradictions.

The different versions of the *De tribus* end rather abruptly, without any real conclusion; some manuscripts end in a draft form, revealing a text in a rough state, put together in a hurry and without careful composition, which corresponds to the circumstances of the development of the dissertation furnished by Müller to Mayer, as we have reported them.

The Atheism of the Traité

The situation is different with respect to the *Traité des trois impos-teurs*, which we shall examine in its original print version, the 1719 *L'Esprit de Spinoza*.[11] Here we are dealing with an organized and ex-panded treatise, which certainly borrows from different authors— Vanini, La Mothe Le Vayer, Naudé, Charron, Hobbes, and of course Spinoza—but does not stop at stitching together the various bits. On the one hand, it gives them a more radical meaning by taking them out of context, and on the other hand, it groups them in such a way as to build an original and percussive synthesis. "It is a question of an explosive collage, a Molotov cocktail of heterodox texts, also heterogeneous texts, but organized in a perfectly coherent fashion," writes Jean-Pierre Cavaillé.[12] The tone is particularly aggressive, in keeping with the title. The book achieves its own originality with re-spect to its sources, especially by accentuating the political aspect of religious imposture, and in turning the borrowings from Hobbes and Spinoza in a materialist direction.[13] The author or authors, in the service of their proof, make use of all the arguments furnished by the learned libertines as well as Hobbes and Spinoza, but shape them so as to make a systematic and uncompromising antireligious demonstration, avoiding the usual ambiguities of the "public" het-erodox writings.

Like the *De tribus*, the *Traité des trois imposteurs* begins with con-siderations on God. Men, it says, have a completely false notion of God because they don't want to take the trouble to use reason. They accept uncritically the opinions and prejudices with which they are raised. Thus, they are brought to believe that the prophets and apos-tles were directly inspired by God, while they were really ignorant, vulgar men incapable of expressing themselves correctly: "Most of what they said is so obscure that no one can understand it, and in such poor order that it's easy to see that they did not understand themselves and that they were extremely ignorant. What gave rise to the belief that people have in them is that they bragged about having straight from God everything they proclaimed to the people. A belief that is absurd and ridiculous."[14]

Just "a little common sense" would suffice, a little use of reason to figure out that these men "were neither smarter nor better educated than other men." Reason should be our only guide, and the *Traité* here displays a certain optimism: the people can be taught. "What is certain is that straightforward reason is the only light that man should follow, and that the people are not so incapable of making use of it as they are persuaded they are."[15] This comment is important, as it is one of the points on which the treatise departs from its sources: from the learned libertines to Spinoza, all were convinced of the incurable character of popular stupidity. Were the authors of the *Traité* ahead of their time on the topic of the possibility of educating the common people? Actually, they appear to hesitate and to contradict themselves. Chapter 15, "On the Superstitious, on Superstition, and on the Credulity of the People," is reminiscent of Naudé and La Mothe Le Vayer: "The common people (and by this I mean the masses, the mob, the dregs of the populace, men of low, servile, and mechanical condition) are a beast of many heads, vagabond, wandering, mad, stupefied, lacking in proper conduct, lacking spirit or judgment."[16] They can be made to believe anything: "Whether they tell them the fables of Mélusine, or of the Witches' Sabbath," they will swallow it all. Here the treatise takes up Naudé's rant word for word. Above all, this credulity is irremediable, because the people are incapable of learning the lessons of the past: "If you fool them today, they will still allow themselves to be surprised tomorrow, learning nothing from past events to guide them in present or future events; and these are the primary signs of their great weakness and imbecility."[17] This pessimism smothers the hopeful sketch of the first chapter, and sets a general tone: the treatise reports the status of things, it does not actually aim to change them. The common people have always thought that God was as petty as men, whence all those superstitions, which the rulers uphold. "The great and powerful, even though they know what it is, do not want to trouble it or prevent it, knowing that it is a very useful tool for leading a people."

Men have thus forged for themselves a completely false idea of God, one that is full of contradictions, by following the teachings of scripture: they say that he is a pure spirit, and they go on representing him in corporeal form, an old man clothed in white, flames, a dove; he speaks, he sits and stands. He is infinitely good, and at the same time formidable, never repents, and yet repents. The treatise has abundant choices to illustrate these contradictions through texts from the Bible, "a book where there is neither order nor method, that nobody understands, it is so confused and ill conceived, and which serves only to stir up discord," because everyone takes from it what they wish. "What is even stranger is that, the more these pieces of nonsense contradict each other and insult common sense, the more the common people venerate them." They are only "impertinent and ridiculous fables, . . . childish tales, . . . a tissue of fragments stitched together at different times and given to the public at the whim of the rabbis."[18] It is upon this book, "which contains only supernatural things, that is to say, things that are impossible," that men have based their beliefs concerning a purely imaginary future world, without fear of contradiction, for "no one has ever returned from the other [world] to bring us news of it."

In chapter 2, which takes up almost word for word the appendix of the first part of the *Ethics* of Spinoza, the treatise develops the psychological and sociological origin of religious beliefs. Ignorance of physical causes gives rise to fear, and pushes the human spirit to imagine the existence of invisible beings, with whom one can make contact to gain their favor. Men imagine these invisible beings necessarily in their own image: anthropomorphic, subject to the same passions, and doing everything for a purpose. Every event is supposed to correspond to a precise goal in the service of men. This is finalism: "There is nothing in nature that is not made for them, and which they cannot dispose of." To explain physical and moral evil, they imagine that it is the manifestation of the anger of the gods over the sins of men, and when they do not manage to find an explanation, they say that the judgments of God are impenetrable and that human reason cannot attain truth. From there, one can believe anything, and the believers wrap themselves up in their beliefs. "They never give up," impermeable to reasoning. "Becoming infatuated with the ridiculous opinion that everything they see was made for them, men made a point of religion to bring together all the things of the world in their interest, and to evaluate their price by the profit they could make from them. Whence they developed these notions, which served to explain to them the nature of things—good, evil, order, chaos, heat, cold, beauty, ugliness—which in reality are not what they imagine. As from another angle they prided themselves on having free will; they believed it was for them to decide on praise or shame, sin, and merit, calling everything good that could be turned to their profit."[19]

For the treatise, "it is thus evident that all the reasons that the vulgar mind is used to using when it tries to explain nature are only ways of imagining." All our ideas come from our sensations. The beautiful and the good are simply whatever gives us pleasurable sensations; the ugly and the bad are whatever is disagreeable to us. Finalism is destroyed by logical reasoning: if God acts with an end in view, then he desires something that he does not have, which is not realized, and therefore he is not perfect.

If men imagine a God who rewards and who punishes, it is also, and perhaps above all, in order to console themselves for the griefs and injustices of this life; this is what "prevents them from despairing over the misery of life." The treatise anticipates the psychological and sociological explanations of Feuerbach, as well as of Marx and Freud, of the origins of religion. Is it atheistic? The question is discussed. "God, that is to say nature, insofar as it is the principle of movement," it declares in chapter 3, "What God Is." A pantheistic formula, appropriate to Spinozism, but a materialist pantheism. In effect, if the treatise retains the name of God, it defines it in a way that covers the material universe, space. God

> is an absolutely infinite being, one of whose attributes is to be of an eternal and infinite substance. The extension or the quantity being finite, or divisible, only when one imagines it as such. Matter being everywhere the same, understanding cannot distinguish parts. . . . Thus, matter and quantity have nothing that would be unworthy of God. For if everything is in God, and if everything flows necessarily from his essence, it is absolutely necessary that he be like what he contains; for it is contradictory that altogether material beings should be contained in a being that is not material.[20]

The treatise returns to the definition of God in chapter 18, which sharpens the materialist orientation: "God is a simple being, or an infinite extension, which resembles what it contains, that is to say, which is material, without being either just, or merciful, or jealous, or anything that we imagine, and who by consequence neither punishes nor rewards."[21] This God makes "no more fuss over a man than an ant, or over a lion than a stone." There is "in his regard no beauty, no ugliness, no good, no evil, no perfection, no imperfection." He is not moved by men's deeds; he desires neither praise nor prayer. At this point, we might well ask why the treatise retains the name of God and attempts to define it. It would be much simpler to say that he does not exist, to erase the word from the vocabulary, like those of heaven, hell, and the soul, all presented purely as products of the imagination. "Any man who makes good use of reason will not believe in heaven or hell, or the soul, or gods, or devils, in the way that we commonly speak of them. All these big words were forged only to blind or to intimidate the people."[22]

The End of Religions

Another question of vocabulary: the word *religion*. "Before this word *religion* was introduced to the world, men were obliged to follow natural laws, that is to say to conform to straightforward reason. . . . But ever since fear made them [men] suspect that there were gods, and invisible powers, they raised altars to these imaginary beings. Renouncing the light of nature and reason, which are the sources of true life, they tied themselves to the phantoms of their imagination by means of vain ceremonies and a superstitious cult."[23] Thus begins chapter 4, "What This Word *Religion* Signifies," which is directly inspired by chapter 12 of Hobbes's *Leviathan*.

Religions, the fruit of fear and hope, are multiple. They make the fortune and power of the clergy. And that is where imposture really begins, according to the treatise—with the deliberate exploitation of a lie. "The honor and large revenues that people attached to the priesthood, as they have since done for the ministry and for ecclesiastical offices, flattered the ambition and the avarice of sly people, who profited by the stupidity of the people, and provided so well in their weakness that they gradually made a weak habit of censing the lie and hating the truth."[24] The clergy then instituted an entire system of beliefs, rites, and ceremonies, and had sumptuous temples built to impress the masses and thus to make religious imposture take root in the countryside. They elaborated a theology, invented spirits, angels, demons, and prophecies—all that, "to better delude the people." By these means, religions became so powerful, and so firmly anchored in the minds of men, that thereafter it seemed impossible to make them disappear. "But even though there is little appearance of success in this enterprise, we must not for all that abandon the cause of truth."[25]

The treatise develops the question of religions in chapters 12 through 17, which owe much to Charron. It distinguishes five great religions, in chronological order of their appearance: natural religion, pagan religion, Judaism, Christianity, and Islam. Each has its variants, its subgroups, its heresies, and its sects that fight against one another. "Each claims its miracles, its saints, its victories; these are the common arms. In particular, each wants to prevail against the others by some right and prerogative." The faithful of each religion "hate each other, despise and disdain each other, with each calling the others blind, cursed, condemned, and lost, even pursuing each other like mad dogs."[26]

However, they are all alike. "All religions find and furnish miracles, prodigies, oracles, mysteries, rites, prophets, feasts, certain articles of faith and belief that are necessary for salvation. All were small, weak, and humble at their origin and commencement, but little by little, by gaining a following and by the contagious acclamation of the peoples, with fictions put forward, they have taken hold and become respectable, such that all are viewed with affirmation and devotion, even the most absurd." Above all, they all affirm that God takes pleasure in the suffering of his faithful, that the best way to appease him is to inflict upon oneself "difficult and painful tasks," "very painful exercises," "to give oneself pain and torment": this surely gives a very wretched notion of their gods, whose "goodness" is repaid by our affliction.

Each religion claims that it is obviously better than the others, and each built itself up by using the preceding one as its jumping-off point. A new religion never completely destroys its predecessor, or else no one would follow it. It retains certain elements and criticizes the rest, which permits it to recover some part of the adherents of the old religion. "[The new religion] comes along to succeed and perfect [the old one], and thus ruins it little by little and grows rich from its spoils, as Judaism did to the gentile and to the Egyptian faith, Christianity to Judaism, Islam to Judaism and Christianity both. In return, the old religions totally condemn the young, and see them as deadly enemies."[27]

To arouse veneration, religions deliberately place their creed outside of ordinary experience, whether in things that are "low, unworthy" (like a God who becomes man and gets himself crucified), or in things that are "exalted, stunning, miraculous, and mysterious," which permit them to amaze and to astonish people. And to better establish their prestige, they will claim "that they are brought and given by extraordinary heavenly revelation, taken and received by divine inspiration, and as if they came from heaven. Thus all those who uphold, and believe, use this language, which comes neither from men nor any other creature, but from God."[28] This allows them to place themselves beyond criticism: one does not debate the word of God. But do the believers truly believe the stories they tell? "Would it be possible to believe in the truth, and hope for this happy immortality, and yet fear death, the necessary passage to this very condition? To fear and apprehend this infernal punishment, and yet to live as one does? These are tales, things that are more incompatible than fire and water. They say that they believe it; they make others believe that they believe it, and they want to make others believe it, but it is nothing, and they do not know what it is to believe. These are mockers and challengers, as an ancient writer said."[29]

One of the essential themes of the treatise is its emphasis on the political exploitation of religions, in the tradition of Naudé. The beginning of chapter 16, "On the Origin of Monarchies," sets the tone. "If we consider what the origins have been of all monarchies, we shall always find that they began by some inventions and deceptions, placing religion and miracles at the head of a long train of barbarisms and acts of cruelty."[30] Take Semiramis, Cyrus, Alexander, Romulus: it is always the same story, an imposture accompanied by the use of force. And all the legislators, the founders of monarchies and empires, resort to religion to establish their domination. Religious imposture is the most effective ally of political imposture. "There have only ever been two effective means of keeping men to their duty, that is to say, the means of torture . . . and fear of the gods."

Political leaders make use of religion in five different ways. The first is to make people believe that they are in direct communication with the divinity. This is what Savonarola did, and yet "the people of Florence are not stupid." But wait—one needs to combine this lie with the use of force, "as Machiavelli says"; as proof, consider the failures of Guillaume Postel, of Campanella, and of Savonarola himself.

The second subterfuge: "to fake miracles, find dreams, invent visions." Take the examples, says the treatise, of Clovis and the Holy Chrism that fell upon him from the sky, or Charles VII and Joan of Arc. The third means involves "false rumors, revelations, and prophecies that they spread intentionally to frighten the people, astonish them, stun them, or else to confirm, embolden, and encourage them." There is no shortage of historical examples, according to the treatise. Beyond Mahomet, a case to which we shall return, Cortés, Pizarro, Charlemagne, and Mehmed II all had recourse to false prophecies to discourage their enemies; it is also by this means that the city of Acosta was taken in 1613. "This is then a major road open to the politicians to deceive and seduce the stupid masses: using these predictions to make people fear or hope, to receive or refuse everything that seems good to them."[31]

The fourth means: to use preachers and skilled orators, for "the force of eloquence ... flows so pleasingly into the ears that one would have to be deaf or cleverer than Ulysses to not be charmed." Illustrations include the sermons of Peter the Hermit or of Saint Bernard, which attracted the masses to the Crusade; the speech of Jean Petit in 1407 justifying the murder of the Duke of Orléans; the sermons of Brother Richard, reported in the *Journal of a Bourgeois of Paris* in the fifteenth century, which persuaded the Parisians to give up games and luxuries.

Finally, "The fifth invention, which has always been the one most used and most skillfully practiced, is to undertake, on the pretext of religion, what no other means could make valuable and legitimate."[32] To illustrate this point, the treatise makes use of the book of the Spanish historian Mariana, from which it draws numerous examples. It concludes this section thus: "It is natural to most princes to make use of religion as charlatans, and to use it like a drug, to uphold the credit and the reputation of their drama."

The Soul and Demons: Subtle Chimeras

Before we turn to the characters of the impostors themselves, we must say a word about two topics the treatise brings up as an annex, in chapters 19 through 21. Chapters 19 and 20 are dedicated to the soul, which clearly poses an embarrassment to the authors. They begin by recalling the definitions given by the ancients. What comes out of this is cacophony—as many opinions as there are philosophers.

Some have said that the soul is a spirit or an immaterial substance, others [that it is] a part of the divinity. Some, that it is a subtle vapor, others a hot wind, others a fire, others a composite of water and fire. These [say it is] a chance assemblage of atoms, and those, a composite of subtle parts, which evaporate and are exhaled when a man dies. There are some who would have it consist of the harmony of all the parts of the body, and others, of the subtlest part of the blood, which separates itself in the brain and is distributed through the nerves. So that the source of the soul, according to these last, is the heart, where it is engendered, and the brain is the place where it has its noblest functions, because there it has been purified of the grosser parts of the blood. Finally, there are some who have denied that there were souls.[33]

Pythagoras and Plato think that the soul is incorporeal, that it can survive outside the body, and that the souls of animals are part of the universal soul of the world, the source of all movement. The human soul exists in the body as in a prison. Aristotle admits a world soul but also a universal understanding; for him, the soul is "what makes us live, feel, conceive, and move," but he does not explain what it is. For Dicaearchus, Asclepiades, and Galen, the soul consists of harmony and equilibrium between all the parts of the body, which "with proper guidance" means that it is corporeal, while others affirm, in contrast, that it is incorporeal. Others openly conceive it as material. For Diogenes, it is air; for Zeno, Leucippus, and Democritus, fire; for Hippocrates, a composite of water and fire; for Empedocles, a composite of the four elements; for Aristoxenus, an agreement of all the parts of the body. All these philosophers, noting that the soul perished with the body, concluded that it was mortal. Xenocrates and Dicaearchus, however, simply deny its existence: it is not even wind; it is a word. "Monsieur Descartes" pitifully maintains that the soul is immaterial. "I say pitifully, because no other philosopher ever reasoned so poorly on this subject as this great man." The treatise highlights this absurd side of the *Cogito* and of methodical doubt. This is not an honest, authentic doubt, it says; it is a deception. To say that I think, all the while doubting my body, thus I am a thinking being, and to conclude from this that the soul is incorporeal, is a conjuror's trick. In fact, at no moment do I doubt the existence of my own body.

What of all this? "It is certain that there exists in the world a very subtle spirit, or a form of matter very detached and always in movement, whose source is in the sun, and the rest is spread among all other bodies, more or less, according to their nature, or their consistency. This is what that soul of the world is, what governs it, what vivifies it, and of which some portion is distributed to all the parts that constitute it."[34] We must acknowledge that the treatise is not very convincing on this subject. Its "very subtle spirit" could just as well be spiritual as corporeal, and we have scarcely advanced at all. For the author, however, "it is certain that this soul, being of the same nature in all animals, is dissipated at the death of a man, just as it is in animals. Whence it follows that what the poets and theologians tell us of the other world is only a chimera they have created and sold for reasons it is easy to guess."[35]

The treatise is more comfortable with demons. We recall that this subject had given rise to lively debates in Holland around 1700. Here we find their echoes. According to the treatise, it was the ancients who invented this foolishness, which Jews and Christians hastened to adopt—"an absurd belief, but ordinary to the ignorant people who imagine that what they do not understand is some infinite power." Spirits, made of subtle matter, which circulate rapidly and have the power to act upon us, are a godsend for the rulers. "This ridiculous opinion was no sooner divulged than the rulers made use of it to buttress their authority, . . . in order that the fear that the people would feel for these invisible powers would hold them in subjection. And to do this with more force, they divided demons into good and bad, the former to incite men to obey their laws, and the latter to restrain them and to prevent them from breaking them."[36]

The Greeks were the inventors of this "foolish imagining." The Jews borrowed it from them, and attributed to the action of demons the behavior of "those whom we call lunatics, crazy, mad, epileptics, and also those who spoke an unknown language. A misshapen or unclean man was, to their mind, possessed by an unclean spirit; a mute, by a mute spirit." Later, Christians adopted these pieces of nonsense in their turn, since "Jesus Christ was Jewish, and as a consequence, strongly imbued with these insipid opinions that his nation had taken from the Greeks."

The devil appears throughout the gospels; he defies God, provokes him, incites men to evil, and God does nothing! He wiped out humanity, his own creation, by drowning it in the Flood for some obscure sins, and then he let Satan walk about and commit all the evil that he can. This is indeed a history of madmen, concludes the treatise.

> How can we conceive that God maintains a creature who not only curses him unceasingly and bears him a mortal hatred, but who takes pains to seduce his friends, in order to have the pleasure of cursing him through an infinite number of mouths? How, I say, can one understand that God maintains and preserves the devil and allows him to survive in order to do the worst to him that he can, to dethrone him if he could, and to turn aside to his service his chosen and his favorites? What is God's goal in this? Or rather, what are they trying to tell us, in speaking to us of devils and hell? If God can do anything, and no one can do anything without him, how did it come about that the devil hates him, that he curses him, and takes away his friends? Either he is complicit, or not: if he is complicit, it is certain that the devil, in cursing him, is doing only what he should, since he can only do what God wishes, and in consequence this is not the devil but God himself who curses himself through the mouth of the devil, a thing that to my mind is very absurd. If he is not complicit, it is not true that he is all-powerful, and if he is not all-powerful, it would be necessary to admit, instead of one sole principle of all things, two, one for good and the other for evil, one who wants one thing, the other who wants and does exactly the contrary. Where does this reasoning lead? To admitting unconditionally that there is no God, no devil, no soul, no heaven, no hell in the manner that it is depicted, and that the theologians, that is to say those who sell fables as divinely revealed truths, are all, except for some ignorant ones, men of bad faith, who maliciously abuse the credulity of the people to insinuate what pleases them, as if the masses were only capable of seeing chimeras, or were to be nourished only by these past-dated foods, where they see only emptiness, nothingness, madness, and not one grain of the salt of truth and wisdom.[37]

Moses the Impostor: Magic and Persecution

Let us get to the heart of the *Traité des trois imposteurs*: the case of the three characters in question, Moses, Jesus, and Mahomet. A frontal attack on these three icons is doubly blasphemous: on the one hand, by accusing each of them of imposture, and on the other hand, by placing them all on the same level. By insulting the three founders of the three great monotheistic religions, the authors of the treatise struck these religions at their most sacred spot. Each of these characters was the object of attacks on the part of the faithful of the other religions, who thereby defended their own champion. But to attack all three at once was an incredibly bold undertaking for that era, when atheism, even if it was not unknown, as we have seen, was generally considered a monstrosity in all public statements. To uphold the thesis of the three impostors around 1700, even secretly, required remarkable strength of character; not only were there legal risks, which could go as far as execution, but also the risk of eternal punishment, if by chance . . . After all, one could never be 100 percent sure, and to knowingly defy all the gods in an environment where they were omnipresent, where no one seemed to doubt their existence, was a deed beyond the reach of the first unbeliever to come along. Recall that for many theologians, the true atheist cannot exist: this would be madness. Such a person might be a libertine, morally corrupt, or oblivious, but he could not truly believe his own claim. "Earth has few such monsters," said Bossuet, "even idolators and infidels regard them with horror."[38] A treatise that argued coldly against the three "impostors" was thus the worst form of defiance imaginable, especially since the little book made no compromise.

Numa Pompilius was evidently no more than an appetizer. He could be shot down without fear: the unhappy man no longer had a defender. The treatise, however, treated him gently, acknowledging that this "wise man," who "worked throughout a reign of more than forty years to soften the savage ways of the Romans," had done useful work. His story of private conversation with the nymph Egeria was a pious lie that permitted him to establish Roman law. He was thus more or less a sympathetic character.

The tone changed when the subject turned to the case of Moses. Of the three impostors, he was the one whose status was most ambiguous. He was venerated by the Jews, of course, but Christians had ambivalent feelings about him: a great prophet, certainly, but a bit too Jewish to be really respectable, as one might say. Besides, before the appearance of Christianity, accusations of magical practices had already taken shape in the Hellenistic environment, as we have seen.

In the second half of the seventeenth century, the very authenticity of his work began to be threatened, as well as its anteriority with respect to ancient civilizations.

Some people began to ask themselves if, far from having been an innovator, Moses had not been a copier or an imitative genius. This was affirmed by the Englishmen John Marsham and, in 1685, John Spencer, of Corpus Christi College, Cambridge. How was it possible that, after several centuries of Egyptian domination, this rude people called the Hebrews had not come under the influence of a stable, dominant civilization? Were the rites of Leviticus not just imitations of Egyptian practices? This thesis, though impious, still had a certain attraction, as Abbé Renaudet admitted regretfully in 1702: the work of John Marsham was

> in its own particular line, . . . perfect; perfect in respect of the orderliness, the method, the precision, the conciseness and the profound scholarship which distinguish it throughout. At the same time, it is difficult not to animadvert on an author, who, either because he has a special leaning towards Egypt, and its antiquities, or for some other reason best known to himself, has so attenuated everything that lends dignity to the Scriptures and their ancient origin, that he has provided the free-thinker with more food for scepticism than the majority of the declared opponents of religion ever did.[39]

The defenders of the Bible who launched themselves into learned studies in order to respond to the attacks only furnished arms to their adversaries. Huet, in his *Demonstratio evangelica* (1678), which claimed to establish a proof by the facts, in relying upon the prophecies of Moses, drew attention in spite of himself to the incoherencies of the Pentateuch, which Richard Simon, that same year, showed could not be the work of the great legislator. The Pentateuch contained many citations, proverbs, turns of phrase, and elements of style of a later period, without even mentioning that it gave a detailed account of Moses' funeral, which was somewhat suspect. Moreover, the redundancies, variants, contradictions, and chronological errors showed that it had several strata of composition.

Huet was a theologian, Simon a philologist, and both were devout Christians, whose sincere work certainly gave more ammunition for doubt than the attacks of Spinoza. One could say as much about the colossal work done by the Benedictine monks on Christian sources.

They rummaged through libraries, going over them with a fine-tooth comb; manuscripts were brought to light, relieved of the dust of centuries. It was obscure and thankless work, which restored the past of the church: lives of saints, history, polemics, linguistics, iconography, archaeology, and numismatics. Between 1680 and 1720 Benedictines and Bollandists, such as Mabillon, Du Cange, Muratori, Montfaucon, Bentley, Puffendorf, Rymer, Leibniz, and many others were all hard at work. The more editorial work they did and the more they piled up the folio volumes, the more people doubted, questioned, and sank into skepticism.

It was thus a weakened Moses whom the treatise attacked in chapter 5. This "grandson of a great magician, who became the chief of the Hebrews and got them to believe that God had appeared to him; that it was by his order that he had taken up their leadership; that God had chosen him to govern them; and that they themselves would be his chosen people, privileged, to the exclusion of all other nations, provided that they believed and that they did what he would tell them. And to convince them of his divine mission, he did some fancy tricks in their presence, which they took for miracles."[40] His method: "He retired into solitude from time to time, on the pretext of going out to confer privately with God; and by this pretence of immediate converse with the divinity, he gained limitless respect and obedience." But he also used force, because—according to the treatise, following Machiavelli in this—"deception without arms has rarely succeeded." Moses eliminated his rivals without mercy; he "administered death without quarter to those strong minds and spared none of those who found fault with his government. With these precautions, and by coloring these torments in the name of divine vengeance, he lived as an absolute ruler."

Jesus the Impostor: A Merchant of Absurd Dreams

The case of Jesus is obviously much more sensitive. This is the true center of the treatise, which devotes lengthy discussions to it. For we are, after all, in the land of Christianity: if attacking Mahomet is a holy enterprise from the point of view of the church, and if to demystify Moses conforms to the beginnings of modern exegesis, to label Jesus an impostor is a major crime. The character is untouchable, erected as a champion of love by theology and hagiography, killed by the blows of Jewish fanaticism. Attacking him is a delicate matter. Anti-Christian criticism attacked the clergy, accusing them of having betrayed the message of the founder, who remained a venerated figure. To attack Jesus himself was a novelty of stunning boldness.

However, he was an impostor like the others, according to the treatise. It was his method that was different: he deliberately took the opposite tack from Moses.

> [Moses] began by making himself terrible and formidable to other nations. Jesus Christ, in contrast, drew men to him by their hope for the delights of another life, which they would obtain, he said, by believing in him. While Moses promised only temporal goods to those who observed his law, Jesus Christ made them hope for eternal goods. The laws of the one concerned only external matters; those of the other concerned the interior. They allotted praise or blame even for thoughts, and in every way were a counterpoise to those of Moses.... But as it is very difficult to get men to resolve to move from one law to another, and as most minds are extremely tenacious in matters of religion, Jesus Christ, imitating other innovators, resorted to miracles, which have always been the trap of the ignorant and the refuge of the ambitious.[41]

Against Jesus, the treatise uses Greco-Roman and Judaic arguments, and especially Celsus. Spinoza provides the basis for the critique of the notion of incarnation. The basic accusation one can make against Jesus is to have spread a false message of hope, to have deceived men by presenting his own wild imaginings as divine revelations, to have been a merchant of dreams, of illusions, who demanded the submission of bodies and spirits in exchange for a false hope of eternal life without any guarantee.

The man was skillful: he presented himself as the Messiah, and to make sure that no one else would come along later to supplant him, he prophesied that all those who would claim to be messiahs after him would be impostors and Antichrists. "Jesus Christ, more adept than the Mosaic prophets, in order to cut the ground out from under those who would rise up against him, predicted that any such man would be the great enemy of God, the delight of demons, the sewer of all vices, and the desolation of the world. After these fine praises, there was, in my opinion, no one who wanted to call himself Anti-christ; and I don't see that anyone could find a better secret than that one to eternalize a law."[42]

Another of Jesus' skills was to address his message to the igno-rant and the poor in spirit, because he knew that those people were the most numerous and that they were resistant to all reasoning. By appealing to this category, Jesus assured himself of the permanence of his doctrine. In addition, it provided, according to the treatise, a powerful argument to his sectarians: if his religion founded on idi-ots managed to triumph, they would say, this was proof that it was divine, because how could idiots prevail without the aid of God?

> A religion that survives on such weak foundations, and whose preachers were men ignorant to the point of stupidity, is a com-pletely divine and supernatural religion; as if one did not know that there was no one better suited to give currency to the most absurd opinions than women and idiots. It is thus nothing to marvel at, that Jesus Christ certainly did not choose wise men and philoso-phers for his apostles. He knew that his law and common sense were diametrically opposed, and that is why he spoke out on so many occasions against the wise and excluded them from his kingdom, to which he admits only the poor in spirit, the simpleminded, and imbeciles.[43]

Jesus was sly: he claimed at the start to want to fulfill the law of Moses, but as his troop of followers grew, he excused himself from observing it, excused his disciples likewise, and made their apolo-gies when they violated it. "He avoided performing miracles in the presence of unbelievers and enlightened folk," knowing that the ignorant are easier to fool. Certainly, in contrast to Moses and Mahomet, Jesus failed on the personal level, since he was crucified, which illustrates yet again that force is necessary to maintain decep-tion. "When he had performed the miracles that are attributed to him, lacking money or an army, he could not fail to perish. But with finances and troops, it is likely that he would have been no less suc-cessful than Moses, Mahomet, and those who have had the ambition to raise themselves up above others. If he was more unfortunate, he was no less adroit, and some parts of his story show that the great weakness of his strategy was to have neglected to provide sufficiently for his own safety."[44] But his disciples, in spiriting away the body, knew how to transform his failure into victory, by putting out the rumor of a resurrection. Because the Jews were hostile, they turned to the pagans; for that, they needed to refine their doctrine somewhat, for the pagans were not as rustic as the Jews. Therefore, they recruited "a young man of a bold and active spirit, a little better educated than the fishermen, or a bigger babbler." This was Saint Paul, who made Jesus pass for a God.

In fact, who was this Jesus? The treatise does not say. It avoids repeating the story of Celsus, which had it that Christ was the adulterous son of the soldier Panther and Mary. The author contents himself with saying that Jesus had the aim of imitating Moses and that "he gained a following of some idiots, whom he persuaded to believe that the Holy Spirit was his father and that a virgin was his mother." The idea of divine incarnation "involves as big a contradiction as if one were to say the circle had taken on the nature of the square, or that the whole had become a part." As for redemption through putting to death the son of God, how could this grave crime in any way redeem lighter sins? How can we conceive that this all-powerful God "should have debased himself to the point of avenging the bites he had received from these ants, these worms, and to take satisfaction as if he could have been injured by them? ... as if, supposing he had really been offended by them, he would not have been the master, either to give up his rights, or to reconcile these sinners with his divinity in some other way, or finally to award them a free pardon?"[45]

Jesus taught a moral doctrine that was utterly impossible to follow, contrary to nature, and would have given rise to the worst disorders if it had actually been applied: not to resist the wicked, to offer oneself to their blows, to live at the expense of others by begging. Moreover, the clergy exempted themselves from following these precepts: "These sellers of air, of wind, of smoke ... seem to have studied solely in order to gain a post that would provide them with bread. A post that they worship and for which they applaud themselves when they have obtained it. Believing that they have arrived at a state of perfection, even though it is only, for those who obtain it, a state of self-love, ease, pride, voluptuousness, where most observe nothing less than the maxims of the religion they preach."[46] The treatise opposed to these "hypocrites" the life of the sages of antiquity. No one was "more austere, more firm, more equal, and more detached from

passions" than Epictetus; Epicurus led a frugal life, and "this philosopher, even though he was a pagan, used to say that it was better
to be out of luck and reasonable than rich and wealthy without having right reason; adding that it was rare for fortune and wisdom to
exist in the same person, and that we only know how to be happy
or to live pleasurably when our happiness is accompanied by prudence, justice, and honesty, which are the qualities of true and last-
ing pleasure."[47]

Christians borrowed most of their beliefs from pagans. "Saint
Augustine acknowledges that he found the entire beginning of the
Gospel of Saint John in some of their writings." The Old Testament,
according to the treatise, is the result of pillaging from Plato and
Greek myth: Eve and the Androgyne, original sin and Pandora's box,
manna in the desert and the ambrosia of the gods, the river of Daniel and the Pyriphlegeton, the sacrifices of Isaac and of Iphigenia,
and so on.

From the beginning, the Christian world tore itself apart, and "it
is truly a strange thing that this Christian religion—which, being
the only true religion in the world, the truth revealed by God, ought
to be united in faith, since there is only one God and one truth—
should always be torn into so many parts and divided into so many
contrary opinions and sects."[48] And these divisions have provoked
unheard-of violence among people who all claim to follow the law of
love and of pardoning offenses, "as if the Christian religion taught
people to hate and to persecute others." "It is permitted only to
Christians to be murderers, betrayers, traitors, and to set themselves
against one another by all kinds of inhumanities, against the living,
the dead, honor, life, memory, spirit, tombs, and ashes, by means of
fire, steel, vicious libels, curses, banishments from heaven and from
earth, exhumations, breakings of bones and monuments, provided
that this was for the security or advancement of one's own party and
the retreat of the other."[49]

All of this is explained, according to the treatise, by the fact that
Christians "neither can nor should carry themselves calmly and
moderately, without betraying God's cause and their own." But one
of the results of these atrocious wars of religion is that many people
lose their faith: "Many, worn out and tired of so many divisions and
contrasts, not knowing what to attach themselves to and uphold,

abandon everything, live blank, and come to despise and abandon religion. For we know only too well that apostasy, atheism, and irreligion are the product and the offspring of heresies."[50]

This is a specific characteristic of Christianity, says the treatise, which is, typical of its period, largely ignorant of the heresies of other religions: "In other false and bastard religions, gentile, pagan, Judaic, Mahometan, one does not find such divisions and partialities. And if there are divisions, they are few in number, light, and unimportant, as in the Judaic and Mahometan religions, or if they have been numerous, as among gentiles, between philosophers, at least they have not produced major and shocking effects and disturbances in the world."[51]

Mahomet the Impostor: The Senses and the Sword

The third impostor is Mahomet. Apparently, the task was an easier one. For centuries, the Prophet was considered in Christian Europe as the prototype of the impostor, the rascal, the deceiver, who owed his success only to the swords of his soldiers. However, the case of Mahomet was reexamined around 1700—with a desire, if not of rehabilitation, at least of relativization—by heterodox intellectuals who thought that Islamic doctrine was probably no worse than Christian. As early as 1671, Henry Stubbs had emphasized the positive aspects of the Prophet in his *Account of the Rise and Progress of Mahometanism*. He especially appreciated the oneness of Allah, for as a good Socinian he rejected the Trinity. Bayle, in the article "Mahomet" in his *Dictionnaire*, tried to take into account history and rumor and gossip, favorable and hostile. Both the orientalist Ludovico Marracci, in his *Prodromus ad refutationem Alcorani*, published at Rome in 1691, and the learned Abraham Hinckelmann, in *Alcoranus s[cilicet] lex islami[ti]ca Muhammedis . . .* (Hamburg, 1697), abandoned an aggressively polemical tone for a reasoned critique. In 1697, Humphrey Prideaux, in *The True Nature of Imposture Fully Displayed in the Life of Mahomet* (London; French translation, Paris, 1699), based his work on more credible historical sources and condemned the violent Christian pamphlets that used only unverified calumnies.

Kindest to Mahomet was Boulainvillier, to the point that a rumor reported by Mathieu Marais said that he had actually converted to

Islam.[52] In any case, he had translated the Qur'ān, in an edition published at Amsterdam in 1731, of which the Duc de Saint-Simon had a copy in his library. Between 1718 and 1721, Boulainvillier wrote a *Life of Mahomet*, which was published in 1731 at London by Hinchcliff. Diego Venturino calls it "the first frankly pro-Islamic text produced by European culture."[53] Boulainvillier took his information from the late seventeenth-century scholars Pocock and Herbélot, and turned the Prophet's biography into a weapon against Christianity. Mahomet was indeed a "notorious and acknowledged" impostor, but also a man endowed with "superior qualities." This had to be admitted, for otherwise his successes could only be explained by the will of God, "which the impious will blame for having brought part of the world into error, and having violently destroyed his own revelation." The case was clearly embarrassing for Christians.

Boulainvillier similarly gave a positive view of the Muslim religion, which rejected the contradictions of Christianity, such as the Incarnation, which would be due simply to an error of interpretation of the disciples. He presented Islam as the religion that was "the simplest in its dogmas, the least absurd in its practices, the most tolerant in its principles," following the expression of Condorcet. To parade the merits of Islam in this way was above all a way of denigrating Christianity and favoring deism.

In fact, no one in Europe actually imagined the rehabilitation of Mahomet. The image of the impostor, of the false prophet who imposes his power by lies and force of arms, was always present, among devout Christian authors as well as among the heterodox. Mahomet inspired unanimity of opinion against him. In 1679, the dean of Lichfield, Rev. Lancelot Addison, in his *Life and Death of Mahumed*, called him a "monstrous impostor."[54] The term *impostor* was likewise used by the *Dictionnaire* of Moréri (1680) and by the *Dictionnaire de l'Académie* (1694). Spinoza, in a letter to Jacob Ostens, wrote that "it clearly follows [from my doctrine] that Mahomet was an impostor.... And if he replies that Mahomet, too, taught the divine law and gave sure signs of his mission as did the other prophets, there is certainly no reason for him to deny that Mahomet was a true prophet."[55] As for Hobbes, he recalled how "Mahomet, to set up his new Religion, pretended to have conferences with the Holy Ghost, in forme of a Dove,"[56] an old chimera from medieval apologetics against Islam.

The *Traité des trois imposteurs* had only to draw from this anti-Islamic tradition, and it did not fail to do so. Gathering all the stories compiled by Christians against the Prophet, it declared that this

> impostor, seeing that he was subject to the falling sickness, decided to make his friends believe that the most violent paroxysms of his epilepsy were moments of ecstasy and signs of the spirit of God that entered into him. He convinced them also that a white pigeon that came to eat grains of wheat from his ear was the angel Gabriel come to announce to him, on God's behalf, what he was to do; afterward, he made use of the monk Sergius to compose a Qur'ān, which he pretended had been dictated to him from God's own mouth; finally, he got hold of a notorious astrologer to predispose the people by the predictions he made about the change of regime that was going to occur and the new law that a great prophet was going to establish, so that they would more easily accept his own when he came to publish it. But when he noticed that his secretary Abdalla Bensalon, against whom he had unjustly taken offense, had begun to discover and to make known such impostures, he cut his throat one night in his house, and set fire to its four corners, with the intention of convincing the people the next day that this had happened by fire from heaven, and in order to punish the said secretary who had taken the initiative of changing and corrupting some passages of the Qur'ān.
>
> However, this scheme was not the end of all the others; there still needed one more that would top off the mystery. He persuaded the most devoted of his servants to descend to the bottom of a well that was near a high road, so that he might cry out, when he was passing by in company with a large crowd of people who ordinarily accompanied him, "Mahomet is the well-beloved of God, Mahomet is the well-beloved of God." And when this happened in the manner that he had proposed, he thanked divine goodness for such a remarkable testimony, and begged the people who followed him to cover up this well then and there, and to build a little mosque above it as the mark of such a miracle. And by this invention this poor servant was buried under a shower of stones that took away the means of ever revealing the falseness of this miracle.[57]

One must recognize the episode drawn from Naudé.

Mahomet, like Moses, had to do with men who were "sensual and vulgar." Also, "this impostor promised them ... a paradise, where the happiness of those who would have observed his law would consist in part of whatever most flatters the senses." This religion is "vulgar and fleshly," and the Qurʾān "stuffed with unbelievable stupidities" that are worth no more than those of the Bible, stories of "the sword, wars, murders, and captivities." Mahomet also made use of an astrologer, "to prepare the people to receive more willingly the religion he wanted to introduce." Finally, as the ultimate argument, he used the sword.

In fact, it was he who had the most success of the three liars, in the opinion of the treatise. "He died peacefully, covered with glory and assured that his doctrine would survive after his death, because he had shaped it to the minds of his sectarians, born and brought up in ignorance and in sensuality." And his religion "is so solid that after more than a thousand years of rule, there is no sign yet that it is ready to fall."[58]

The *Traité des trois imposteurs* draws a lesson from these hoaxes: "Here you have it, readers, whatever is most notable about these four (with Numa Pompilius) famous legislators. They are such as we have depicted them for you. It is for you to see if they deserve to have you imitate them, and if you are to be pardoned for allowing yourself to be led by guides that ambition raised up and ignorance made immortal." It ends with a call to reason and to the search for truth:

> For a long time people have favored the absurd maxim that truth is not made for the people and that the people are not capable of knowing it; but in all times, also, there have been sincere spirits, who have rejected such an injustice, as we have done in this little treatise.
>
> Those who love the truth will no doubt find great consolation in it; and it is those alone whom we wish to please, without troubling ourselves in any way with those for whom prejudices serve as infallible oracles.[59]

The tone appears to be cautiously optimistic. However, the appeal, spread by means of very few copies, smothered by censorship and by the flood of religious apologies, did not reach far. In the eighteenth century, this incendiary, provocative text, too radical for its time, caused divisions in the ranks of the heterodox and the enemies of the church. It provoked fear, and burned the hands of the philosophers, most of whom tried to dissociate themselves from it, except for the boldest, like La Mettrie or d'Holbach. Having just emerged from myth, the *Three Impostors* plunged into clandestinity. Read only by a few initiates, by minds already convinced, it remained for the vast majority a simple expression, that of an integral blasphemy, a sort of slogan of the radical Enlightenment.

The *Three Impostors* in the Antireligious Literature of the Eighteenth Century

In the years from 1719 to 1721, the *Traité des trois imposteurs* officially entered into the large family of clandestine literature so character-istic of the intellectual production of the eighteenth century. Ev-erywhere in Europe, to various degrees, the censors of the church and state were watching. The boldest works, produced anonymously and in secret, were passed surreptitiously from hand to hand. They were sought out by the police, seized, and burned when they were discovered. The subterranean commerce of forbidden books was all the more prosperous as the spirit of the Enlightenment gained ground, won over larger and larger circles, and gave rise to bolder ideas. The little "red book" was one of the flowers of this literature. But its radical thesis divided even the most disputatious minds: while d'Holbach approved of it, even publishing an edition of the text in 1768, Voltaire took offense at it, and went so far as to write a refutation.

An odd man, this Paul Henri Thiry, Baron d'Holbach. Born in the Palatinate in 1723, he died in Paris in 1789. He owed his title of baron of the empire, along with his fortune, to his uncle, who sub-sidized his education in Paris. From 1744 to 1749, he was in Hol-land, studying law in Leiden. He moved to Paris in 1749, became a French citizen, and bought a post as councilor secretary to the king. His absorbing occupation was to publish clandestine texts, and for more than thirty-five years, starting in 1753, he held a salon in the rue Royale-Saint-Roch, which rapidly became known for its very free atmosphere.

D'Holbach was a likable man, discreet, sociable, and virtuous; a good father and a good husband, as even his enemies acknowledged. He had many enemies, for this scholar, who published nothing un-der his own name, was a complete atheist, materialist, and fatalist, who spent his life publishing the most antireligious clandestine works. He wrote formidable treatises against belief systems, notably what might be considered the first great materialist synthesis, the *Système de la nature* (1770). D'Holbach embodied peaceful atheism.

In his view, the propensity to believe is especially strong in ignorant people, and this is the basis for religious imposture. D'Holbach devoted an entire treatise to the topic in 1766: *Le Christianisme dévoilé ou Examen des principes et des effets de la religion chrétienne [Christianity Unveiled; Being, An Examination of the Principles and Effects of the Christian Religion]*. "Founded on imposture, ignorance and credulity, [religion] can never be useful but to men who wish to deceive their fellow-creatures. We shall find, that it will never cease to generate the greatest evils among mankind, and that instead of producing the felicity it promises, it is formed to cover the earth with outrages, and deluge it in blood; that it will plunge the human race in delirium and vice, and blind their eyes to their truest interests and their plainest duties."[1] All the founders of religions are thus necessarily impostors, Moses, Jesus, and Mahomet at the head.

D'Holbach's propositions are very close to those of the *Traité des trois imposteurs*, and the baron could not help but take an interest in this mysterious work. In 1768, he arranged an edition of it that became a standard reference. As he did for the *Histoire critique de Jésus-Christ* and *Le Bon Sens du curé Meslier*, other clandestine manuscripts whose publication he arranged (in 1770 and 1772), d'Holbach made certain modifications to the text, modernized its language, and added notes, but he felt no need to change its contents, with which he was fully in agreement. It is impossible to know which manuscript of the treatise he worked with. A great variety of them circulated in this period, and were altered along the way, intentionally and unintentionally, by the copyists. D'Holbach's version, once readied, was sent secretly, via Sedan and Liège, to Amsterdam, to the bookseller-publisher Marc-Michel Rey, a native of Geneva living in Holland, who published virtually all the *philosophes* and many of the clandestine works. Rousseau, his compatriot, was one of his principal clients from *La Nouvelle Héloïse* to the *Contrat social*, but Diderot, Voltaire, Jacobi, and many others also entrusted their works to him. D'Holbach regularly had recourse to him. Once printed, the books arrived in France by the same routes, and sold for higher prices because of the limited size of the editions, which rarely reached a thousand copies. A small book like *Le Christianisme dévoilé* cost 10 ecus, and a big book, like *Le Système de la nature*, cost 5 louis.[2]

This 1768 edition of the *Traité des trois imposteurs* by Marc-Michel Rey, in d'Holbach's version, may be said to mark its entry into the great classics of clandestine literature, and would gain it the honor of the *Index* in 1783 (after the reprints of 1775, 1776, and 1777 and before those of 1793 and 1796). Before this semi-public life, the treatise had had a secret life since its first publications in 1719 and 1721. For this almost half century, it is very difficult to follow its trace. Copies of the printed editions are extremely rare. The first edition, that of 1719, under the title *L'Esprit de Spinoza*, of which only four extant copies are known, must have been extremely limited: seventy copies, "after the example of the seventy apostles," according to a note in *La Vie et l'Esprit* in a manuscript now in Göttingen.[3] A fantastic figure, since Prosper Marchand stated that he himself had burned three hundred copies of this edition in 1734, at the request of Levier's heirs. But after this auto-da-fé, extant copies had to be few in number. Of the mysterious edition of 1721, no surviving example has been found. And from 1721 to 1768, no new edition has been noted. Only the *Life* of Spinoza was republished, but from then on it led an independent existence, as a simple biography. The *Traité des trois imposteurs*, on the other hand, circulated only in manuscript form, along with a few print survivors from 1719 and 1721.

Attempts were made to publish it, motivated by the desire for gain. In 1736, Mortier, who had a copy of *L'Esprit*, wanted to have it printed in order to pass it off as a translation of the thirteenth-century *De tribus*. This was reported by Caspar Fritsch in a letter of 17 January 1740 to Marchand: "It is four years since Mortier brought a [copy] of it, which he wanted to sell dear to the little masters following the Court. This made some noise. I was informed of it by reasonable men. I showed them mine. They found it to be *una et eadem [one and the same]*: to counter the charlatanism of Mortier, I allowed them to freely make as many copies as they wanted." Fritsch thus contributed to the spread of the treatise in manuscript form. Marchand, in the article "Impostoribus" of his *Dictionnaire historique*, mentioned yet another abortive attempt: "In addition to these two extremely rare and almost unknown editions [those of 1719 and 1721], we might have seen a third, made after the manuscript of Mr. Hulst mentioned above and procured by a certain academician, reproducer, and what is worse, secondhand dealer in these sorts of literary curiosities, if the Dutch publisher, to whom he made the proposition, had not been a more honest man than he, and had not flatly refused to accept such a criminal commission."

The treatise thus circulated essentially in manuscript form before 1768. Copies had to be fairly numerous, because they were reproduced in series, as shown by the interrogation in 1725 of a certain Jérôme Lecouteux, a specialist in the distribution of news by hand, who had as many as fifty clerks working under his orders. At the home of one of them, named Bonnet, a search turned up "a manuscript containing 302 folio rolls having for a title *La Vie et l'Esprit de Spinoza.*" Interrogated, Bonnet responded "that he had made five or six copies of it for the account of Sieur Le Coutuels."[4] The latter did his best to minimize the affair: "With regard to Spinoza, it was agreed to have made three complete copies, a year or eighteen months ago by Sieur Bonnet, which were sold by him to M. le comte de Toulouse, to M. the bishop of Blois and to M. de Caraman, but that then he had ceased this work, Monsieur Dargenson having so ordered him." Imprisoned in the Bastille, he admitted in the course of a second interrogation "to have had copied a part of the said manuscript last summer by the said Sieur Bonnet, which copy was delivered by him to M. Daguesseau de Valjouin, who had asked him for it." The investigation revealed the existence of a veritable network of copyists and salesmen, which suggests that dozens of copies flowed, benefiting from complicity and protections. The affair equally reveals that the treatise was much sought after and read among the aristocracy and even by ecclesiastical dignitaries. This explains the assurance of Lecouteux, who swore "to have in his possession no bad manuscripts" and had his friends intervene to get him released from the Bastille. The police seem to have been more interested in the seizure of works of Boulainvillier than in *L'Esprit de Spinoza.*

The extent of the spread of the treatise was confirmed in 1739 when authorities discovered thirty-four copies of the *Vie de Spinoza*, forty-one of *Spinoza [L'Esprit?]*, and fifty-eight of the *Réfutations de Spinoza* (Boulainvillier) at the home of one Stella, who had been arrested and imprisoned in the Bastille. Stella was a maître d'hôtel of the Venetian ambassador.[5] In 1746, they arrested a certain Claude Lapalu, a former

Latin teacher, who was part of a team of copyist-salesmen specializing in "infamous books full of obscenities." The search made on 23 March at his home revealed, in addition to pornographic works, "in manuscript, the treatise of the three impostors." He stated that "this manuscript was entrusted to his wife by the said Lefevre mixed up in the book business who is at present in Italy."[6] It seems that the band, under the direction of a certain Clermont, did an active trade in the treatise. In 1747, another affair revealed the growing concern of the police in the face of the circulation of the three impostors: for several months, the exempt Dadvenel put a watch on the movements of a former *valet de chambre* and innkeeper, Pierre Guillier, in Paris; informers bought copies of the *Traité des trois imposteurs* from him, which were entrusted to the director of the Librairie, Maurepas, as trial exhibits. The arrest of Pierre Guillier followed, and a thorough search was made of his lodging, where investigators found several pornographic manuscripts. He was asked "if in the past year he had not given for sale four copies of the three impostors, six copies of a manuscript entitled *Le Jean Foutre puny [John Fuckoff Punished]* and two copies of another entitled *Paris foutant [Paris Fucking]*." Guillier admitted that he "had given to an individual who came to him to ask on behalf of someone two or three copies of the three impostors and the same number of *Jean Foutre puny*, with the three impostors at 6 livres apiece, *Le Jean Foutre puny*, 3 livres."[7] Imprisoned in the Grand Châtelet and then in the Bicêtre in July 1747, he was exiled in August 1748. In 1759, again, the police seized from Durey de Morsan a *Dissertation sur les trois imposteurs*.[8]

These several affairs suffice to convince us that the manuscripts of the treatise were secretly in great demand and circulated covertly in large numbers, in spite of their high price. Their mention alongside pornographic best sellers such as *Jean Foutre* and *Portier des Chartreux* is rather flattering: it reveals that the work was greatly sought after in France.

The demand seemed no less in other countries. In the United Provinces, the location of the print editions of 1719 and 1721, many printed copies were seized and destroyed, but thanks to the activity of copyists in French immigrant circles, hundreds of manuscripts circulated. Fritsch allowed copies to be made freely. The correspondence of Marchand confirms the popularity of the work commonly called "the red book."[9] In 1753, Durey wrote to him to offer "some

French manuscripts, copied secretly after those of the king's library in Paris, or those of the library of Abbé Bignon," including the *Mémoire* of Meslier and various clandestine antireligious writings.[10]

In Germany, interest in the three impostors was no less strong. According to the pastor A. G. Masch, people trafficked in it at Halle. He wrote in 1757: "In my day there was a man at Halle, a disciple of Edelmann in his doctrines and a swine of Epicurus in his conduct, who did an unholy business in this manuscript. Passions pushed me to buy a copy from him at 8 grl., and although he told me that he frequently got 10 Reichsthalers for it. For each copy, I figure however that I am not buying repentance so dearly."[11] Lessing consulted several copies of the work in Latin, which he borrowed from the library of Reimarus. In a letter of 10 April 1770 accompanying the return of several volumes, he mentioned among them "two manuscripts *'De tribus impostoribus,'*" which indicates that Reimarus father and son had themselves bought manuscripts or had them copied. In the inventory of the library of Heinrich Friedrich von Diez, who died in 1817, we find no fewer than eight copies of the *Traité*, five of them in Latin. The library in Dresden included ten copies of *L'Esprit de Spinoza*, and four of the *De tribus impostoribus*.[12] Manuscripts have been located in the public libraries of Berlin, Celle, Gotha, Göttingen, Hamburg, Oldenburg (four copies), Hanover, Kiel, Munich, Tübingen, Wolfenbüttel (two copies), Constance, and Lübeck. In neighboring Denmark, the work was equally sought after, like all the clandestine antireligious works, as witnessed in 1750 by *La Spectatrice danoise*: "The license of the presses of Holland and England has spawned several works against Christianity. The books are read greedily. There is one circulating in this city which sells at so high a price that some people have preferred to copy it in their own hand than to give 20 ecus for it. On the basis of the price, I figured that it had to be very long and very interesting."[13] In England, in contrast, the treatise enjoyed less success. Only four copies have been found there: one at Manchester, one near Barnard Castle in Yorkshire, and two in London. This could be due to the fact that in the native land of Hobbes, Toland, and Harrington, the heterodox sought not to suppress religion, but to purify it, in order to make it conform to reason and nature, by creating a civil religion. The three "impostors" were seen more as three "legislators." This is the explanation put forth by Justin Champion: "The specifically English reading suggests that

since all religion is a social, political, and ultimately historical phenomenon with an inherent tendency to imposture, then it is necessary for the wise and rational (those proponents of right reason) to
reform religion to 'the gentle yoke of reason and nature.' This second embedded reading ... suggests that while religious leaders have
ordinarily been impostors, they can become 'true legislators.'"[14]
Supporting this interpretation, we may adduce the fact that the only
English translation of the *De tribus*, which is found in the British
Library, omits the passage on Mahomet. The copyist explains this in
a note, stating that since the writer consulted only "bad authors (apparently only lying Greeks)," for his chapter on Mahomet, the copyist chose to omit it, as unworthy of translation, "for we already have
many accounts of this famous Arab legislator that are much better
and more authentic."[15]

Apart from this exception, the *Traité des trois imposteurs* had a remarkable success in continental Europe in the eighteenth century.
It was undeniably one of the most sought-after works—by the police,
by curious readers, and by the champions of the radical Enlightenment. And it aroused the fury of Voltaire, which confirms the atheistic interpretation of the work.

Voltaire's position with regard to religions is ambiguous. Religions
are human creations, and thus their founders, who make claims of
divine revelation, are necessarily either impostors or visionaries.
Religions are agents of fanaticism. But they are necessary to the people, for they help preserve the social order. Atheism is harmful. What
is needed is a moderate religion, tolerant, without dogmas, a serene
deism as a guarantee of good morality. This is why he had no sym-
pathy for Moses and his "ridiculous prodigies": according to him,
Moses was a butcher, and his terrorist doctrine never speaks of the
immortality of the soul.[16] Peter the Great was far superior to him as a
legislator. With regard to Jesus, Voltaire is quite discreet. His official
position, which he displays in his works destined for the public, is
respectful and reserved; he pays homage to him through lip service
and in passing, throwing all the imposture onto the priests, who have
betrayed his message. But in his private correspondence, he shows
much less respect for "the lover of the Magdalen, [who] changed
pure water into bad wine."[17] Jesus may not be an impostor, properly
speaking, but he was a poor man, one whom Voltaire himself, no
doubt, would not receive at Ferney. He is quite easy with regard to

the "cousin of John the Baptist," who "let his leg be kissed by the Magdalen." He oscillates, in this respect, between sly commiseration and mocking humor. Jesus was only a man, and not even a man of good company. But Voltaire hesitates to label him an impostor.

There is no hesitation, however, on the subject of Mahomet, who according to Voltaire was the archetype of the impostor and the fanatic. Voltaire here places himself in the classical Christian tradition. Mahomet is "whatever trickery can invent that is most atrocious, and whatever fanaticism can accomplish that is most horrifying. Mahomet here is nothing other than Tartuffe with armies at his command," he wrote on 20 January 1742 to the Prussian King Frederick II, in announcing his intention to compose a play on the Prophet in order to combat religious imposture. Mahomet represents the height of fanaticism, of superstition, and of imposture: "But that a camel driver should stir up insurrection in his village; that in league with some miserable followers he persuades them that he talks with the angel Gabriel; that he boasts of having been carried off to heaven and having received there a part of this unintelligible book, which makes common sense shudder on every page; that, to forcibly ensure that this book will be respected, he brings fire and sword into his own country; that he cuts the throats of fathers and rapes daughters; that he lets the defeated choose between his religion or death: this is assuredly what no man can excuse, at least if he was not born a Turk, or if superstition has not extinguished all natural light in him."[18] In the same letter, Voltaire displays indignation over Boulainvillier's attempt to partially rehabilitate Mahomet: "He tried to pass him off as a great man whom Providence chose to punish the Christians and change the face of a portion of the world."

The play, entitled *Le Fanatisme ou Mahomet le Prophète*, appeared in 1742. It was anything but a masterpiece. Reading it, one quickly grows bored, except for the interest of some passages castigating virulently the "false prophet."

The play was a failure. The only one to find it good was . . . the pope, Benedict XIV, who thanked "his dear son" Voltaire for the gift of his "admirable tragedy of Mahomet." The *philosophe* would have preferred other forms of praise. He did not understand why his play was not a success. His correspondence is full of recriminations against the bad taste of the public. One more plot of the priests, he thought. But how could the devout be scandalized by a play attacking Mahomet? They ought to have been pleased, he wrote to Marie-Louise Denis: "Frankly, I have never understood how the Prophet of Mecca scandalized the devout folk in Paris. I can well imagine that in Constantinople one would find fault with my having so treated the great prophet of the Ottoman Turks; but what interest can your rigorists take in this? In truth, it is a ridiculous example of what the cabal and envy can do. Who could ever believe that a man such as Abbé Desfontaines would have persuaded some poorly informed men of the cloth that this tragedy was dangerous to religion?"[19]

When d'Holbach's edition of the *Traité des trois imposteurs* appeared in 1768 in Amsterdam, Voltaire immediately received a copy of it, which is not at all surprising, since the publisher, Marc-Michel Rey, was also the publisher of Voltaire's own works. From his first reading, his opinion was extremely negative. He wrote on 11 April, from Ferney, to Daniel-Marc-Antoine Chardon: "Holland has been infected for some years with defrocked monks, Capuchins, friars, Mathurins, whom Marc-Michel Rey of Amsterdam puts to work at so much the sheet and who write as much as they can against the Roman religion in order to earn their bread. There is one especially, named Maubert, who has flooded Europe with brochures of this type. It is he who produced the little book of the *Trois imposteurs*, a fairly insipid work that Marc-Michel Rey impudently gives out as a translation of the so-called book of Emperor Frederick II."[20] We do not know why he attributed the work to Jean-Henri Maubert de Gouvest, an ex-Capuchin and the author of several books of political history. His opinion with regard to the treatise was about to change rapidly; if he called it "insipid" in his letter, he wrote in his own copy, "dangerous book,"[21] and began to fear that people would attribute its paternity to him. "My name unfortunately is on the tip of their tongue," he wrote on 16 April to the comte d'Argental, and on the same day to Michel-Paul-Guy de Chabanon: "They never stop attributing to me the brochures of Mathurin Laurent, and the Batavian insolence of Marc-Michel Rey . . . and the little book of the *Trois imposteurs* so many times renewed and so often despised."[22]

Voltaire himself kept on talking about this "despised" book, commenting on it with his correspondents, and thereby contributing to the spread of the little work, which clearly many people had procured for themselves. On 9 May, he wrote to Henri Rieu, a man of letters of Geneva: "You said it very well, my dear pirate, that the book of the *Trois imposteurs* was a flat work."[23] This "flat work" pre-occupied him to such an extent that he decided to respond to it, as he announced on 12 March 1769 to Marie-Louise Denis: "I amused myself this morning by writing an epistle against the book of the *Trois imposteurs*. I have just finished it. I shall send it to you. I believe that atheism is as pernicious as superstition."[24] He sent off his epistle, "of which one part is edifying and the other a bit playful," as he himself said, to several people for critique: Mme du Deffand (15 March), Jacques Lacombe (27 March), the royal censor and journalist François-Louis-Claude Marin. Together with the *Épître de M. de Saint-Lambert* and the *Épître à Boileau*, the *Épître à l'auteur des trois imposteurs* was published at Paris under the title *Les Trois épîtres*, in 1769. Mme du Deffand had already replied to him by 21 March: "I have just reread your writing on the *Trois imposteurs*; one cannot prevent oneself from bursting into laughter on finishing it; nothing is better reasoned than the beginning and the middle, and nothing so humorous as the end; as you always say so well, and I repeat it with you: *Let us toss aside these novels that people call systems, / and in order to raise ourselves up, let us descend into ourselves.* If we don't find truth there, we will seek it fruitlessly elsewhere: *This God, of whom you, better than I, conceive the existence, / ought indeed to give me your belief, as he did you.*"[25]

What Voltaire could not stand in the *Trois imposteurs* was atheism, which he pursued with fanatical zeal in all the works where he detected it. It is in this *Épître à l'auteur des Trois imposteurs* that we find his famous adage, "If God did not exist, it would be necessary to invent him." If he himself felt little love for Moses, Jesus, and Mahomet and their doctrines, Voltaire could not permit them to be completely demystified: "I think that it is always very good to uphold the doctrine of the existence of a God who rewards and punishes; society needs this opinion,"[26] he wrote to the duc de Richelieu. This was to say that society needed imposture, and that Voltaire was ready to uphold it, behaving like an impostor himself.

The publication of the *Traité des trois imposteurs* by the efforts of d'Holbach in 1768 made a sensation. While the work had circulated almost entirely in manuscript form up to that point, with everything that implies about fragility and volatility, the printing press gave it a kind of consecration and certainly increased the number of readers. Marc-Michel Rey had a good distribution network. We have just seen that Voltaire and his friends got their copies immediately. We might say that the treatise emerged publicly in the official clandestine literature—and reactions were not lacking. The defenders of the faith threw themselves at their desks, and orthodox pens scratched frantically. One of the most prolix and most capable was that of Abbé Bergier, a canon of Paris and a collaborator on the *Encyclopédie*, who devoted a long section to the *Trois imposteurs* as early as 1769 in his *Apologie de la religion chrétienne*. He came back to it in a more systematic fashion in his *Traité historique et dogmatique de la vraie religion*, in twelve volumes, published in 1780.

The founders of religions, he said, were not, properly speaking, impostors. They did not invent religion, which existed well before them and was the natural tendency of men to explain natural phenomena by the will of the gods. Thereafter,

> if people's imaginations, once overheated by this error, believed they saw what they did not see; if some imbeciles dreamed a dream; if some rascals invented fake miracles in an attempt to accredit a particular faith: they were subordinate to the support of the general error already established on the basis of false reasoning.... The so-called inspired ones, who came afterward, were not the first authors of idolatry. At most, they only formalized the external cult; they said they had been sent to give laws and not to create religion: it existed before them; it was the work of peoples that were still savage and barbarous.[27]

In reality, "the only proven impostors we know of, in fact, of religion, are Zoroaster and Mahomet; both employed violence more than inspiration; their so-called miracles were forged by their disciples. Many may have been true and natural facts, unfortunately mistaken for prodigies."[28]

Here was a hue and cry against Mahomet; Bergier devoted fifty pages of accusations to him. "The treachery, the cruelty, the hypocrisy, the vindictive and bloody character of this false prophet" were softened by some writers of this century, who "wanted to rehabilitate the memory of the impostor, soften the absurdity of his doctrine and his laws, cause people to forget the evils they had caused and which still endure." These oblivious people were Boulainvillier, Sales, and

Doctor Morgan, the author of the *Questions sur l'Encyclopédie*. At least, "the author of the book of the *Trois imposteurs* was not of their way of thinking"—the only positive point of the treatise.

In contrast, Bergier undertook to show that the treatise blackened Moses and Jesus. Taking up once again all the traditions that made Moses an impostor, an Egyptian priest using magic to seduce the Hebrews, he attempted to show the falsity of this, all the while repeating the worst stereotypes of medieval anti-Semitism, heaping abuse on the Jews in order to save Moses.

With regard to Jesus, Bergier showed that it was psychologically impossible that he could have been an impostor: "It is impossible that a man should be the proselyte of his own fiction, that he should seriously believe an imposture that he himself created, at least unless his mind were seriously troubled; in that state, he is no longer able to seduce anyone. We pity the mad, we shut them up, but we place no faith in their fantasies. It is impossible that an impostor should see as a holy and worthy cause a tissue of lies and cheats of which he himself was the author."[29]

Bergier was evidently not the only one to fly to the aid of Moses and Jesus. The following year, 1781, the Abbé Laurent Terrasson, in his *Raisons de la foi*, also set out to refute the thesis of imposture. Plenty of others followed. The *Traité des trois imposteurs* itself was reprinted in 1775, 1776, 1777, and 1780. With the French Revolution and freedom of the press, what had been a subversive idea became almost banal. As reworked by Hébert, the "sans-culotte Jesus" became a Jacobin patriot. The treatise was reprinted again in 1793, and updated to the current taste in 1796 in a pirated edition made, according to the title page, at "Philadelphia, under the auspices of General Washingthon [*sic*]."

Did the *Trois imposteurs* reach the New World in the baggage of Lafayette and Rochambeau? In fact, the publisher was Claude-François-Xavier Mercier de Compiègne (1763–1800), a secretary in the office of the navy, who specialized in fantasy places of publication, such as "Frivolipolis, 1788," "Cythera, 1240," "Lutipolis, 2496," or "Memphis, 5800." He published popular works, in the spirit of the times, patriotic, erotic, humorous, such as the *Manuel des boudoirs [Bedroom Manual]* (Cythera, 1240), or *La Calotine, ou La tentation de saint Antoine, poème épi-satyri-héroï-comique et burlesque* (Memphis, 5800).[30] This is to say that for him, the *Trois imposteurs* was a good subject for jest and an occasion for patriotic propaganda, as indicated by the title he gave the work: *Traité des trois imposteurs, des religions dominantes et du culte, d'après l'analyse conforme à l'histoire: contenant nombre d'observations morales, analogues à celles mises à l'ordre du jour pour l'affermissement de la République, sa gloire et l'édification des peuples de tous les pays [Treatise of the Three Impostors, of the Dominant Religions and Religious Cult, after an Analysis Conforming to History: Containing numerous moral observations, analogous to those put forth for affirming the Republic, its glory, and the edification of peoples of all nations].*

It reproduced the text of d'Holbach's 1768 edition, with some light changes, and added to it poems on the glory of the Revolution and the Supreme Being, in a Rousseauist and Robespierrist spirit, avoiding atheism.[31]

After this last imposture on the *Trois imposteurs,* the treatise soon fell into oblivion. Freedom of the press and the progress of exegesis, as well as scientific atheism, relegated it to the rank of a banal, outdated pamphlet of merely historical interest. In the nineteenth and twentieth centuries, reprintings were the work of anarchist movements, freethinkers, or communists who recognized in it a pioneering text, a sort of symbol of the rationalist revolt against religious imposture. In 1844 there appeared at Amsterdam and Dundee an English translation, *The Three Impostors,* followed in 1846 by an American edition published in New York. In 1863, some Italians published in Milan *Mosè, Gesù e Maometto del barone d'Orbach.* Then, for the next seventy years, nothing. The treatise surfaced again in the context of the ideological conflicts of the years between 1930 and 1970: the French edition by L'Idée Libre in 1932; the German edition at Bern, *Das Buch von der drei Betrügern,* in 1936; a Soviet edition in 1969, *Anonimnye ateisticskie,* published in Moscow; an Italian anarchist edition of 1970, *I tre impostori, Mosè, Gesù Cristo, Maometto,* at Ragusa. In 1973, J. Rétat published at Saint-Étienne an anastatic facsimile of the 1777 edition.

We enter the era of scholarly publications with the *Trattato dei tre impostori* (Milan, 1981); the *Traktat über die drei Betrüger* (Hamburg, 1992); the Franco-Italian critical edition of Silvia Berti, *Trattato dei tre impostori: La vita e lo spirito del Signor Benedetto de Spinoza* (Turin, 1994). Finally, the early twenty-first century has already seen two republications in paperback, intended for a wider audience, which testify to a rebirth of interest in this work in the context of an aggressive and intolerant turn of religions: the *Traité des trois imposteurs* of Max Milo in 2001; the *Livre des trois imposteurs* of Payot and Rivages in 2002. In parallel, historians of the first rank, among whom we may mention Françoise Charles-Daubert, Silvia Berti, and Miguel Benitez, have made the treatise a central subject of their research. A major international conference was held at Leiden in 1990 on the subject.[32] The *Trois imposteurs*, like the Bible, the gospels, and the Qur'ān, have their exegetes ...

APPENDIX 1

Hypothesized Origin of the *Traité des trois imposteurs*

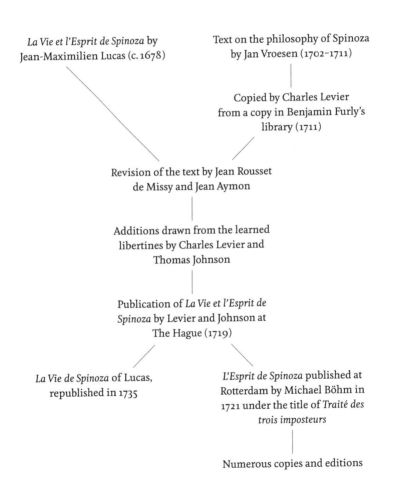

La Vie et l'Esprit de Spinoza by
Jean-Maximilien Lucas (c. 1678)

Text on the philosophy of Spinoza
by Jan Vroesen (1702-1711)

Copied by Charles Levier
from a copy in Benjamin Furly's
library (1711)

Revision of the text by Jean Rousset
de Missy and Jean Aymon

Additions drawn from the learned
libertines by Charles Levier and
Thomas Johnson

Publication of La Vie et l'Esprit de
Spinoza by Levier and Johnson at
The Hague (1719)

La Vie de Spinoza of Lucas,
republished in 1735

L'Esprit de Spinoza published at
Rotterdam by Michael Böhm in
1721 under the title of Traité des
trois imposteurs

Numerous copies and editions

APPENDIX 2

Hypothesized Origin of the *De tribus impostoribus*

1688: Johann Joachim Müller, at Kiel, gives Johan Friedrich
Mayer a manuscript, partially compiled by himself, entitled
De tribus impostoribus.

Multiple copies of this manuscript are made at Mayer's
library, including one by Peter Friedrich Arpe.

1716: Leibniz examines the manuscript at Mayer's son's
house, on behalf of Baron von Hohendorf.

Von Hohendorf purchases the manuscript, by then entitled
De imposturis religionum breve compendium, for the library of
Prince Eugen of Savoy.

1753: The manuscript is published at Vienna, by Straub, with
the fictitious date of 1598 and the title *De tribus impostoribus.*

Manuscript passes into the collection of the National
Library in Vienna.

NOTES

PREFACE TO THE ENGLISH-LANGUAGE EDITION

1. Heather Blair, "Impostors and Revolution: On the 'Philadelphie' 1796 edition of the *Traité des trois imposteurs*," in *Heterodoxy, Spinozism, and Free Thought in Early-Eighteenth-Century Europe: Studies on the "Traité des trois imposteurs*," ed. Silvia Berti, Françoise Charles-Daubert, and Richard H. Popkin (Dordrecht: Kluwer Academic Publishers, 1996), 297-304.

CHAPTER ONE

1. *Monumenta Germaniae historica, Epistolae pontificum* (1883), 1:645.

2. The authoritative work on Frederick II is still Ernst Kantorowicz, *Frederick the Second, 1194-1250* (1927; Eng. trans. 1931).

3. *Épitres de Pierre des Vignes*, book 1, letter 31, cited by François Berriot, *Athéisme et athéistes au XVIe siècle en France* (diss., Université de Lille-III, 1976), 1:316.

4. C. H. Haskins, *Studies in the History of Medieval Science* (Cambridge, Mass., 1924), 292.

5. Published by Miguele Amari, "Livre des questions siciliennes concernant les recherches sur l'âme," *Journal asiatique*, 5th ser., vol. 1 (1853): 240ff.

6. See, for example, Michel Onfray, *Atheist Manifesto: The Case against Christianity, Judaism, and Islam* (New York: Arcade Publishing, 2007-2008).

7. Quoted by Claude Fleury, *Histoire ecclésiastique* (1772 ed.), 17:256.

8. Ibid., 252.

9. Prosper Marchand, *Dictionnaire historique, ou Mémoires critiques et littéraires, concernant la vie et les ouvrages de divers personnages distingués, particulièrement dans la République des Lettres* (The Hague, 1758), article "Impostoribus."

10. Herodotus, *Histories*, 4.95; translated into English by A. D. Godley, Loeb Classical Library, 4 vols. (New York: G. P. Putnam's Sons, 1921), 2:297.

11. Livy, *History of Rome*, 1.19; translated into English by B. O. Foster, Loeb Classical Library, 13 vols. (New York: G. P. Putnam's Sons, 1925), 1:69.

12. Lucretius, *De natura rerum*, 5.1218; translated into English by W. H. D. Rouse, revised by Martin Ferguson Smith, Loeb Classical Library (Cambridge, Mass.: Harvard University Press, 1925), 473.

13. Examples given by Diogenes Laertius, *Lives of Famous Philosophers*. On athe-

ism in the ancient world, see Georges Minois, *Histoire de l'athéisme* (Paris: Fayard, 1998), chap. 2.

14. Cicero, *De natura deorum*, 1.6.14; translated into English by H. Rackham, Loeb Classical Library (New York: G. P. Putnam's Sons, 1933), 17.

15. On this subject, see the collective work *Moïse: L'homme de l'Alliance* (Paris: Desclée de Brouwer, 1955).

16. Celsus, *True Doctrine*, quoted by Origen, *Against Celsus*, 1.23, 1.26; translated into English by Henry Chadwick: *Origen: Contra Celsum* (Cambridge: Cambridge University Press, 1953), 22, 26.

17. Ibid., 4.36–41, pp. 211–12.

18. Ibid., 1.27 and 1.68, p. 63.

19. Ibid., 1.71, pp. 64–65; 2.8, p. 71; 3.44, p. 158.

20. Ibid., 2.55, p. 109.

21. Ibid., 2.63, p. 114; 2.72, p. 121; 2.70, p. 120.

22. Ibid., 2.70, p. 120.

23. Ibid., 2.73, p. 122.

24. Ibid., 2.78, p. 126.

25. Ibid., 1.9, p. 12.

26. Ibid., 1.10, p. 13.

27. Ibid., 1.9, p. 12.

28. Cyril of Alexandria, *Against Julian*, Sources chrétiennes 322 (Paris, 1985), 213.

29. Jean-Pierre Osier, *L'Évangile du ghetto* (Paris: Berg International, 1984). For a recent study of the image of Jesus in the Talmud, see Peter Schafer, *Jesus in the Talmud* (Princeton: Princeton University Press, 2007).

30. Hugh Schonfield, *According to the Hebrews: A New Translation of the Jewish Life of Jesus, the Toledot Jeshu* (London: Duckworth, 1937).

31. Mishneh Torah, "Laws of Kings and of War," chap. 11, sections 10–13; English translation quoted from http://www.chabad.org.

32. Robert Chazan, *Daggers of Faith: Thirteenth-Century Christian Missionizing and Jewish Response* (Berkeley: University of California Press, 1989).

33. See M. Gaudefroy-Demonbynes, *Mahomet* (Paris: Albin Michel, 1957); M. Rodinson, *Mahomet* (Paris, 1963); P. Boz, *L'Islam* (Paris: Desclée de Brouwer, 1993). A good presentation is found in F. Lenoir and Y. Tardan-Masquelier, eds., *Encyclopédie des religions* (Paris: Bayard, 1997), 1:731–43.

34. Paulus Alvarus, *Indiculus luminosus*, 21–35, Corpus Scriptorum Muzarabicorum (Madrid: Instituto Antonio de Nebrija, 1973), 293–315.

35. Guibert de Nogent, *Dei gesta per Francos*, ed. R. B. C. Huygens (Turnhout: Brepols, 1996), 94.

36. Norman Cohn, *The Pursuit of the Millennium* (London: Secker and Warburg, 1957). The subject has been treated more recently by Yves-Marie Bercé, *Le Roi caché: Sauveurs et imposteurs; Mythes politiques populaires dans l'Europe moderne* (Paris: Fayard, 1990); and Jean Delumeau, *History of Paradise: The Garden of Eden in Myth and Tradition* (Champaign-Urbana: University of Illinois Press, 2000).

37. Gilles Lecuppre, *L'Imposture politique au Moyen Âge: La seconde vie des rois* (Paris: PUF, 2005).

38. On these predictions, see Cohn, *Pursuit of the Millennium*; J. Delumeau, *History of Paradise*; and Georges Minois, *Histoire de l'avenir: Des prophètes à la prospective* (Paris: Fayard, 1996).

39. Max Horten, *Die Philosophie des Islams* (Munich, 1934).

40. Émile Bréhier, *La philosophie du Moyen Âge* (Paris: Albin Michel, 1937; rpt., 1971), 94.

41. Louis Massignon, "La Légende *De tribus impostoribus* et ses origines islamiques," *Revue d'histoire des religions* 82 (July 1920): 74–78.

42. Cited by Ernest Renan, *Averroès et l'averroïsme* (1852; Paris: Calmann-Lévy, 1949), 228. See also on this topic Patrick Marcolini, "Le *De tribus impostoribus* et les origines arabes de l'athéisme européen," *Les Cahiers de l'ATP* (October 2003).

43. Ahmad Gunny, "Le *Traité des trois imposteurs* et ses origines arabes," *Dix-huitième siècle* 28 (1996): 169–74.

44. Cited by A. de Libéra, introduction to Averroes, *Le Livre du discours décisif* (Paris: Garnier-Flammarion, 1996), 80–81.

45. L. Gauthier, *La Théorie d'Ibn Roschd Averroès sur les rapports de la religion et de la philosophie* (Paris, 1909).

46. Tayyib Tizini, *Projet pour une vision nouvelle de la pensée arabe au Moyen Âge* (Damascus, 1971).

47. Cited by Renan, *Averroès et l'averroïsme*, 229.

48. Jean Gerson, *Tractatus super Magnificat*, vol. 4, col. 400.

49. Petrarch, "On His Own Ignorance and That of Many Others," in *Francesco Petrarca: Invectives*, ed. and trans. David Marsh, The I Tatti Renaissance Library (Cambridge, Mass.: Harvard University Press, 2003), 299.

50. Honorius of Autun, *Elucidarium*, 2.18. On the Goliards, see O. Dobiache-Rojdestvensky, *Les Poésies des goliards* (Paris, 1931).

51. J. Warichez, *Les "Disputationes" de Simon de Tournai* (Louvain, 1933).

52. Thomas of Cantimpré, *Bonum universale de apibus*, translated into French by J. Cousin, *Histoire de Tournai* (Douai, 1620).

CHAPTER TWO

1. Lecuppre, *L'Imposture politique au Moyen Âge*.

2. Ibid., 373.

3. For all these millenarian movements, see J. Delumeau, *History of Paradise*.

4. J. A. F. Thomson, *The Later Lollards* (London: Oxford University Press, 1965), 27, 36–37, 76, 80, 82, 160.

5. G. G. Coulton, "The Plain Man's Religion in the Middle Ages," *Medieval Studies* 13 (1916).

6. Keith Thomas, *Religion and the Decline of Magic* (New York: Charles Scribner's Sons, 1971), 168–69.

7. Cited by Hervé Martin, *Le Métier de prédicateur à la fin du Moyen Âge, 1350-1520* (Paris: Le Cerf, 1988), 359.

8. Ibid., 359-60.

9. Vatican, Ms. Reg. Lat. 1129. Cited by Mario Esposito, "Una Manifestatione d'incredulità religiosa nel medioevo: Il detto dei 'Tre impostori' e la sua trasmissione da Federico a Pomponazzi," *Archivio storico italiano*, ser. 6, vol. 16 (1931): 39-40.

10. Marchand, *Dictionnaire historique*, article "Impostoribus."

11. Odoric Rinaldi, cited by Bernard de La Monnoye, *De tribus impostoribus* (1861), 30.

12. Marchand, *Dictionnaire historique*, 315.

13. Dante, *Divine Comedy, Inferno*, 28.1-63.

14. *Chrétiens et musulmans à la Renaissance*, Acts of the 37th International Colloquium of the Center for Economic and Social Rights, 1994.

15. Cited by Berriot, *Athéismes et athéistes*, 1:312.

16. Ibid., 1:582.

17. Georges Minois, *Censure et culture sous l'Ancien Régime* (Paris: Fayard, 1995), 52-53.

18. Compare Berriot, *Athéismes et athéistes*, 1:128-29; and Alain Cabantous, *Histoire du blasphème en Occident, XVIe-milieu XIXe siècle* (Paris: Albin Michel, 1998).

19. *Mémoire de l'estat de France sous Charles neuvième* (Meidelburg, 1578).

20. Gabriel Dupréau Prateolus, *Nostrorum temporum calamitas* (1559), fol. 210.

21. Jean Sleidan, *Histoire entière déduite depuis le Déluge jusqu'au temps présent en XXIX livres* (Geneva: G. Crespin, 1563), book 25.

22. Henri Busson, "Les Noms des incrédules au XVIe siècle (athées, déistes, achristes, libertins)," *Bibliothèque d'humanisme et Renaissance* 16 (1954): 282.

23. Nicolas Lefèvre, in a note to his translation of Thomas Browne's *Religio medici*.

24. Frederick II, *Anti-Machiavelli* (The Hague, 1740), chap. 6.

25. Machiavelli, *Discourses on the First Decade of Titus Livius*, book 1, chap. 11. English translation by Harvey C. Mansfield and Nathan Tarcov, *Niccolò Machiavelli: Discourses on Livy* (Chicago: University of Chicago Press, 1996), pp. 34-36.

26. Ibid., chap. 12, p. 37.

27. Ibid.

28. Ibid., chap. 11, p. 35

29. Ibid., book 3, chap. 30, p. 280.

30. Innocent Gentillet, *Discours sur les moyens de bien gouverner et maintenir en bonne paix un royaume*, . . . *contre Nicolas Machiavel, Florentin* (1576), part 2, maxims 8-9.

31. Florimond de Raemond, *Histoire de la naissance, progrez et decadence de l'hérésie de ce siècle, divisée en huit livres* (Paris, 1610).

32. Melchior de Flavin, *De l'estat des âmes après le trépas, et comment elles vivent estant des corps séparées, et des purgatoires qu'elles souffrent en ce monde et en l'autre, après icelle séparation* (Paris, 1595).

33. J.-L. Vivaldo de Mondovi, *De duodecim persecutionibus ecclesiae dei*, 1506.

34. Antonio Doni, *La Libraria del Doni Fiorentino* (Venice, 1551), fol. 60.

35. Thomas Browne, *Religio Medici* (1643), part 1, sec. 20, in *Sir Thomas Browne: Religio Medici, Hydriotaphia, and the Garden of Cyrus*, ed. R. H. A. Robins (Oxford: Clarendon Press, 1972), 23.

36. Sir Kenelm Digby, cited by Marchand, *Dictionnaire historique*, article "Impostoribus."

37. Compare Berriot, *Athéismes et athéistes*, 1:540–45.

38. Marchard, *Dictionnaire historique*.

39. P.-H. Michel, "L'atomisme de Giordano Bruno," in *La Science au XVIe siècle*, symposium of Royaumont, Paris, 1960.

40. Angelo Mercati, *Il Sommario del processo di Giordano Bruno* (Bibliotheca Apostolica Vaticana, 1842), 86–87.

41. Ibid., 83, 73, 69.

42. Cited by Berriot, *Athéismes et athéistes*, 522.

43. Jean Henri Ursin, *Tractatus de Zoroastro* (1661).

44. Mathurin Veyssière de La Croze, *Entretiens sur divers sujets d'histoire* (Cologne, 1711; London ed., 1770), 287.

45. Delio Cantimori, *Eretici italiani del Cinquecento* (Florence: Sansoni, 1939).

46. Silvana Seidel Menchi, *Erasmo in Italia, 1520–1580* (Turin: Bollati Boringhieri, 1987).

47. Ibid., 219.

48. H. Pommier, "L'itinéraire religieux d'un moine vagabond au XVIe siècle," *Mélanges d'archéologie et d'histoire de l'École française de Rome* 66 (1954): 293–322.

49. Erasmus, *Praise of Folly*, in *Desiderius Erasmus: The Praise of Folly and Other Writings*, selected, translated, and edited by Robert M. Adams (New York: W. W. Norton, 1989), 45.

50. Bernard de La Monnoye, *Lettre à Bouhier*, in *Oeuvres complètes* (The Hague, 1770), 37.

51. Berriot, *Athéismes et athéistes*, 1:448–52, and 2:849–65.

52. Ibid., 865.

53. Ibid., 450.

54. Ibid., 862–64.

55. Guillaume Postel, *De orbis terrae concordia* (1543), 72.

56. Michael Servetus, *Christianismi restitutio* (1553), book 3, p. 100.

57. Florimond de Raemond, *Histoire de la naissance, progrez et décadence de l'hérésie de ce siècle . . .*, chap. xv, p. 228.

58. Cited in A. Roget, *Le Procès de Michel Servet* (Geneva, 1877), 57.

59. Cited by F. Secret, *Kabbalistes chrétiens de la Renaissance* (Dunod, 1964), 171.

60. Guillaume Postel, *Absconditorum clavis*.

61. Ibid.

62. Guillaume Postel, *Orientales histoires* (Paris, 1560), part 2, pp. 42–43.

63. Henri Estienne, *Apologie pour Hérodote* (The Hague, 1730), 1:182.

64. Marchand, *Dictionnaire historique,* article "Impostoribus."

65. Antoine Sabatier de Castres, *Les Trois Siècles de la littérature* . . . (Paris, 1772), 3:102.

66. Cited by Bernard La Monnoye in *Menagiana, ou Les bons mots et remarques critiques, historiques, morales et d'érudition de Monsieur Ménage recueillies par ses amis,* new ed. (Paris, 1729), 4:293–94.

67. Ibid. The allusion is said to be found on p. 39 of Genebrard's response.

68. Montaigne, *Essays,* 2:12; English translation by M. A. Screech, *Michel de Montaigne: The Complete Essays* (London: Penguin, 1991), 578.

69. Ibid., 2:12, p. 495.

70. Jean Bodin, *Colloquium heptaplomeres,* French translation of De Conrart, mid-seventeenth century, *Colloque de Jean Bodin entre sept scavans qui sont de différens sentimens,* Bibliothèque de l'Arsenal, ms. 6026, fols. 247–48.

71. Ibid., fol. 222.

72. The classic story of a faked miracle, a child born with a gold tooth—*Trans.*

CHAPTER THREE

1. Wolfgang Gericke, *Das Buch von den drei Betrügern* (1983), 44.

2. Susanna Akerman, "Johan Adler Salvius, Questions to Baruch de Castro concerning 'De tribus impostoribus,'" in *Heterodoxy, Spinozism, and Free Thought,* ed. Berti, Charles-Daubert, and Popkin, 399.

3. Berriot, *Athéismes et athéistes,* 1:588.

4. Jacques Severt, *De atheismo et haeresibus* (Lyon, 1621), 44–48, 428–29.

5. Robert Burton, *The Anatomy of Melancholy,* ed. Thomas C. Faulkner, Nicolas K. Kiessling, and Rhonda L. Blair, 6 vols. (Oxford: Clarendon Press, 1989–2000), vol. 3 (1994), 405.

6. Marin Mersenne, *Quaestiones celeberrimae in Genesim, in quibus Athei et Deistae impugnantur* (1623), cols. 533, 672, 1829, 1830.

7. Tommaso Campanella, *De gentilismo non retinendo,* 21.

8. German Ernst, "Campanella and the *De tribus impostoribus,*" *Nouvelles de la République des Lettres* 2 (1986): 143–70.

9. Thomas Browne, *Religio medici,* part 1, sec. 20, in *Sir Thomas Browne,* ed. Robbins, 23.

10. Cited by Antoine Adam, *Les Libertins au XVIIe siècle* (Paris: Buchet-Chastel, 1964), 112.

11. Ibid., 114–15.

12. Gericke, *Das Buch von den drei Betrügern.*

13. C. de Baillon, "La Suède en 1653 . . . ," *Le Correspondant* (1878).

14. Letter from Colvius to Saumaise, 6 June 1652, cited in F. F. Blok, *Caspar Barleus* (Leiden, 1978), 185n29.

15. Lucien Bély, *Espions et ambassadeurs au temps de Louis XIV* (Paris: Fayard, 1990), 338–40.

16. Friedrich Niewöhner, *Veritas sive varietas: Lessings Toleranzparabel und das Buch von den drei Betrügern* (Heidelberg: L. Schneider, 1988), 356.

17. Akerman, "Johan Adler Salvius," 408.

18. Ibid., 404n12: "Femmellarum etiam, insuavis conugii sui taedio, amoribus obnoxius valde ac dedisti fuit."

19. Johann Christoph Harenberg, *Dissertationibus de secta non timentium Deum* (Brunswick, 1756).

20. Gabriel Harvey, *A New Letter of Notable Contents* (London, 1593).

21. Jan W. Wojcik, "Behold the Fear of the Lord: The Erastianism of Stillingfleet, Wolseley and Tillotson," in *Heterodoxy, Spinozism, and Free Thought*, ed. Berti, Charles-Daubert, and Popkin, 361n12.

22. G. B. Harrison, *Willobie his avisa* (London, 1926), app. 1, p. 256.

23. Richard Hooker, *Of the Laws of Ecclesiastical Polity*, book 5, chap. 2, in *The Folger Library Edition of the Works of Richard Hooker*, vol. 2, ed. W. Speed Hill (Cambridge, Mass.: Belknap Press of Harvard University Press, 1977), 25–26.

24. L. Stone, review, *English Historical Review* 77, no. 303 (1962): 328.

25. David Riggs, *The World of Christopher Marlowe* (London: Faber and Faber, 2004), 113.

26. Pierre Lefranc, *Sir Walter Raleigh écrivain* (Paris: Armand Colin, 1968), 381.

27. Francis Bacon, "Of Atheism," in *Essays; The Moral and Historical Works of Lord Bacon . . .*, ed. Joseph Devey (London: Henry G. Bohn, 1854), 45–46.

28. Francis Bacon, "Of Atheisme," in *Religious Meditations*, in *A Harmony of the Essays etc. of Francis Bacon*, ed. Edward Arber (London, 1871), 123–25.

29. "Of the Kinds of Imposture," ibid., 121.

30. Francis Bacon, "On Temerity," in *Essays*, ed. Devey, 32.

31. Burton, *Anatomy of Melancholy*, ed. Faulkner, Kiessling, and Blair, vol. 3 (1994), 369–70.

32. Ibid., 3:348. The citation comes from Vanini's treatise *On the Secrets of Nature*, dialogue 50.

33. Ibid., 3:356–57.

34. We rely in particular on the biography by David Riggs, *The World of Christopher Marlowe*.

35. Christopher Marlowe, *Doctor Faustus*, 1.1.47–50.

36. Cited by Riggs, *World of Christopher Marlowe*, 229–30.

37. Henry Wright, *The First Part of the Disquisition of Truth, concerning Political Affairs* (London, 1616), 2.

38. Gerrard Winstanley, *The Law of Freedom in a Platform; Or, True Magistracy Restored* (London, 1652), 61.

39. René Pintard, *Le Libertinage érudit dans la première moitié du XVIIe siècle* (Paris: Boivin, 1943; rpt. Geneva: Slatkine, 1983).

40. Françoise Charles-Daubert, *Les Libertins érudits en France au XVIIe siècle* (Paris: PUF, 1998).

41. Pierre Charron, *De la sagesse*, 2:5.

42. Ibid.

43. Lucilio Vanini, *L'Amphithéâtre de l'éternelle providence*, in *Oeuvres philosophiques de Vanini*, French translation by M. X. Rousselot (Paris: Gosselin, 1842), 36.

44. Ibid., 33.

45. Ibid., 52.

46. In 1572—*Trans.*

47. François La Mothe Le Vayer, *Lettres de l'autheur*, introduction to the *Dialogues d'Orasius Tubero.*

CHAPTER FOUR

1. Thomas Hobbes, *Leviathan*, edited by Richard Tuck (Cambridge: Cambridge University Press, 1991), 78–79, 305.

2. Deposition of Isaac Pacheco, cited in Yosef Kaplan, *From Christianity to Judaism: The Story of Isaac Orobio de Castro* (Oxford University Press, 1989), 142–43.

3. I. S. Révah, "Aux origines de la rupture spinozienne," *Revue des études juives* 123 (1964): 404.

4. Kaplan, *From Christianity to Judaism*, 142.

5. Richard Popkin, "Spinoza and the *Three Impostors*," in *Spinoza: Issues and Directions, the Proceedings of the Chicago Spinoza Conference*, ed. Edwin Curley and Patricia Fetzer Moreau (Leiden: E. J. Brill, 1990).

6. Quoted in Jonathan I. Israel, *The Dutch Republic, Its Rise, Greatness and Fall, 1477–1806* (Oxford, Clarendon Press, 1998), 917.

7. Quoted in ibid., 921.

8. Spinoza, *Tractatus*, preface, in *The Chief Works of Benedict de Spinoza*, ed. Elwes, 1:4.

9. Ibid., 7.

10. Ibid., 5.

11. Ibid.

12. Ibid., 6.

13. Ibid., 98.

14. An excellent study is the recent work edited by Catherine Secrétan, Tristan Dagron, and Laurent Bove, *Qu'est-ce que les Lumières radicales? Libertinage, athéisme et spinozisme dans le tournant philosophique de l'âge classique* (Paris: Éditions Amsterdam, 2007).

15. Pierre Bayle, *Continuation des Pensées diverses sur la comète*, 110.

16. Gianni Paganini, "L'apport des courants sceptiques à la naissance des Lumières radicales," in *Qu'est-ce que les Lumières radicales?*, ed. Secrétan, Dagron, and Bove, 88–89.

17. Cited by Élisabeth Labrousse, *Pierre Bayle* (Paris: Albin Michel, 1996), 203.

18. Ibid., 328.

19. Pierre Bayle, *Nouvelles de la République des Lettres*, July 1686.

20. Alfred R. Hall and Marie B. Hall, eds., *The Correspondence of Henry Oldenburg* (Madison: University of Wisconsin Press, 1973), 1:89–92.

21. Ibid., 91.

22. J. C. Jeaffresen, ed., *Middlesex Sessions Rolls, 1667–1668*, 4 vols. (1886–1892), 3:29.

23. British Library, MS Sloane 388.

24. Bossuet, *Panégyrique de saint Pierre Nolasque*, in *Oeuvres complètes*, vol. 5 (Brussels: Greuse and de Mat, 1848), 94–95.

25. Henry Stubbe, *An Account of the Rise and Progress of Mahometanism*, ed. H. M. K. Shairani (1911).

26. Ibid., 159.

27. Ibid., 167, 163.

28. Quoted in Justin A. I. Champion, "Legislators, Impostors and the Politic Origins of Religion: English Theories of 'Imposture' from Stubbe to Toland," in *Heterodoxy, Spinozism, and Free Thought*, ed. Berti, Charles-Daubert, and Popkin, 349.

29. *Correspondence of Henry Oldenburg*, ed. Hall and Hall, 144.

30. J. Crossley, ed., *The Diary and Correspondence of John Worthington*, Chetham Society Series 13 (1847), 168.

31. Rob Iliffe, "'Jesus Nazarenus legislator': Adam Borel's Defence of Christianity," in *Heterodoxy, Spinozism, and Free Thought*, ed. Berti, Charles-Daubert, and Popkin, 394.

32. Françoise Charles-Daubert, "Le *Tractatus theologico-politicus*, une réponse au *Traité des trois imposteurs?*" *Les Études philosophiques* 4 (1987): 385–91.

33. Sir Charles Wolseley, *The Unreasonableness of Atheism Made Manifest* (London, 1669), 198.

34. Marchand, *Dictionnaire historique*, article "Impostoribus."

CHAPTER FIVE

1. Jean Chapelain, *Lettres*, ed. L. Tamizey de Larroque (Paris, 1883).

2. Theophili Spizelii, *Scrutinium atheismi historico-aetiologicum* (Augsburg, 1663), 55. A rare book, of which one copy exists at Münster. We thank Martin Rudolph for this information.

3. Jean Deckherus, *De scriptis adespotis* (1681), 114.

4. Martin Lipenius, *Bibliotheca philosophica* (1682).

5. These questions have been examined by Wolfgang Gericke, *Das Buch de tribus impostoribus* (Berlin, 1982); and by Friedrich Niewöhner, *Veritas sive varietas: Lessings Toleranzparabel und das Buch von den drei Betrügern* (Heidelberg, 1988).

6. Gericke, *Das Buch de tribus impostoribus*.

7. Martin Mulsow, "Freethinking in Early Eighteenth-Century Protestant Germany: Peter Friedrich Arpe and the *Traité des trois imposteurs*," in *Heterodoxy, Spinozism, and Free Thought*, ed. Berti, Charles-Daubert, and Popkin, 208.

8. This is stated in a letter of Kortholt of 30 December 1715, cited by Mulsow, "Freethinking in Early Eighteenth-Century Protestant Germany," 207.

9. Cited by Mulsow, ibid., 209n52.

10. *Journal des savants*, March 1713, 319–26.

11. Saint-Simon, *Mémoires*, Éditions de la Pléiade (Paris: Gallimard, 1986), 6:186.

12. Albert-Henri de Sallengre, *Mémoires de littérature*, ed. H. Sauzet (The Hague, 1715), 1:282.

13. A catalogue of Hohendorf's library was published after his death: *Bibliotheca Hohendorfiana ou Catalogue des livres de la bibliothèque de feu Monsieur George Guillaume Baron de Hohendorf*, 3 vols. (The Hague, 1720).

14. A. Kobuch, "Aspekte des aufgeklärten bürgerlichen Denkers in Kurschsen in der ersten hälfte des 18. Jh. im Lichte der Bücherzensur," *Jahrbuch für Geschichte* 19 (1979): 251–93.

15. B. de La Monnoye, *Sentimens sur le prétendu traité des trois imposteurs* (Amsterdam, 1715), 33.

16. Leibniz, manuscript letter, Codex vindobonensis 10450, National Library of Vienna.

17. *Viri illustris Godefri Guil. Leibnitii Epistolae ad diversos*, ed. C. Kortholt, 4 vols. (Leipzig, 1734–1742), 1:443.

18. *Thesauri epistolici Lacroziani tomus I* (Leipzig, 1742), 106.

19. Ibid., 2:107.

20. Ibid., 3:205.

21. Ibid., 1:276.

22. Ibid., 3:208.

23. Hamburg, Staats et Universitätsbibliothek, Cod. Theol. 1222.

24. Staatsbibliothek de Berlin, MS Diez C 40 37, fol. 42v.

25. H. Schröder, *Lexikon der hamburgischen Schriftsteller* (Hamburg, 1851), no. 122.

26. Cited by W. E. Tentzel, *Curieuse Bibliothec, oder Foertsetzung der Monatlichen Unterredungen einiger guten Freunde von allerhand Büchern und andern ännehlichen Geschichten, von anno 1689 bis 1698* (Frankfurt and Leipzig, 1704), 493.

27. W. E. Tentzel, *Monatliche Unterredungen einiger guten Freunde . . . herausgegeben von A. B. Januarius 1689* (Thoren and Leipzig, 1690), 44.

28. B. G. Struve, *Dissertatio historico litteraria de doctis impostoribus* (Jena, 1704), 18.

29. W. E. Tentzel, *Curieuse Bibliothec*, 494.

30. Miguel Benitez, "La diffusion du *Traité des trois imposteurs* au XVIIIe siècle," *Revue d'histoire moderne et contemporaine* 40–41 (1993): 137–51.

31. Ibid., 140–41.

32. Cited in ibid., 141–42.

33. Miguel Benitez, "Une histoire interminable: Origines et développement du *Traité des trois imposteurs*," in *Heterodoxy, Spinozism, and Free Thought*, ed. Berti, Charles-Daubert, and Popkin, 53–74.

34. Ibid., 60.

35. Codex Vindobonensis 10450 2, item 3.

36. Ms Latin L 160.

37. Raoul Vaneigem, ed., *L'Art de ne croire en rien, suivi du Livre des trois impos-teurs* (Payot and Rivages, 2002).

38. Françoise Charles-Daubert, "Le *Tractatus theologico-politicus*, une réponse au *Traité des trois imposteurs?*" *Études philosophiques* 4 (October–December 1987): 385–91.

39. *Menagiana*, 303.

40. *Correspondance de l'abbé Nicaise*, Bibliothèque Nationale, Ms. 9359–9363, fol. 193.

41. Letter from Fritsch to Marchand, Leipzig, 7 November 1737, Leiden, Bibliothèque RU, MS March.2.

42. B. E. Schwarzbach and A. W. Fairbairn, "History and Structure of Our *Traité des trois imposteurs*," in *Heterodoxy, Spinozism, and Free Thought*, ed. Berti, Charles-Daubert, and Popkin, 100.

43. Text transcribed by Prosper Marchand, *Dictionnaire historique*, article "Impostoribus."

44. Wiep Van Bunge, "Échos des Lumières radicales dans la République de Hollande: Justus van Effen; La raison et la vertu," in *Qu'est-ce que les Lumières radicales?*, ed. Secrétan, Dagron, and Bove, 151–76.

45. Brom Anderson, "Sallengre, La Monnoye and the *Traité des trois imposteurs*," in *Heterodoxy, Spinozism, and Free Thought*, ed. Berti, Charles-Daubert, and Popkin, 268.

46. University Research Library, special collections, A4 L96.

47. Bibliothèque Royale, reserve, II 86730.

48. Biblioteca Marucelliana, R.U.1.

49. Staatsbibliothek, R7.

50. Silvia Berti, "*L'Esprit de Spinoza*: Ses origines et sa première édition dans leur contexte spinozien," in *Heterodoxy, Spinozism, and Free Thought*, ed. Berti, Charles-Daubert, and Popkin, 49.

51. Voltaire, *Correspondance*, La Pléiade (Paris: Gallimard, 1980), 5:145.

52. Ibid., 137.

53. Marchand, *Dictionnaire historique*.

54. C. Berkvens-Stevelinck, *Prosper Marchand: La vie et l'oeuvre (1678–1756)* (Leiden, 1987).

55. Cited by Berti, "*L'Esprit de Spinoza*," 26.

56. Ibid., 21.

57. *Reimmannismae bibliothecae theologicae catalogus systematico-criticas continuatus* (Hildesheim, 1731), 1029–30.

58. *Nouvelles Littéraires* 10 (July 1719): 41.

59. Marchand, *Dictionnaire historique*, article "Impostoribus."

60. Ibid.

61. Ibid.

62. Letter of Prosper Marchand to Fritsch and Böhm, 2 November 1711, Leiden, Bibliothèque RU, MS March.2.

63. Letter of 13 August 1730, ibid.

64. Leiden, Bibliothèque RU, MS March.39.

65. John Christian Laursen, "The Politics of a Publishing Event: The Marchand Milieu and *The Life and Spirit of Spinoza* of 1719," in *Heterodoxy, Spinozism, and Free Thought*, ed. Berti, Charles-Daubert, and Popkin, 273–96.

66. Françoise Charles-Daubert, "*L'Esprit de Spinoza* et les *Traités des trois imposteurs*: Rappel des différentes familles et de leurs principales caractéristiques," in *Heterodoxy, Spinozism, and Free Thought*, ed. Berti, Charles-Daubert, and Popkin, 185.

67. Louis Moréri, *Le Grand Dictionnaire historique* (Paris, 1759), 2:132.

68. *Journal et mémoires de Mathieu Marais sur la régence et le règne de Louis XV* (Paris: Didot, 1863–1868), 2:237.

69. Saint-Simon, *Memoirs*, 8:453.

70. This was the case for Ira O. Wade, *Clandestine Organization and Diffusion of Philosophic Ideas in France from 1700 to 1750* (Princeton: Princeton University Press, 1938).

71. Boulainvillier, *Essai de métaphysique*, in *Oeuvres philosophiques* (The Hague: Nijhoff, 1973), 146, 149.

72. Manuscripts BN fr. 12242–43; Mazarine 3558; Auxerre 235–36, 237; Laon 514; Fécamp 24–25; Arsenal 2236; Périgueux 36; Rouen 1769; and Carpentras 1275.

73. *Voyages et aventures de Jacques Massé* (Geneva: Slatkine, 1979).

74. Joseph Almagor, *Pierre des Maizeaux (1673–1745), Journalist and English Correspondent for Franco-Dutch Periodicals, 1700–1720* (Amsterdam: Holland University Press, 1989).

75. M. Iofrida, "Matérialisme et hétérogénéité dans la philosophie de John Toland," *Dix-huitième siècle* 24 (1992).

76. Thomas Brett, *Tradition Necessary to Explain and Interpret the Holy Scriptures* (London, 1718), iv.

77. Françoise Charles-Daubert, "Les principales sources de l'*Esprit de Spinoza*," in *Groupe de recherches spinozistes: Travaux et documents* 1 (Paris, 1989), 82.

78. Giuseppe Ricuperati, "Libertinismo a desimo a Vienna: Spinoza, Toland e il Triregno," *Rivista Storica Italiana* 79 (1967): 628–95.

79. John Toland, *Origines Judicae*, 1709, para. 6.

80. Giovanni Aquilecchia, "Nota su John Toland traduttore di Giordano Bruno," *English Miscellany* 9 (1958): 85.

81. Justin Champion, "Toland and the *Traité des trois imposteurs*," *International Archives of the History of Ideas* 148 (1990): 333–56.

CHAPTER SIX

1. Because of its availability, we shall make use of the edition by Raoul Vaneigem, *L'Art de ne croire en rien, suivi du Livre des trois imposteurs* (Paris: Rivages Poche, 2002). The *De tribus impostoribus* takes up no more than forty-three pages (49–92).

2. Ibid., 50

3. Ibid., 54.

4. Ibid.

5. Ibid., 55–56.

6. Ibid., 57–58.

7. Ibid., 59.

8. Ibid., 62.

9. Ibid., 65.

10. Ibid., 66.

11. For reasons of availability, we shall cite the text from the edition of Max Milo, *L'Esprit de Spinoza: Traité des trois imposteurs; Moïse, Jésus, Mahomet* (Paris: Max Milo Éditions, 2001).

12. Jean-Pierre Cavaillé, "Libertinage ou Lumières radicales?," in *Qu'est-ce que les Lumières radicales?*, ed. Secrétan, Dagron, and Bove, 69.

13. On this subject, see the illuminating pages of Silvia Berti, "*L'Esprit de Spinoza*: Ses origines et sa première édition dans leur contexte spinozien," in *Heterodoxy, Spinozism, and Free Thought*, ed. Berti, Charles-Daubert, and Popkin, 3–52.

14. Milo, *L'Esprit de Spinoza*, I.V, p. 27.

15. Ibid., I.III, p. 26.

16. Ibid., XV.V, p. 108.

17. Ibid.

18. Ibid., III.II, pp. 45–46.

19. Ibid., II.VII, pp. 38–39.

20. Ibid., III.I, pp. 43–44.

21. Ibid., XVIII.II, p. 131.

22. Ibid., XVIII.IV, pp. 132–33.

23. Ibid., IV.I, pp. 48–49.

24. Ibid., IV.V, p. 52.

25. Ibid., IV.I, p. 49.

26. Ibid., XII.III, p. 91.

27. Ibid., XIII.IV, p. 96.

28. Ibid., XIII.VII, p. 97.

29. Ibid., XIII.VIII, p. 99.

30. Ibid., XVI.I, p. 112.

31. Ibid., XVII.V, p. 125.

32. Ibid., XVII.VII, p. 127.

33. Ibid., XIX.I, pp. 135–36.

34. Ibid., XX.I, p. 143.

35. Ibid., XX.III, p. 144.

36. Ibid., XXI.V, p. 147.

37. Ibid., XXI.IX, pp. 150–51.

38. Bossuet, *Premier Sermon pour le premier dimanche de l'Avent*, in Oeuvres complètes, vol. 1, pp. 127–44.

39. Cited by Paul Hazard, *The European Mind (1680–1715)* (Cleveland: Meridian Books, World Publishing Company, 1963), 46.

40. *Traité*, V.II, p. 57.

41. Ibid., VIII.IV, pp. 67–68.

42. Ibid., VIII.V, p. 69.

43. Ibid., VIII.VI, p. 70.

44. Ibid., VII.I, p. 64.

45. Ibid., VIII.II, p. 81.

46. Ibid., IX.III, p. 77.

47. Ibid., IX.III, p. 75.

48. Ibid., XIV.I, p. 101.

49. Ibid., XIV.II, p. 103.

50. Ibid., XIV.II, p. 105.

51. Ibid., XIV.I, p. 102.

52. Mathieu Marais, *Journal*, 2:227.

53. Diego Venturino, "Un prophète 'philosophe'? Une Vie de Mohammed à l'aube des Lumières," *Dix-huitième siècle* 24 (1992).

54. Lancelot Addison, *The Life and Death of Mahumet, the Author of the Turkish Religion* (London, 1679), 32.

55. Spinoza, *Letters*, trans. Samuel Shirley (Indianapolis: Hackett Publishing Company, 1995), 241.

56. Hobbes, *Leviathan*, chap. 12; ed. Richard Tuck (Cambridge: Cambridge University Press, 1991), 82.

57. *Traité*, XVI.I, pp. 117–18.

58. Ibid., XI.II, XI.III, pp. 84–85.

59. Ibid., XXI.IX, p. 152.

EPILOGUE

1. D'Holbach, *Christianity Unveiled; Being, An Examination of the Principles and Effects of the Christian Religion*, trans. W. M. Johnson (New York: Columbian Press, 1795), 34–35.

2. J. Vercruysse, "Voltaire et Marc-Michel Rey," *Studies on Voltaire and the Eighteenth Century* 58 (1967): 1707–63. See also the notice "Marc-Michel Rey, libraire des Lumières," in *Histoire de l'édition française*, under the direction of Roger Chartier and Henri-Jean Martin, vol. 2, *Le Livre triomphant, 1660–1830* (Paris: Fayard-Cercle de la Librairie, 1990), 413–17.

3. Göttingen, Uu LB, Hist. Lit. 42.

4. Bibliothèque de l'Arsenal 10889, Report of d'Ombreval to d'Argenson, fols. 112–13.

5. Bibliothèque de la Ville de Paris, CP 3997.

6. Bibliothèque de l'Arsenal 11597, dossier Lapalu, fol. 63.

7. Bibliothèque de l'Arsenal 11616, dossier Guillier, fol. 579.

8. Benitez, "La diffusion du *Traité des trois imposteurs* au XVIIIe siècle," 149.

9. Universiteits Bibliotheek, Leiden, March.47, letter from Heinzelmann to Marchand, 23 March 1749.

10. Benitez, "La diffusion du *Traité des trois imposteurs* au XVIIIe siècle," 150.

11. A. G. Masch, "Nachrichten von den Buche *De tribus impostoribus*" (Hamburg: Brem und Verdische Bibliothek, 1757), 837.

12. On the *De tribus* in Germany, see Wolfgang Gericke, "Über Handschriften des Budhes *De tribus impostoribus*," *Marginalien, Zeitschrift für Buchkunst und Bibliophilie* 24 (1954): 24.

13. *La Spectatrice danoise* 2 (1750): 467.

14. Justin A. I. Champion, "Legislators, Impostors and the Politic Origins of Religion: English Theories of Imposture from Stubbe to Toland," in *Heterodoxy, Spinozism, and Free Thought*, ed. Berti, Charles-Daubert, and Popkin, 340.

15. British Library, MS Stowe 47, fol. 54.

16. Voltaire, *Lettre sur les juifs*, in *Mélanges*, Pléiade ed. (Paris: Gallimard, 1961), 1211–15.

17. Voltaire, *Correspondance*, Pléiade ed. (Paris: Gallimard, 1980), 3:442.

18. Voltaire, letter of 20 January 1742 to Frederick II, in *Oeuvres complètes* (1784), fol. 3.

19. Voltaire, letter of 20 February 1751, *Correspondance*, 3:358.

20. Ibid., 9:431.

21. Catalogue Ferney, B406, BV3330.

22. Voltaire, *Correspondance*, 9:444.

23. Ibid., 479.

24. Ibid., 822.

25. *Lettres de Madame du Deffand*, 1742–1780 (Paris: Mercure de France, 2002), 278.

26. Voltaire, *Correspondance*, 10:463.

27. Abbé Bergier, *Traité historique et dogmatique de la vraie religion* (Paris, 1780), 4:380–81.

28. Ibid.

29. Ibid., 592.

30. Gustave Brunet, *Imprimeurs imaginaires et librairies supposés* (Paris, 1866), 244 and 280.

31. Heather Blair, "Impostors and Revolution: On the "Philadelphie" 1796 edition of the *Traité des trois imposteurs*," in *Heterodoxy, Spinozism, and Free Thought*, ed. Berti, Charles-Daubert, and Popkin, 297–304.

32. The *Acts* of the conference were published in *Heterodoxy, Spinozism, and Free Thought*, ed. Berti, Charles-Daubert, and Popkin.

GLOSSARY OF NAMES

Abelard, Peter. 1079-1142. French. Major twelfth-century philosopher, author of works on logic and theology, notably *Sic et non [Yes and No]*, using the approach of dialectics.

Abudiente, Moses Gideon. d. 1688. Portuguese poet and grammarian, known for his *Grammatica hebraica* and *Fin de los dias*.

Abū Ṭāhir al-Djannābī. 907-943/4. Chief of small Karmatian state of Bahrain.

Addison, Rev. Lancelot. 1632-1703. English clergyman, dean of Lichfield, father of essayist Joseph Addison.

Alberic of Trois-Fontaines. Thirteenth-century Cistercian chronicler.

Albert Behaim. c. 1180-c. 1260. Papal legate and anti-imperialist; advisor to Pope Innocent IV.

al-Bukhārī, Muḥammad ibn Ismāʾīl. 810-870. Eminent Sunni legal scholar and collector of traditions, best known for his *Ṣaḥīḥ al-Bukhārī*.

Allamand, Johannes Nicolaas Sebastiaan. 1713 (or 1716)-1787. Dutch scholar and professor of mathematics and philosophy at University of Leiden, known for his work in natural history.

al-Maʿarrī, Abu ʾl-ʿAlāʾ. 973-1058. Arabic poet and prose author of late ʿAbbāsid period.

al-Malik al-Kāmil. c. 1177/80-1238. Ayyūbid Sultan, ceded Jerusalem to Frederick II, 11 February 1229.

Amenhotep. Name of three ancient Egyptian kings: Amenhotep I, founder of the Eighteenth Dynasty, ruled 1514-1493 BCE; Amenhotep II, r. 1426-1400 BCE; Amenhotep III, r. 1390-1353 BCE.

Anatoli, Jacob ben Abba Mari ben Samson. Thirteenth century. Physician, preacher, and translator of Arabic works into Hebrew; physician to Frederick II.

Anaxagoras of Clazomenae. Probably 500-428 BCE. First philosopher known to have settled in Athens. His work survives only in fragments.

Aretino, Pietro. 1492-1556. Italian author of poems, plays, and dialogues; best known for his letters, published in six volumes, 1538-1557.

Arius. c. 250-336. Alexandrian priest and heresiarch who denied the divinity of Christ. His doctrines were condemned by the first Council of Nicaea (325).

Arnauld, Antoine. 1612-1694. French Jansenist theologian, called "The Great
   Arnauld."
Arpe, Peter Friedrich. 1682-1740. German freethinker.
Asclepiades. fl. first century BCE. Greek physician.
Averroes. *See* Ibn Rushd
Aymon, Jean. 1661-1734. Priest who embraced Calvinism; author of several
   works against the papacy.
Baldwin IX, Count of Flanders, and Emperor Baldwin I of Constantinople.
   1172-c. 1205. A leader of the Fourth Crusade, resulting in capture of
   Constantinople.
Basnage, Jacques. 1653-1725. French Protestant theologian and historian.
Bayle, Pierre. 1647-1706. French Protestant writer; publisher of *Nouvelles de la
   République des Lettres*. Best known for his *Dictionnaire historique et critique*
   (1697).
Beauregard, Claude. 1578-1664. French physician and philosopher; author of
   Circulus pisanus.
Bekker, Balthasar. 1634-1698. Dutch theologian and pastor. Condemned belief
   in witchcraft.
Bembo, Pietro. 1470-1547. Italian scholar and poet, known for his work in liter-
   ary theory; Catholic churchman, made a cardinal by Pope Paul III.
Benedict XIV (Prospero Lambertini). 1675-1758; pope, 1740-1758. Born in
   Bologna. One of the most learned of all popes and most important pope of
   his century.
Bentley, Richard. 1662-1742. Master of Trinity College, Cambridge, vice
   chancellor of the university, and Regius Professor of Divinity. Classics
   scholar who gave the first Boyle Lectures (1692), attacking materialism and
   atheism.
Benvenuto da Imola. 1320?-1388. Contemporary and acquaintance of Boccac-
   cio; author of a commentary on Dante's *Divine Comedy.*
Bergier, Abbé. Canon of Paris and a collaborator on Diderot's *Encyclopédie.*
Bernard, Jean-Frédéric. 1683-1744. Author of *Cérémonies et coutumes religieuses
   de tous les peuples du monde [Religious Ceremonies and Customs of All the Peoples
   of the World].*
Bernard le Trésorier. Thirteenth century. Chronicler.
Bernard of Clairvaux. 1090/91-1153. French cleric of the Cistercian order.
   Founded monastery of Clairvaux, and presided over expansion of Cistercian
   order. Canonized 1174.
Beverland, Adrian. 1650-1716. Dutch philosopher who settled in England;
   secretary to Isaac Vossius
Beza, Theodore. 1519-1605. French Protestant biblical scholar and theologian.
   Professor at Calvin's Geneva Academy, 1558-1595. Produced critical edition
   of Greek New Testament.
Blanche of Castile. 1188-1252. Daughter of Alfonso VIII of Castile. Married

Prince Louis of France, who became Louis VII (r. 1223-26). Regent during minority of her son, Louis IX.

Blount, Charles. 1654-1693. English deist and author of freethinking books.

Boccaccio, Giovanni. 1313-1375. Italian writer and scholar, considered father of Italian prose, best known for his *Decameron*.

Bodin, Jean. 1529/30-1596. French political theorist, known for emphasizing the concept of sovereignty; author of *Six Books of the Republic*.

Boerhaave, Hermann. 1668-1738. Famous physician at Leiden. Strong influence on teaching of medicine.

Bossuet, Jacques Bénigne. 1627-1704. French Catholic clergyman and orator; bishop of Meaux.

Boulainvillier, Henri de, comte de Saint-Saire. 1658-1722. French philosopher, influenced by Spinoza.

Bourdelot, Pierre. 1610-1685. French physician in the service of Louis XIII and members of the French court.

Bracciolini, Poggio. 1380-1459. Italian humanist and Latinist; served eight popes in succession as part of papal secretariat.

Brenz, John. 1499-1580. German Lutheran reformer; institutionalized the Reformation in several German states.

Bruno, Giordano. 1548-1600. Italian Renaissance neoplatonist and magician. Became a Dominican monk, but abandoned the order. Traveled throughout Europe. Imprisoned in Rome by the Inquisition, he refused to recant and was burned for heresy.

Calepino, Ambrogio. c. 1435-1509/10. Italian lexicographer.

Calvin, John. 1509-1564. French theologian and dominant figure of Protestant Reformation, based in Geneva but influenced all of Europe.

Campanella, Tommaso. 1568-1639. Italian poet, philosopher, and utopian.

Cardano, Girolamo. 1501-1576. Italian writer, best known for his medical and mathematical works.

Castel, Charles-Irénée, abbé de Saint-Pierre. 1658-1743. French legal and social reformer.

Castro, Bendito de (also called Baruch). 1597-1684. German doctor; physician to Queen Christina of Sweden. An adherent of Shabbetai Ẓevi.

Chabanon, Michel-Paul-Guy de. 1730-1792. French writer and musician.

Chapelain, Jean. 1595-1674. French poet and critic; founding member of the Académie Française.

Chardon, Daniel-Marc-Antoine. 1730-1795. French magistrate and author.

Charlemagne. 742-814. Frankish king, later emperor, ruler of Carolingian empire. Crowned emperor in 800.

Charles VII. 1403-1461. King of France, crowned July 1429 thanks to victories of Joan of Arc.

Charron, Pierre. 1541-1603. French lawyer turned theologian and moral philosopher; friend of Montaigne.

Chateillon, Sébastien. Also known as Castalion or Castellion. 1515-1563. French Protestant theologian.

Chevaliers de la Jubilation. Dutch Protestant organization in the early eighteenth century, said to have been the first Masonic Lodge in Europe.

Cholmeley, Richard. Sixteenth century. English government spy and associate of Christopher Marlowe.

Clovis I. c. 466-511. Most important of the Merovingian kings of Gaul. First Christian king of the Franks.

Collins, Anthony. 1676-1729. English Deist and freethinker; friend of John Locke.

Conscientiaries. Atheistic sect founded by Matthias Knützen.

Cooper, Anthony Ashley, 3rd Earl of Shaftesbury. 1671-1713. English moral philosopher.

Cortés, Hernán. 1485-1547. Spanish Conquistador, conqueror of Mexico.

Costa, Uriel da. 1583/4-1640. Philosopher and freethinker, born in Oporto, Portugal, into a *converso* (New Christian) family. Converted himself and family to his own version of Judaism. Fled first to Amsterdam, then to Hamburg and Utrecht. Excommunicated. Seen as precursor and inspirer of Spinoza.

Coste, Pierre. 1668-1747. French Protestant printer and translator.

Critias. Fifth century BCE. Greek philosopher. An associate of Socrates, and often included among the Sophists.

Curio, Jacques. 1497-1572. Saxon physician, professor at University of Heidelberg.

Danaeus, Lambertus. c. 1535-c. 1590. French Huguenot pastor; fled France to settle in Geneva.

De Bure, Guillaume-François. 1732-1782. French bookseller and bibliographer.

Deffand, Marie de Vichy, Marquise du. 1697-1780. French aristocrat and *saloniste*.

Democritus. Fifth century BCE (born 460-57). Greek philosopher, born in Thrace, known for his atomic theory of the universe.

Denis, Marie-Louise (Marie Louise Mignot). 1712-1790. Voltaire's niece, housekeeper, and companion.

Des Barreaux, Sieur (Jacques Vallée). 1599-1673. French poet and skeptic.

Descartes, René. 1596-1650. French philosopher and scientist.

Desmaizeaux, Pierre. 1666? (or 1673)-1745. Huguenot writer and man of letters active in London.

Des Périers, Bonaventure. c. 1510-1544. French writer, poet, and translator of Plato. Author of *Cymbalum mundi*. Served as valet de chambre to Queen Marguerite de Navarre.

Des Vignes, Pierre. *See* Pierre des Vignes

De Witt, Jan. 1625-1672. Dutch statesman, chief minister of United Provinces of the Netherlands.

Diagoras of Melos (the Atheist). Late fifth century BCE. Greek lyric poet, active in Athens, known for his atheism; his work survives only in fragments.

Dicaearchus. fl. c. 320-300 BCE. Greek scholar and writer, pupil of Aristotle.

Diez, Heinrich Friedrich von. 1751-1817. Prussian official, orientalist, and bibliophile.

Digby, Sir Kenelm. 1603-1665. English author, naval commander, and diplomat.

Diodati, Giovanni. Swiss Protestant theologian. Published Italian and French translations of the Bible.

Diogenes of Apollonia. Fifth century BCE. Greek philosopher, considered the last of the Greek Presocratics.

Diopeithes. Fifth century BCE. Athenian legislator. The "decree of Diopeithes" attacked impiety.

Dolet, Étienne. 1509-1546. French writer and publisher. A freethinker accused of publishing heretical works, he was burned to death in Paris in 1546, along with a pile of his books.

Du Bellay, Joachim. 1522-1560. French poet of Pléiade school, best known for his *Defense and Illustration of the French Language*.

Du Cange, Charles du Fresne, Seigneur. 1610-1688. French scholar and parliamentary advocate.

Duijkerius, Johannes. 1661/2-1702. Dutch Reform writer and Spinozist.

Duns Scotus, John. c. 1266-1308. Scottish philosopher and theologian; member of the Franciscan order. He studied at Oxford and taught at both Oxford and University of Paris.

Duplessis-Mornay, Philippe (Seigneur du Plessis-Marly). 1549-1623. French Protestant (Huguenot) leader and spokesman during the French Wars of Religion (1562-1598).

Dupuy, Pierre and Jacques. Pierre: 1582-1651; Jacques: 1586-1656. French historians and curators of Royal Library, Paris.

Dury, John. 1596-1680. Scottish Calvinist minister and intellectual of the Civil War period.

Du Sauzet, Henri. 1686?-1754. French journalist and publisher, based in Netherlands. Publisher of *Nouvelles Littéraires*.

Du Verdier, Antoine. 1544-1600. French politician and writer, best known as a bibliographer.

Effen, Justus van. 1684-1735. Dutch writer and essayist.

Empedocles. Fifth century BCE. Greek philosopher from Sicily.

Epicurus. 341-270 BCE. Greek moral and natural philosopher.

Epiphanius of Salamis. c. 310-403. Bishop of Constantia (Salamis) and Father of the Church.

Erasmus, Desiderius. 1467-1536. Dutch humanist, scholar and writer. Greatest classicist of the northern European Renaissance. A Catholic himself, his many works influenced both Catholics and Reformers.

Estienne (Stephanus), Henri the Younger. 1531-1598. French printer, lexicographer, and traveler. Born into the Estienne family of French scholar-printers active in Paris and Geneva; succeeded his father as head of the shop in Geneva.

Eugen of Savoy (Prince Eugen Francis of Savoy-Carignan). 1663-1736. Military strategist who helped bring about rise of Austrian Habsburgs; also a patron of the arts.

Euhemerus. fl. fourth-third century BCE. Greek Sophist and mythographer.

Eymeric, Nicolás. c. 1320-1399. Spanish theologian; member of the Dominican order. Became grand inquisitor (1357-1360). Author of *Directorium inquisitorum* (1376).

Fausto da Longiano, Sebastiano. c. 1502-1565. Italian translator and editor.

Fénelon, François de Salignac de la Mothe. 1651-1715. French theologian, defender of quietism.

Flavin, Melchior de. d. 1580. French theologian and linguist.

Francis of Assisi. c. 1181-1226. Founder of Franciscan order; canonized 1228.

Frederick II. 1195-1250. King of Germany, Holy Roman Emperor (from 1220), king of Sicily (from 1198), and King of Jerusalem (1229); one of the most brilliant medieval rulers.

Frederick II (the Great). 1712-1786. King of Prussia.

Fritsch, Caspar (Gaspar). Eighteenth century. Publisher, Leipzig.

Furly, Benjamin. 1636-1714. English Quaker and friend of John Locke.

Galen. AD 129-199/216? Physician from Pergamum; became court physician to Emperor Marcus Aurelius in Rome.

Garasse, Francis. 1585-1631. French Jesuit; author of several works. Focus of "war" between Jesuits and Jansenists.

Gassendi (Pierre Gassend). 1592-1655. French philosopher; revived Epicureanism.

Genebrard, Gilbert. 1537-1597. Benedictine cleric, scholar, and linguist.

Gentillet, Innocent. 1535-1588. French Huguenot and anti-Machiavellian. Published *Discourse against Machiavelli* in 1576.

Gerson, Jean (Jean Charlier). 1363-1429. Theologian, scholar, teacher, poet, mystic, humanist. Chancellor of the University of Paris.

Goliards. Twelfth-thirteenth centuries. Mostly wandering scholars and clerics; writers of secular Latin lyric poetry. The largest collection of their work is known as the *Carmina burana*.

Gravesande, Wilhem Jacob 's. 1688-1742. Dutch philosopher and mathematician.

Green Ribbon Club. Active c. 1674-c. 1683. London political club. Membership composed of lawyers, city politicians, and members of Parliament. Espoused antipapist views and opposed James II.

Gregory IX (Ugolino di Conti). c. 1170-1241. Became pope 1227. Twice excommunicated Frederick II, whom he had anointed at his imperial coronation in 1220.

Gruet, Jacques. d. 1547. Freethinker tortured and executed in Geneva for criticizing Calvin.

Gustav II Adolf (Gustavus Adolphus). 1594-1632. King of Sweden.

Hardy, Claude. 1598-1678. French lawyer and mathematician, friend of Descartes.

Harriot, Thomas. 1560-1621. English mathematician, astronomer, and natural philosopher. Tutor to Sir Walter Raleigh.

Hartlib, Samuel. c. 1600-1662. English reformer; friend of poet John Milton.

Harvey, Gabriel. 1550-1631. English writer and scholar; friend of poet Edmund Spenser.

Herbert (of Cherbury), Edward, Baron. 1583-1648. English soldier, statesman, and philosopher.

Hermes Trismegistus. Mythical author of esoteric texts in Greco-Egyptian tradition: the Hellenistic Hermes combined with the Egyptian god Thoth.

Hinckelmann, Abraham. 1652-1694. German Protestant theologian and Islamic scholar; published an edition of the Qur'ān at Hamburg.

Hippocrates. Fifth century BCE. Greek physician from Cos, contemporary of Socrates. Most important physician of the ancient world.

Hobbes, Thomas. 1588-1679. English philosopher, best known for his work *Leviathan*.

Hohendorf, Baron Wilhelm von. d. 1719. In the service of Prince Eugen of Savoy; bibliophile who compiled a notable collection of books.

Holbach, Paul Henri Thiry, Baron d'. 1723-1789. French philosopher of German birth. *Saloniste* and contributor to Diderot's *Encyclopédie*.

Honorius of Autun. d. c. 1156. Benedictine monk, of Regensburg. Best known for his *Elucidarium*, a popular manual of theology.

Hosius, Stanislaus. 1504-1579. Polish Catholic leader and cardinal, best known for his *Confessio catholicae fidei*, opposing Protestantism.

Huet, Pierre-Daniel. 1630-1721. French prelate and scholar; bishop of Avranches.

Humbert of Romans. d. 1277. Dominican friar and head of Dominican order.

Huygens, Christiaan. 1629-1695. Dutch physicist and astronomer.

Ibn al-Djawzī, Sibṭ. c. 1185-1256. Writer, preacher, and historian who wrote *Universal History [Marʾāt al-zamān]*.

Ibn Hishām, Abū Muḥammad ʿAbd al-Malik. d. 834 at Bassorah; biographer of Muhammad.

Ibn Rushd, Abu 'l-Walīd al-Ḥafid (Averroes). 1126-1198. Born in Córdoba. Physician and philosopher, known for his commentaries on Aristotle.

Ibn Sabʿīn ʿAbd al-Ḥaḳḳ. c. 1217-1269. Author of *Sicilian Questions*.

Ibn Tūmart al-Mahdī, Muḥammad. d. 1130. Berber; founder of Almohad movement.

Ibn Wāṣil, Abū ʿAbd Allāh. 1208-1298. Arabic historian and man of letters.

Ignatius of Loyola. 1491-1556. Founder of the Catholic order of Society of Jesus (Jesuits); canonized 1622.

Index librorum prohibitorum [List of Forbidden Books]. List of prohibited publications, issued by the Catholic Church beginning in 1559 with Pope Paul IV and abolished in 1966 by Pope Paul VI.

Jelles, Jarrig. c. 1620-1683. Merchant of Amsterdam, part of Spinoza's circle.

Joachim of Fiore. d. 1201/2. Catholic mystic of the Cistercian order; philosopher of history.

Joan of Arc. c. 1412-1431. French peasant girl called "Maid of Orléans." Led French army to victories in Hundred Years' War; captured by Burgundians, turned over to English. Tried in an episcopal court on charges of witchcraft and heresy; convicted and burned at stake. Canonized 1920.

Johnson, Thomas. d. 1735. Scottish publisher at The Hague.

Journal of a Bourgeois of Paris. Diary kept by an anonymous French priest, 1409-1431; continued by another to 1449.

Judah ben Salomon ha-Cohen Matqa. b. c. 1215. Jewish philosopher of Toledo, from a famous family of astrologers. Student of celebrated Spanish rabbi Meir Abulafia; author of *Inquisitio sapientiae.*

Kettner, Friedrich Ernst. 1671-1722. Saxon Protestant theologian.

Knuttel, Matthias. German atheist [possibly same as Matthias Knützen?].

Knützen, Matthias. 1646-after 1674. German critic of religion, said to have founded Conscientiaries.

Koch, Johannes (Johannes Cocceius). 1603-1669. German theologian; professor at University of Leiden.

Koerbagh, Adriaan. 1632-1669. Dutch scholar and writer; critic of religion.

Kortholt, Christian (the Elder). 1633-1694. German Protestant theologian.

Kuyper, Frans. 1629-1691. Dutch Socinian writer and publisher.

La Mettrie, Julien Offray de. 1709-1751. French physician and philosopher, known as an extreme materialist.

La Monnoye, Bernard de. 1641-1728. French lawyer, poet, and philologist; contributor to Bayle's *Dictionnaire historique.*

La Mothe Le Vayer, François de. 1588-1672. French skeptical philosopher; tutor to Louis XIV.

Lamy, Bernard. 1640-1715. French Catholic clergyman and scholar; Oratorian.

La Noue, François de. 1531-1591. French soldier, historian, and Huguenot leader.

La Rochefoucauld, François, duc de. 1613-1680. French classical writer, known for his *Maxims.*

Lau, Theodor Ludwig. 1670-1740. German lawyer, known for his antireligious works.

Laukhard, J. C. Pastor in Lower Palatinate, discovered after his death to have been a fervent Spinozan.

Le Clerc, Jean. 1657-1736. Swiss theologian and scholar.

Leibniz, Gottfried Wilhelm. 1646-1716. German philosopher and mathematician.

Le Loyer, Pierre. 1572-1634. French lawyer, scholar, and orientalist; friend of the French classical poet Ronsard.

Leti, Gregorio. 1630-1701. Italian historian satirist, known for works about the Catholic Church; all his works were placed on the *Index.*

Leucippus. Second half fifth century BCE. Greek philosopher, originator of atomic theory.

Levier, Charles. d. 1734. Publisher at The Hague.

Lipenius, Martin. 1630-1692. German teacher and bibliographer.

Locke, John. 1632-1704. English philosopher, best known for his *Essay Concerning Human Understanding.*

Lucas, Jean-Maximilien. 1646-1697. Acquaintance of Spinoza; compiled his biography in French, published anonymously in 1719.

Lucretius. c. 94-55 or 51 BCE. Epicurean poet, author of *De rerum natura.*

Lull, Raymond. c. 1232-1315. Mystic of Catalonia, prolific writer on science, theology, and other subjects; also poet.

Mabillon, Jean. 1632-1707. French scholar and Benedictine; antiquarian, considered the most learned man of his time.

Madre de Dios, Geronimo de la (Jerome Gracian Dantisco). 1545-1614. Spanish Carmelite monk and author of several religious works.

Malebranche, Nicolas. 1638-1715. French philosopher.

Marais, Mathieu. 1664-1737. French jurist and writer; contributor to Bayle's *Dictionnaire historique.*

Marchand, Prosper. c. 1675-1756. French bibliographer; author of several works including a *Dictionnaire historique* following upon Bayle's.

Maréchal, Pierre-Sylvain. 1750-1803. French antireligious writer.

Mariana, Juan de. 1535/36-1624. Castilian humanist, historian, and Jesuit.

Marin, François-Louis-Claude. 1721-1809. French man of letters and journalist; became royal censor.

Marlowe, Christopher. 1564-1593. English Elizabethan playwright.

Marracci, Ludovico. 1612-1700. Italian Catholic priest; made a Latin translation of the Qur'ān.

Marsham, Sir John. 1602-1685. English historian and Egyptologist.

Matthew Paris. d. 1259. Monk of St. Albans, and major English chronicler of the Middle Ages.

Maubert de Gouvest, Jean-Henri. 1721-1767. Adventurer known for his colorful career as, among other things, Capuchin friar, spy, military officer, historian, theatrical impresario, and man of letters; author of several books of political history.

Mayer, Johan Friedrich. 1650-1712. German Lutheran theologian; advisor to King Charles XII of Sweden.

Medici, Giulio de' (Pope Clement VII). 1478-1534; became pope in 1523. Taken prisoner in the sack of Rome, 1527. Has been called "probably the most disastrous of all the popes" (by German historian von Ranke).

Mehmed II (the Conqueror). 1432-1481. Ottoman sultan and military strategist.

Meijer, Lodewijk. 1629-1681. Dutch physician and philosopher; friend of Spinoza.

Mersenne, Marin. 1588-1648. French mathematician and scientist.

Merula (also known as Joannes Andreae). d. 1557. Spanish apostate Muslim, known for his *Confusio sectae mahometanae.*

Michael Scot. 1175?-1234? Scottish scholar and astrologer in court of Emperor Frederick II.

Montaigne, Michel Eyquem de. 1533-1592. French writer best known for his essays, a literary genre that he largely invented. Served as mayor of Bordeaux and was a friend of King Henri IV of France.

Montfaucon, Bernard de. 1655-1741. French scholar and monk; founder of paleography.

Moréri, Louis. 1653-1680. French priest and savant.

Morin, Jean-Baptiste. 1583-1656. French mathematician and astrologer.

Morteira, Saul Levi. c. 1596-1660. Rabbi and scholar. Born in Venice, settled in Amsterdam. Author of the *Tratado da verdade da Lei de Moisès* among other works.

Moses ben Solomon of Salerno, Rabbi. Fourteenth century. Commentator on Maimonides' *Guide of the Perplexed.*

Mosheim, Johann Lorenz von. 1694-1755. German theologian.

Müller, Johann Joachim. 1661-1733. German jurist.

Muratori, Ludovico Antonio. 1672-1750. Italian historian and priest; librarian of Duke of Modena.

Muret, Marc-Antoine. 1526-1585. French humanist; teacher of Montaigne; member of French poetic group Pléiade.

Musaeus, Johannes. 1613-1681. German Protestant theologian.

Nancel, Nicolas de. 1539-1610. French physician and humanist.

Naudé, Gabriel. 1600-1653. French physician; bibliophile and collector of the 40,000-volume Bibliothèque Mazarine.

Nayler, James. 1617?-1660. English Quaker who claimed to be Christ.

Neef, Pieter (Naevius). 1667-1731. Dutch writer who made his living writing funeral speeches; related by marriage to Adrian Beverland.

Nieuwentyt, Bernard. 1654-1718. Dutch philosopher; a follower of Descartes and opponent of Spinoza. Also known as a mathematician, physician, and theologian.

Noodt, Gerard. 1647-1725. Dutch lawyer and university professor.

Ochino, Bernardino. 1487-1564. Italian theologian and preacher; became vicar-general of the Capuchin order in 1538. Converted to Protestantism and influenced radical reformers.

Oldenbarnevelt, Johan Van. 1547-1619. Dutch statesman and Protestant leader.

Oldenburg, Henry. 1619-1677. German theologian, diplomat, and natural philosopher; served as first secretary of Royal Society.

Oratorians. French religious order founded 1611 by Cardinal Pierre de Bérulle. Based on order founded in Italy in 1575 by St. Philip Neri.

Orpheus. Figure of Greek myth; singer and poet. His myth gave rise to a large body of "Orphic" literature.

Osborne, Francis. 1593-1659. English author and friend of Hobbes.

Ottomano, Padre. Seventeenth century. Impostor who claimed to be the first-born son of Sultan Ibrahim.

Parsons (or Persons), Robert. 1564-1610. English Jesuit missionary and controversialist.

Patin, Guy. 1601-1672. French physician and man of letters.

Peiresc, Nicole-Claude-Fabri de. 1580-1637. French humanist, botanist, and gardener.

Pelayo, Alvaro. d. 1353. Portuguese Franciscan; defender of the Catholic faith.

Pennini, Ricoldo (Ricoldo da Monte di Croce). 1243-1320. Italian Dominican monk; writer, traveler, and missionary; Christian apologist.

Peter I (Peter the Great). 1672-1725. Tsar of Russia (1682-1725), who Westernized Russia.

Peter of Vinea. *See* Pierre des Vignes

Peter the Hermit (of Amiens). d. 1115. Most eloquent preacher of First Crusade.

Peter the Venerable. c. 1092-1156. Abbot of the Benedictine abbey of Cluny.

Petit, Jean. 1360-1411. French theologian and professor at University of Paris.

Petrus Alfonsi. Twelfth-century Jewish convert to Christianity; author of *Dialogue against the Jews*, c. 1109.

Philip of Novara. c. 1200-c. 1270. Italian soldier, diplomat, musician, writer, and lawyer.

Pierre des Vignes. d. 1249. Peter of Vinea. Notary and judge in service of Frederick II; became his chief councilor (logothete)

Pizarro, Francisco. 1476-1541. Spanish conquistador, conqueror of Peru.

Plato. c. 429-347 BCE. Greek philosopher of Athens; student of Socrates; teacher of Aristotle.

Plutarch. Born before 50 CE, d. after 120 CE. Greek philosopher and biographer.

Pompilius, Numa. 715-673 BCE. According to legend, the second King of Rome, a reformer who established the institutions of Roman public religion.

Pomponazzi, Pietro. 1462-1525. Italian Aristotelian philosopher.

Postel, Guillaume. 1510-1581. French scholar and orientalist who advocated peace through universal religion.

Prado, Juan de. Spanish Jew. A friend of Spinoza; like Spinoza, excommunicated by the Portuguese Jewish community of Amsterdam, c. 1656.

Prideaux, Humphrey. 1648-1724. English orientalist known for his polemical biography of Mahomet, *The True Nature of Imposture* (1697).

Pucci, Francesco. 1543-1597. Italian philosopher and humanist.

Puffendorf, Samuel, Freiherr von. 1632-1694. German jurist and historian.

Pythagoras. Sixth century BCE. Major but mysterious figure of Greek intellectual history, known for his doctrine of transmigration of souls.

Rabelais, François. 1494-1553. French humanist and major figure in French Renaissance. Best known for his satirical novel *Gargantua and Pantagruel*.

Raemond, Florimond de. 1540-1601. French jurist and historian. In the eighteenth century, his name was often erroneously believed to be a pseudonym used by Louis Richeome, q. v.

Ramus, Petrus (Pierre de la Ramée). 1515-1572. French humanist and
  philosopher.
Ranelagh, Lady (Katherine Jones, Viscountess Ranelagh). 1615-1691. Anglo-Irish
  intellectual; sister of Robert Boyle; friend of Milton. Socially and politically
  influential figure, associated with Hartlib.
Rapin de Thoyras (Paul Rapin, Sieur de Thoyras). 1661-1725. French Protestant
  historian and soldier, active in England and the Netherlands. Author of a
  multivolume history of England.
Reimmann, Jacob Friedrich. 1668-1743. German Lutheran theologian, teacher,
  historian, and philosopher.
Renaudet, Abbé. French agent in England; author of a "Memorandum on the
  Affairs of England" (1698).
Renaudot, Théophraste. 1586-1653. French physician and journalist; founder of
  first French newspaper.
Rey, Marc-Michel. 1720-1780. A native of Geneva, active in the United Prov-
  inces as a French-language publisher; published works of French *philosophes*.
Richeome, Louis. 1544-1625. Jesuit theologian and man of letters, defender of
  the Catholic faith against Protestantism.
Ristwyk, Herman. d. 1512. Dutchman, burned to death at The Hague.
Romulus. Along with Remus, mythical founder of Rome.
Rousset de Missy, Jean. 1686-1762. Former soldier who became a journalist at
  The Hague and Amsterdam.
Rycaut, Sir Paul. 1629-1700. British diplomat and historian; authority on the
  Ottoman Empire.
Rymer, Thomas. 1641-1713. English critic and historian; royal historiographer.
Sabatier de Castres, Antoine. 1742-1817. French journalist and man of letters.
Saint-Hyacinthe, Thémiseul de (Hyacinthe Cordonnier). 1684-1746. French
  satirical writer.
Saint-Simon, Louis de Rouvroy, duc de. 1675-1755. French memoirist.
Salimbene. d. after 1288. Italian Franciscan and author of chronicle containing
  information on Emperor Frederick II.
Sallengre, Albert-Henri de. 1694-1723. Dutch lawyer, councilor, and man of let-
  ters, from a French Huguenot family.
Salvius, Johan Adler. 1589-1652, Swedish diplomat.
Salzmann, Thomas. d. 1540. German, executed at Strasbourg.
Sanchoniatus Phaenicius. c. 700-500 BCE. Probably Sanchuniathon, known for
  his *Phoenician History*.
Savonarola, Girolamo. d. 1498. Born in Ferrara, became Dominican monk. Held
  leading position in Florence as head of San Marco priory. Eventually tried
  and convicted of heresy and schism, and executed.
Scaliger, Joseph Justus. 1540-1609. French philologist and historian.
Scaliger, Julius Caesar (Jules César de l'Escale de Bordonis). 1484-1558. Italian
  physician and humanist. Wrote diatribes against Erasmus.

Schoppe, Caspar (Gaspar Scioppius). 1576-1649. German controversialist and scholar.

Schweigger, Salomon. fl. late sixteenth century. German Lutheran, who translated the Qur'ān into German.

Scot. *see* Michael Scot

Scoto, Thomas. Early fourteenth century. First a Dominican, then a Franciscan friar. Accused of heresy.

Servetus, Michael (Miguel). 1511-1553. Spanish physician who questioned the Trinity, believing that God is unitary. Founding figure of Unitarianism. Burned at stake on orders of John Calvin.

Shabbetai Ẓevi. 1626-1676. Born in Smyrna. Self-proclaimed messiah and central figure of Shabbateanism, a messianic movement named for him.

Shaftesbury, 3rd Earl of. *See* Cooper, Anthony Ashley

Simon of Tournai. c. 1130-c. 1201. At Paris from 1153. Teacher at Paris; falsely accused of heresy.

Socinus, Faustus (Fausto Paolo Sozzini). 1539-1604. Italian Protestant reformer. Born in Siena, spent his later years in Poland. His name became associated with a heresy, but he never led a heretical sect. Maintained the sanctity of human life.

Spencer, John. 1630-1693. English scholar of comparative religion.

Spinoza, Baruch (Bento, Benedictus). 1632-1677. Jewish philosopher born in Amsterdam of Portuguese ancestry. Excommunicated in 1656. Exponent of rationalist thought.

Spitzel (Spizel), Théophile Gottlieb. 1639-1691. German Protestant theologian and scholar.

Staphorst, Nikolaus. fl. early eighteenth century. Pastor of Hamburg.

Stillingfleet, Edward. 1635-1699. English clergyman, bishop of Worcester.

Stouppe, Jean-Baptiste (Giovanni Batista Stoppa). fl. 1651-1673. Pastor of the French Church in London; spy.

Struve, B. G. (Burkhard Gotthelf Struve). 1671-1738. Jurist and professor of history at Jena.

Stubbs, Stubbes, or Stubbe, Henry. 1632-1676. English physician and author; close friend of Hobbes.

Tentzel, W. E. (Wilhelm Ernst). 1659-1707. German historian and writer; author of the *Curieuse Bibliothec.*

Theodorus of Cyrene. Late fifth century BCE. Greek mathematician; friend of Socrates.

Theseus. Legendary king of Athens and figure of Greek myth.

Thomasius, Christian. 1655-1728. German jurist, philosopher, and educator.

Thomas of Cantimpré. c. 1200/1201-1270/1272. Born in Brabant; joined Dominican order. Preacher and writer, author of an encyclopedia of natural history, of which the long chapter on bees (*Bonum universale de apibus*) was dedicated to Humbert of Romans.

Tillotson, John. 1630-1694. English clergyman, archbishop of Canterbury.

Toland, John. 1670-1722. Irish antireligious writer.

Turretini, Jean Alphonse. 1671-1737. Swiss theologian.

Ursin, Jean Henri. 1608-1667. Lutheran pastor and author.

Valdemar II. 1170-1241. King of Denmark.

Vallée, Geoffroy. d. 1574. Author of *La Béatitude des chrestiens*, who was burned at the stake at Paris in 1574

Van Dale, Anton. 1638-1708. Dutch Mennonite physician, preacher, and writer on religious subject; critic of witch-hunting.

Van den Enden, Franciscus. 1602-1674. Former Jesuit; teacher of Spinoza. Also known as a Neo-Latin poet, physician, art dealer, philosopher, and political schemer (who plotted against Louis XIV of France).

Vanini, Lucilio (Giulio Cesare Vanini). 1584-1619. Italian cleric and philosopher. Burned at stake.

Van Limborch, Philippus. 1633-1712. Dutch Remonstrant professor; author of *Historia inquisitionis*.

Vere, Edward de, 17th Earl of Oxford. 1550-1604. Poet and prominent figure in court of Queen Elizabeth I.

Veyssière de La Croze, Mathurin. 1661-1739. French Benedictine historian and orientalist who converted to Protestantism.

Vignes, Pierre des. *See* Pierre des Vignes

Villani, Giovanni. c. 1276-1348. Florentine chronicler and merchant-banker.

Vincent of Beauvais. d. 1264. Scholar considered the greatest of medieval encyclopedists.

Viret, Pierre. 1511-1571. Swiss theologian.

Voet, Gijsbert (Gisbertus Voetius). 1589-1676. Dutch Calvinist theologian.

von Ahlefeld, Johann Heinrich. 1656-1720. Danish diplomat.

von Frankenau, Gerhard Ernst Franck. 1676-1749. Danish diplomat.

Vossius, Isaac. 1618-1689. Dutch scholar; tutor and librarian to Queen Christina of Sweden.

Vroesen, Jan. 1672-1725. Dutch diplomat.

Walten, Ericus. 1663-1697. Dutch pamphleteer.

Wechel, Christian. fl. 1520-1554. Parisian printer, of a dynasty of German humanist printers.

William of Nangis (Guillaume de Nangis). d. 1300. French monastic chronicler.

Winstanley, Gerrard. fl. 1648-1652. English activist said to have been the real founder of the Quaker sect.

Wolf, Johann Christoph. 1683-1739. German scholar of Hebrew; bibliophile and book collector.

Wolseley, Sir Charles. c. 1630-1714. English politician and ecclesiastical pamphleteer.

Worm, Christen. 1672-1737. Danish theologian and scholar; bishop of Zeeland.

Worthington, John. 1618-1671. English clergyman and vice chancellor of Cambridge University.

Wright, Henry. fl. 1616. Author of *Disquisition of Truth.*

Xenocrates. Fourth century BCE. Greek philosopher; disciple of Plato, and head of the Platonic Academy 339-314.

Zalmoxis. Ancient Greek figure. According to Herodotus, either a god of the Thracians or a charlatan.

Zeno. b. c. 150 BCE. Epicurean philosopher.

Zoroaster. Probably c. 1000 BCE. Greek name for Iranian Zarathustra. Either a religious reformer or founder of a new religion.

INDEX OF NAMES

Note: Entries for Jesus, Moses, and Muhammad are here briefly summarized under those names. However, their intertwined legends wind through every page of the book, often inseparably.

Collins, Anthony, 156–57
Colvius, Andreas, 75
Condorcet, Nicolas de (Marie Jean
  Antoine Nicolas de Caritat, Mar-
  quis de Condorcet), 186
Confucius, 120, 132, 159
Constantine, Emperor, 109
Cooper, Anthony Ashley. *See* Shaftes-
  bury, Earl of
Cortés, Hernán, 174
Costa, C. D. N., 16
Costa, Uriel da, 76, 79, 110
Coste, Pierre, 158
Cotin, Abbé, 46
Coulton, G. G., 38
Critias, 11
Cromwell, Oliver, 87, 96, 113, 120
Curio, Jacques, 66
Cyril of Alexandria, 16, 119

Danaeus, Lambertus, 63, 67
Daniel (biblical figure), 17, 19, 22
Dante Alighieri, 3, 29, 42
De Bure, Guillaume-François, 142
Deffand, Marie de Vichy, Marquise
  du, 200
Dekker, Jean, 120, 124
Democritus, 175
Denis, Marie-Louise (Marie Louise
  Mignot), 199–200
Dennett, Daniel C., ix
Des Barreaux, Sieur (Jacques Vallée),
  59
Descartes, René, 70, 74, 98, 124, 175
Desfontaines, Abbé, 199
Desmaizeaux, Pierre, 157–58
Des Périers, Bonaventure, 65, 127
Devereux, Robert. *See* Essex, Earl of
De Witt, Jan, 101
Diagoras of Melos (the Atheist), 11
Dicaearchus, 175
Diderot, Denis, ix, 192
Diez, Heinrich Friedrich von, 196
Digby, Sir Kenelm, 52
Diodati, Giovanni, 93

Diogenes of Apollonia, 11, 175
Diopeithes, 12
Dolet, Étienne, 58–59, 139
Dorsche, Johann Georg, 77
Drejer (theologian), 77
Du Bellay, Joachim, 46, 64
Du Cange, Charles du Fresne, Sei-
  gneur, 180
Duijkerius, Johannes, 105
Duns Scotus, John, 29, 61
Duplessis-Mornay, Philippe (Sei-
  gneur du Plessis-Marly), 50
Dupréau, Gabriel, 45
Dupuy, Pierre and Jacques, 92
Dury, John, 113, 117
Du Sauzet, Henri, 157
Du Verdier, Antoine, 64

Effen, Justus van, 141–42
Elijah (biblical figure), 124
Elizabeth I, Queen of England, 79–81,
  86
Elwes, R. H. M., 103
Emmerich, Count of Leiningen, 22
Empedocles, 175
Epictetus, 184
Epicurus, 11, 51, 142, 184, 196
Epiphanius of Salamis, 10
Erasmus, Desiderius, 57–58
Erntius, Henri, 59, 64
Essex, Earl of (Robert Devereux, 2nd
  Earl of Essex), 81
Estienne (Stephanus), Henri the
  Younger, 44, 62, 64
Eugen of Savoy (Prince Eugen Francis
  of Savoy-Carignan), 124, 127, 129,
  137, 140–41, 157, 159
Euhemerus, 11
Eymeric, Nicolás, 29

Fairbairn, A. W., 139
Fausto da Longiano, Sebastiano, 52
Fénelon, François de Salignac de la
  Mothe, 106, 111
Fernandez, Alvarao, 39

246 *Index of Names*